THE SHUL WITHOUT A CLOCK

Second Thoughts from a Rabbi's Notebook

THE SHUL WITHOUT A CLOCK

EMANUEL FELDMAN

JERUSALEM FELDHEIM PUBLISHERS NEW YORK

First published 2001

Copyright © 2001 by Emanuel Feldman

ISBN 1-58330-499-1

All rights reserved.

No part of this publication may be translated, reproduced, stored ia a retrieval system or transmitted, in any form or by any means, electronic, mechanical, photocopying, recording or otherwise, without permission in writing from the publishers.

FELDHEIM PUBLISHERS

POB 35002 / Jerusalem, Israel

202 Airport Executive Park
Nanuet, NY 10954

www.feldheim.com

Printed in Israel

לע"נ

עמרם הלל בן מנחם ז"ל

Dedicated to the memory of
our beloved son
Amram Hillel ז"ל
who dwells in the serenity
of a clockless realm.

ת.נ.צ.ב.ה.

Other Books by Emanuel Feldman

The 28th of Iyar
Law as Theology
The Biblical Echo
On Judaism
Tales Out of Shul
One Plus One Equals One

Preface

TO BEGIN WITH THE GENESIS of this book: for many years I have been writing short essays and sketches for a number of journals, primarily for *Tradition* magazine, where I have served as editor for the past thirteen years. The positive reaction of many readers has encouraged me to gather them together in this collection.

While some of the material in this book has never before been published, many articles appeared in *Tradition, Jewish Action, Jerusalem Post,* and *Jerusalem Report,* whose publishers I hereby thank for their permission to utilize them here.

I am grateful to my dear wife Estelle for her editorial contributions to these essays. Her finely honed sense of style and her perceptive editing are evident on every page. My esteemed brother, HaRav Aharon Feldman, gave unstintingly of his time and erudition in reviewing many of these essays. His insights and keen analysis were always on the mark. Obviously, I claim exclusive rights to the weaknesses in this work, and share them with no one else.

Both the editorial and graphics departments at Feldheim Publishers were highly professional, supportive, and creative. And my old friend Ben Gasner used his world-class talents to produce a cover that is creative, distinctive, and elegant.

> Emanuel Feldman
> Jerusalem
> Tishrei 5762 / September 2001

While some of the essays in this book have never been published before, many have appeared in *Tradition, Jewish Action, The Jerusalem Post,* and *The Jerusalem Report,* whom I hereby thank for their permission to utilize them here.

I am grateful to my dear wife Estelle for her editorial contribution to these essays. Her finely honed sense of style and her perceptive editing are evident on every page. My esteemed brother, HaRav Aharon Feldman, gave unstintingly of his time and erudition, and his insights and keen analysis were always on the mark. Obviously, I claim exclusive rights to the weaknesses in this work.

The editorial, design, and production staff at Feldheim Publishers in Jerusalem were highly professional, supportive, and creative. And my old friend Ben Gasner used his world-class talents to produce a cover that is striking, distinctive, and elegant.

Emanuel Feldman
Jerusalem
Tishrei 5762 / September 2001

Contents

PART ONE: REACHING FOR GOD ... 1

   God and Mrs. Cooperman ... 3

   The Shul Without a Clock ... 7

   The Local Is Faster than the Express ... 12

   To Think unto the Lord a New Song ... 18

   The Stranger Among Us ... 22

   Observant Jews and Religious Jews ... 27

   A Helicopter Crashes ... 31

   Dailyness and the Daily Ness ... 34

   A Death in Jerusalem: The Real World ... 38

PART TWO: LIVING IN JERUSALEM ... 43

   Yaakov and Jay: A Tale of Two Worlds ... 45

   A Bar-Mitsvah and a Funeral ... 50

   Redeployment & Hare Krishna:
      Re-engineering the Jewish State ... 54

   Violence in Littleton and Jerusalem ... 60

   A Tale of Two Cities ... 64

   Why I Miss Yerushalayim ... 68

Mountain Musings	71
McDonald's and the Newest Commandment	74
The Shulhan Arukh, Hidden Verses, and the Israeli Elections	77
Elections and Pipe Dreams	83
Street Smart in Jerusalem	89
On Rolling Black Hats and Snowmen – Images of Jerusalem	92
The Scrawl on the Siddur Page	96
An Unreal Interview: Israel After Fifty	101
Overtaken by History	114
Strange Bedfellows	119
Believers and Unbelievers in the Land that Defies Belief	122
A Jerusalem Lament	130
PART THREE: OBSERVING JEWS	135
Tefillin in a Brown Paper Bag	137
Jewish Continuity: More and Less	142
"Buddha Is Not As Bad ...": The Floundering of American Jewry	147
A Ten Coarse Affair	152
Abbreviations	156
Not a Jewish Princess	161

The Hebron Murders: Enemies and Friends	164
Into the Looking Glass: The Rabin Assasination	169
The Old Man and the Secularists	174
Melanie, Not Moses	181
A Talmud by Any Other Name	184
Talmud Happily Ever After	189
Cellular Kavannah	194
The German Soldier	197

PART FOUR: THINKING ABOUT JUDAISM — 201

HaMakom, the Place of the World	203
Life's Second Chances: The Second Passover	208
The Holiday in Hiding	216
Why I Like Tish'a B'Av	220
Uncommon Connections in the Halakhot of Mourning	223
Orthodox Feminism or Feminist Orthodoxy	235
Vice and Virtue: Today's Vice-Versa	248
Reform of Reform? A Talmudic Reading	254

PART FIVE: SMILING AT OURSELVES — 265

First Class Musings, Second Class Conclusions	267
Of Pennants and Penitents	272

A Simple Driving Test	278
An Imagined Symposium	281
Haim and Ita and the Communications Revolution	285
The Heavenly Editor	288
The Cruelest Month	291
The Last Bus Stop	294
In Any Image Createth He Them	297
Prime Minister Jones and the New Middle East	299
Glossary	303

Abbreviations

Ber.	Berakhot	Jer.	Jeremiah
Deut.	Deuteronomy	Lev.	Leviticus
Ex.	Exodus	Num.	Numbers
Gen.	Genesis	Ps.	Psalms

PART ONE

Reaching for God

God and Mrs. Cooperman

MRS. COOPERMAN, THE ELDERLY WIDOW who attended my father's synagogue in Baltimore, was every rabbi's ideal congregant: she never spoke during services, she davened meticulously, caressing every word, she listened avidly to the rabbi's sermons, gave charity generously, observed Shabbat and kashrut, and honored those who studied Torah.

There was only one problem. Other than her ability to read Hebrew, she was completely unlettered and unlearned. That is why, in fact, she never skipped a word of davening: she was unable to distinguish between prayers that are recited on a regular Shabbat and those that are recited only when Shabbat coincides with Rosh Hodesh, or Yom Tov, or Hanukah. The net result was that on every single Shabbat of the year she recited every single prayer on every single page of the service.

My mother, who always sat next to her, would gently remind her, "This you don't have say today because today is not Rosh Hodesh."

Mrs. Cooperman would smile: "I ask you, what is so terrible if I do say it? If it isn't Rosh Hodesh today, soon it will be. So it really makes no difference."

We three pre-teen brothers, growing up in our father's shul, were more than a little amused by Mrs. Cooperman. After all, we were already studying Humash and Rashi and knew a little bit of Shulhan Arukh, and we found it absurd that an old lady could not make distinctions between Shabbat and Yom Tov. The mere thought of Mrs. Cooperman reading the *shemone esrei* or the *birkat hamazon* straight through without distinguishing one section from the next was enough to brighten up the dullest of days.

One year, Rosh Hodesh Tevet happened to coincide with the Shabbat of Hanukah. During the davening we recited *ya-aleh veyavo* and *al hanissim* and *hallel,* and at the *birkat hamazon* after our meal we omitted nothing, reciting everything from beginning to end: the *al hanissim* for Hanukah, the *retze* for Shabbat and the *ya-ale veyavo* for Rosh Hodesh. Suddenly it dawned on us that this was the one time that Mrs. Cooperman was right: on this one Shabbat of the year you simply opened up the *siddur* and kept going, reciting everything, omitting practically nothing. "Today is her day," we laughed, and from that moment and forevermore the wondrous conflation of Shabbat, Hanukah and Rosh Hodesh became known among us as Mrs. Cooperman's Shabbat. That such a Shabbat occurs just once every few years only intensified the wicked anticipation of the recurrence of that magical moment in time.

Many Hanukahs, many Roshei Hodashim, many Mrs.-Cooperman-Shabbatot have flown by since then. Mrs. Cooperman is no longer among the living, nor are her favorite rabbi and rebbetzin. We have passed her story down to our children and grandchildren, and whenever that special Shabbat occurs I still call my brothers across continents and oceans to remember the light-hearted mirth she unwittingly created for us when we were young.

A recent Hanukah provided us once again with one of her enchanted Shabbatot. We recited all the prayers consecutively: *ya-aleh veyavo* for Rosh Hodesh, *al hanisim* for Hanukah, the entire *hallel,* and we read from three different *sifrei Torah.* We passed over nothing: quintessential, vintage Cooperman.

But while we still chuckle at the memories which her name evokes, our laughter is of a different kind now. She no longer provokes the giggles of mischievous young boys, but rather smiles of appreciation and illumination. Now we realize that while she may have been ignorant of the subtleties and nuances of Torah learning, she possessed something that we utterly lacked then, and probably still lack now: devotion, surrender, and child-like innocence before the Presence of God.

We were too young to understand that in the torrent of words she poured out before the Creator every Shabbat morning there lay a key ingredient of worship. She didn't know the translation of those words, but in a much deeper sense she understood their meaning. She brought to her praying a total submission of the self before the Presence of God, a love for her Creator so consuming that she could not bear to pass over a single word of His holy *siddur*.

She worshiped God not from knowledge or intellect, but from an inner spirit that transcends the mind. She did not know the proofs for the existence of God, but she needed none, for God was not an abstraction but a reality. She had no idea of the philosophical underpinnings of prayers, but when she said *barukh atah*, she knew she was talking to her personal Creator and that He was listening. She did not know the subtle differences between faith and trust and belief, and her prayer calendar was a seamless web which did not distinguish between one kind of holiness and the next, and she thanked God for the miracle of the Hanukah oil every Shabbat, and ushered in the new moon every week of the year. But she loved God, and her greatest joy was to engage in conversation with Him.

It occurs to me that in our restless society, when a synagogue's worth is often measured by the rapidity with which it runs through its Shabbat service, and when insufficient velocity of prayer is considered sufficient cause to break away and begin a *shtiebel* of one's own; when omitting a *tahanun* prayer is a cause for joy at a minyan, and we are irritated by a *baal tefilla* who keeps us in Shul five extra minutes; when our prayers are often a robotic, mechanical service of the lips, in an unhappy fulfillment of the *mitsvat anashim melumadah* of Isaiah 29:13 – in such a hurried time, the picture of a Mrs. Cooperman lovingly whispering every word of prayer is a striking counterpoint.

Yes, her davening was halakhically out of joint. Certainly God is addressed differently on a Shabbat Hanukah than on a normative Shabbat. Granted, our relationship to God is different on Pesah than it is on Rosh Hodesh, and we may not arrogate to our transient moods the right to transform different approaches to God into one happy mishmash of words – which is why we don't recite *hallel* every day of the year. And while we certainly may approach God at any time with any words of our own, the words of the *siddur* are sacred because, stemming from the Men of the Great Assembly, they reflect the changing divine-human connectedness of different religious seasons of the year that may not be shifted and molded according to our momentary whims.

But when Mrs. Cooperman appeared before her Maker Who is not constrained by the mortal boundaries and limitations of clocks and calendars, and for Whom Time is an indivisible entity, I like to think that perhaps He did not look with disfavor upon the seamless, timeless universe of His loyal servant Mrs. Cooperman.

The Shul Without a Clock

I OFTEN FIND MYSELF WISHING that synagogues would not have clocks on their walls. After all, this is the sacred sphere of the Timeless One. This is where finite man seeks to enter that infinite realm of public and private prayer, the study of Torah, thoughts of God and our relationship to Him — those moments when time stands still and relinquishes its dominion to the One Who is beyond time. A clock in a shul is somehow a discordant note, a temporal intrusion in an other-worldly realm. A clockless shul would represent a timeless, eternal place.

But when non-transcendental reality sets in, I realize how inextricably woven into our service of the Timeless One are the elements of mundane time. Wherever one turns in the religious realm, one is confronted by the relentlessly pointing finger of time and its handmaidens: numbers and counting.

Consider prayer itself. Paradoxically, the act of communing with the Most High is enveloped by the constrictions of the clock. One must pray before the fourth hour of the day, recite the morning *shema* before the third hour, *mussaf* before the seventh hour, *minhah* after the sixth hour but before the sunset, and the evening *shema* before midnight.

The fact is that a consciousness of the passage of time — manifested in the ubiquitous requirement to count — pervades our entire religious life.

- On the eighth day after birth comes the requirement of *berit mila,* and after thirty days, the requirement for *pidyon ha-ben.*
- After giving birth, the mother counts her days of purity: seven days, fourteen days, thirty-three days, sixty-six days (Lev. 15:28); and the married woman counts during every menstrual cycle.
- The courts count the days between new moons, and at the twenty-ninth day they await eagerly the moon-sighting of the witnesses.
- The Paschal lamb must be slaughtered after the sixth hour of the day.
- The daily offerings must be inspected for defects for four days prior to the sacrifice.
- The Biblical months have no names of their own, but are numbered: the first month, the second month....

Not only do we reckon hours, days, weeks, and months, we also count the years: in the first and second years, and the fourth and fifth years of the seven year cycle, we are required to give the First Tithe and the Second Tithe; in the third year and the sixth year, the First Tithe to the Poor; in the seventh year, the fields must lie fallow, open to everyone alike. And Lev. 25:28 commands that the courts count seven times seven sabbatical years in order to arrive at the year of Jubilee.

Before creation, all is chaos. At creation, time and counting and numbers enter the universe, and with them come order and regularity. Time separates and classifies, maintains boundaries and limitations: the first day, the second day, the third day, culminating in the holy seventh day. The sun rises and sets, the moon waxes and wanes, the tides advance and recede, the seasons come and go, all according to the clock established at creation and affirmed to Noah: *Zera ve-katsir, kor va-hom, kayyits va-horef, yom va-lailah lo yishbotu* / "... Seed time and harvest, cold and heat, summer and winter, day and night shall not cease" (Gen. 8:22; Jer. 33:20).

This is the pulse of the universe. Thus it is that, in Exodus 12, the very first commandment given to the Jewish people concerns the basis for religious times and seasons — the fixing of the new moon. The rhythm of numbers and the choreography of the clock are implanted in our genes, and man, the microcosm of the universe, cannot escape it. His very own heartbeat is a paradigm of time, a sign both of his creation and his mortality: when its pulse comes to an end, time for him comes to an end.

※※※

A striking fact: although time is universal, there is a zone of religious time that exists only when man creates it. Certain numbers have no life unless man does the counting. Lev. 27:32, for example, require us to tithe our cattle. How is this done? The Mishnah (Bekhorot 9:7) describes the procedure explicitly:

> How do we tithe animals? We bring them to a shed and make for them a small opening [in the fence] so that two shall not be able to go out simultaneously. We count [with the rod]: one, two, three, four, five, six, seven, eight, nine. He marks every tenth lamb that goes out and says, "This is [the tithe]." If he failed to mark it or did not count [the lambs] with a rod, or if he counted them while they were crouching or standing, they are still considered tithed.

A fascinating question is addressed by the Mishnah: What if a man wishes to give ten percent of his cattle at random but chooses not to engage in the act of counting? The answer is that this will not suffice. If he owns one hundred lambs and offers ten at random, this is not a valid tithe, even though he has given ten percent of his flock. The reason: the Torah explicitly requires that "the tenth shall be holy" — that is, he must physically count every tenth animal. If the count has not taken place, the tithe has not taken place. The act of counting by the owner is the crucial element in the tithing of cattle.

A similar insistence on human counting is found in Lev. 23:15 concerning the counting of the days between Pesach and Shavuot: *U-sefartem lakhem sheva shabbatot temimot/* "You shall count seven full weeks ... they are to be fifty days...." The festival of Shavuot and its offerings will take place whether or not we count the days, but the Torah insists that we nevertheless engage in the act of counting.

More obligatory counting: As part of the Yom Kippur *avodah*, Lev. 16 requires the *kohen gadol* to enter the Holy of Holies and sprinkle the blood of the bull offering upon the Ark cover, once with an upward motion and seven times with a downward motion. The *Mishnah* (Yoma 5:3) describes the procedure, which we recide in the *mussaf* of Yom Kippur: *Ve-kakh haya mone:* / "This is how he would count: 'one; one plus one; one plus two; one plus three; one plus four; one plus five; one plus six; one plus seven.'" Sprinkling alone is insufficient. He must engage in the act of counting.

Through such mandatory counting, God takes man by the hand and, in effect, says: "Come, I Who am the *Me-kadesh Yisrael veha-zemanim* will teach you how to elevate the ephemeral moment into something eternal, how to number your days (*li-mnot yameinu ken hoda...* Ps. 90:12) In the celebration of every seventh day, you attach yourself to the Infinite, and time, though it continues to move, is brought under your control. So, too, in *Yom Tov*. So, too, in every aspect of religious time. By enveloping your hours in the cloak of holiness, you soar upward to a sphere where time has no dominion. Although time is Mine, you can sanctify it with Me. Through your counting, the potential holiness in My universe is actualized."

※❈※

But despite the full realization that the world-to-come is the only timeless realm, it nevertheless seems to me that it would be felicitous if, in the one place on this earth which is an adumbration of that realm — the house of God — one would not confronted by that relentlessly ticking reminder of this world's temporality. That is why I still find myself wistfully looking for a clockless shul.

The Local Is Faster than the Express

I ASKED SOMEONE WHAT TIME his morning *minyan* begins. "We start at 7 A.M.," he replied. "*Barekhu* is at 7:11, and *shemoneh esrei* is at 7:18. We finish at 7:35, except for Monday and Thursday when we finish at 7:45."

While I appreciated the detailed response, it reminded me of one of the disconcerting facts of shul life: there are few *minyanim* in the world where the times of *barekhu*, *shema* and the *amidah* are not predictable up to the split second.

On one level this is quite natural. We are creatures of time, and schedules and responsibilities are part of our daily routine. After all, we are not of the spiritual quality of the *hasidim harishonim* who would spend one hour preparing for *tefillah* (the *amidah*), then recite it for one hour, and after praying would wait another hour to come down from the summit (Ber. 32b). We do not even comprehend such concepts, much less practice them. We who have not reached such rarefied height are fortunate if in our daily davening we are able to attain an occasional moment of *kavannah*.

But even on our ordinary level it is mildly incongruous that *tefillah*, the quintessential attempt to connect with God — *avodah shebalev* — should be quantifiable. Can one know in advance how long it will take to establish such a connection? Can a stop watch be placed on the service of the heart?

One keeps thinking of the fascinating pericope in *Berakhot* 34a.:

> A certain disciple led the prayers before R. Eliezer, and drew out the prayers to great length. The disciples said to him: Master, what a drawer-out (*arkhan*) is this one! He said to them: Is he drawing out (*maarikh*) any more than Moshe Rabbeinu of whom it is written, "The forty days and forty nights that I prayed. . ." (Deut. 9:25). In another incident, a disciple led the prayers before R. Eliezer and was very brief. The disciples said to him: Master, how brief (*katzran*) is this one! He replied to them: Is he any briefer than Moshe Rabbeinu, who prayed (only five words), as is written: "*el na, refa na lah*/God, I beseech, heal her now." (Num. 12:13).

There are many layers of meaning within this episode, but one key point is clear: no one could ever predict with precision the exact moment when the *minyan* of R. Eliezer would be reciting the *shema*. Some days it was later; some days it was earlier. This might have played havoc with their personal schedules, but it was good prayer.

For good prayer means to lose one's self in God's presence, to become as one with Him. (See Rashi at Bereishit 30:8 where the root of *tefillah* — *pll*, which bears the same root as the name *Naftali* — is translated as "intertwine," or "bond," or "connect." See also Targum Onkelos *ad loc*.) Ideally, we enter another realm where time has no dominion over our lives. Time, after all, is this worldly thing, a reminder of mortality. The rhythmic pulsebeat of the human heart is a reminder that we are alive - and also that we will not always be. But during *tefillah* we can catch intimations of eternity and immortality, and at such moments the clock becomes irrelevant.

Further, do all the members of a *minyan* approach God in the identical way, with the same feelings and emotions, on every single day of the year? There must be some mornings when the pull of a certain phrase in *pesukei dezimrah* tugs at the heart and calls for a momentary reflection; surely there is a word in the *shema* or the *amidah* that resonates differently on some days than on others. But no member of the *minyan* dares pause or meditate or ponder. (I know: occasionally I attend such *minyanim* here in Jerusalem.) All aboooard! The train is pulling out of the station, and he who hesitates will miss the *barekhu* stop, and then he will certainly not arrive at the other stops together with his fellow passengers. All aboard! No lingering. We must arrive at the *shemoneh esrei* station promptly at 7:18. No pious Jew wants to *daven shemoneh esrei* without the *minyan*.

So it is with most *minyanim* in the world, and, I suppose, so must it be. The individual in a *minyan* loses his individuality and becomes as one with the community. And though he is part of that newly created *minyan* community, he has no control over it. The community is a separate entity with a life of its own. One's personal desire to proceed at his own pace must yield to the right of the community to impose its own discipline on the participants. No *minyan* can long endure half spontaneous and half scheduled. Communal prayer requires order and regularity, and while each individual retains the right to personal expressions of spontaneity during the *tefillah*, the needs of the community to proceed with its prayers takes precedence. Obviously, this mitigates against sustained emotional peaks. The incident of R. Akiva in Berakhot 31a is telling: when he was in private, R. Akiva would daven with ecstatic and fiery emotion, but when he was part of the *minyan* he would follow the norms of the community.

All true. But one nagging thought keeps recurring: it is only when worship is disconnected from feelings and emotions, and consists simply of reciting a set amount of words at a certain rate of speed, that it is possible to know in advance how long the entire drill will last. Such an exercise can strip prayer of soul and spirit and transform it into mechanical rote, a chore that takes 32.5 mumbling minutes out of our time every morning before we get it over with.

To be sure, even *davening* without *kavannah* — as happens to all of us frequently — has value. *Vehayu hadevarim ha-eileh... al levavekha*, states the *shema*. "Let these words be on (*al*) your heart..." Why "on your heart"? Would not "in your heart" be more appropriate? No, explains a great hasidic sage, for we cannot always attain the high level of having the holy words enter our hearts. Shall we, then, not ever pray? Not at all. Be not discouraged, let the words be recited, and let them rest temporarily on the outside of the heart, *al levavekha*. Ultimately, at certain moments of divine favor, the heart will open up and those words will then slip inside the heart.

In brief, it would be an error to pray only spontaneously, when the spirit moves us, and to disregard the set order and liturgy of prayer. There is a *seder ha-tefillah*, and we may not edit or streamline according to our whims of the moment. In addition, relationship with God requires constancy and steadiness, and we are required to *daven* whether or not we are in the mood. There is room for spontaneity in *tefillah*, certainly, but there is also a precise liturgy that must be followed. In public prayer, the individual heart cannot be allowed to run away with itself, lest chaos result.

Furthermore, while there must be order to public prayer, the set liturgy, far from stultifying our spirits, helps lift them. The liturgy is a spiritual symphony that speaks to the soul. Beneath every phrase, within the order and the uniformity, there lie infinite possibilities for the flashes of illumination and cognition that enable us to reach out to the Object of our prayer. This is eminently doable - as long as we remember that the object of our prayer is not to reach *shemoneh esrei* by 7:18, but to reach our God at any time.

Nor is it a solution to our dilemma to abandon the *minyan* in favor of solitary and isolated prayer. It is a special *mitsvah* to *daven* with the *minyan*, and this *mitsvah* and its long-term benefits are so significant that it must be attended to even at cost to one's personal intensity and *kavannah*. Ideally, of course, public prayer engages each Jew as a lonely individual and also as a member of the *minyan* community. We stand alone before our God, but we stand alone together with the *minyan* community, each member of which also stands alone.

So we are faced with a perplexing dilemma: On the one hand, the need for the set liturgy and the *minyan*; on the other hand, our craving for individual spontaneity and personal reflection.

While it may not be possible for a *minyan* to accommodate the spiritual needs of each individual member, all members can be accommodated their occasional need to reflect by instituting a very simple procedure: the addition of another few minutes to the normal davening time. The allocation of, say, only one or two extra minutes to *pesukei dezimrah*, another minute or two to the *shema*, and another minute or two to the *shemoneh esrei* — a net addition of some five minutes — could have a powerful effect on *kavannah*. And if there is a practical need to conclude by a certain time, one can always begin the *davening* five minutes earlier. The express can become a local, giving even the most seasoned commuter a chance to appreciate the scenery. And in this case, the local may reach God faster than the express.

Even if we are not spiritually constituted to spend three hours in a weekday *shaharit*, and even if circumstances prevent us from kicking the habits of rote, it is valuable to bear in mind that the habits we are engaged in are far from ideal. That we may be incapable of scaling the peaks of the spiritual Mount Everest is not reason to lose sight of the fact that the summit exists, and that some rare souls attain it.

Yes, I realize that time and prayer cannot be totally separated from one another, and that time is an integral element in our reaching out to God. We must recite the *shema* by the third hour, the *amidah* by the fourth hour, *musaf* before the seventh hour, *minhah* between the sixth hour and sunset, the evening *shema* before midnight, and those who *daven* "vatikin" must calculate their davening precisely to the minute every single day.

But despite the relentless power of the halakhic clock, I still find myself waiting for the day after the Messiah comes, when conversation such as this will take place:

> *What time does your Shul daven in the morning?*
> We daven at seven.
>
> *And what time do you finish davening?*
> I can't answer that. Sometimes we end at 7:45, sometimes at 8. It all depends.
>
> *Depends on what?*
> Depends on how the spirit moves us, on how well we fit into the mood of davening. Sometimes it takes less time, sometimes more. We never know for sure.

Come to think of it, even before Messiah comes I'd like to find a Shul like that.

To Think unto the Lord a New Song

I AM SITTING IN MY Jerusalem Shul on a Friday night, listening to a *shiur* on the fine points of *sefirat ha-omer*: Rambam, Rashba, Rabbeinu Nissim, Rosh, and Beit Yosef all make their appearance, and their views are meticulously probed and examined. It is an exciting and stimulating exercise in halakhic analysis and classification, a treat for the mind.

Through the open windows a lovely melody edges in on my concentration. The hasidic shul next door is greeting the Shabbat queen with a lovely and evocative *Lekha Dodi niggun*, redolent of the serenity and joy of the Shabbat day. It tugs at the heart.

I try to hum along with the melody, but it interferes with my ability to concentrate on the analysis. I try to concentrate on the analysis, but cannot hear the melody. I want both, but I can have only one. I must make a wrenching choice: either the heart or the mind.

❦

Mine is not a new dilemma. It is as old as Jewish history. There are two major paths leading toward God. One is the path of the mind; the other is the path of the heart.

We are required to think before Him and to serve Him with the intellect through the study of His Torah; and we are required to sing before Him, to express our joy and our love for Him through the medium of prayer.

Thus has it always been: the path of Torah and the path of *avodah*. We are commanded, *ve-hagita bo yomam va-lailah*; and we are commanded *le-avdo bekhol levavkhem*. We are required to study the Torah and we are required to pray and bring offerings to the Author of that Torah.

But study and prayer are very different from one other. In the act of study, one stands alone before God and before His Word. The mind thinks, contemplates, reasons, analyzes. It must be dispassionate and objective as it strives to plumb the depths and subtle nuances of the text.

Not so prayer. It is not restricted by the limits of the intellect, nor controlled by the rigorous axioms of logic, analysis, whys and therefores. Good prayer is never dispassionate. It is filled with exuberance and ecstasy, and expresses itself in song and in dance. It does not engage in cold, cerebral matters; it pulsates with emotion and with affect.

Magen Avraham (R. Avraham Gombiner, 1637-1683), in his commentary to Orah Hayyim 50:2, delineates the difference between study and prayer in the eyes of God: while it is best to understand what one is praying,

> . . . Nevertheless [even if one does not understand what he is saying] the Holy One Blessed Be He knows one's intention and He understands. But [in the matter of Torah study] if one recites [a text] but does not understand it, it is not considered [a fulfillment of the mitsvah of Torah] study. Therefore, one must learn the meaning.

Two paths: not only "I think, therefore I am," but also "I feel, therefore I am." They are parallel paths, but, paradoxically, we are required to walk on both of them.

They are not forever mutually exclusive. Occasionally, in adumbration of their ultimate convergence, the two paths intersect for a brief moment. In the midst of prayer, for example, we study the Torah. Conversely, whenever we conclude the study of the Torah, we recite the hymn of praise that we call the *kaddish*. We wear *tefillin* on the head adjacent to the brain, the source of the intellect; and we also wear *tefillin* on the arm adjacent to the heart, the source of the affect. And the student of Talmud, engaged in rigorous analysis and logical formulations, often finds himself singing and humming as he contemplates a subtle text.

Two paths, but here and there they converge in brief encounters. The Jew, as he pours out his heart in prayer, is constrained by *halakhot* of time and place and thus must think and consider: am I required or not required at this moment to don *tefillin* and *tsitsit*? May I or may I not pronounce the *shema* and the *amidah* and the *mussaf*? At what hour may I or may I not recite certain *tefillot*? Which prayers must precede other prayers and which must follow? When may I insert a personal petition in the *amidah* and when may I not? And always the Jew, though he prays in the communal setting of the *minyan*, stands alone before God.

There are paths with the paths. There is the worship of God that is hidden in the recesses of the heart, and there is the worship of God that sings resounding hymns of praise. There is worship which is structured and controlled, faithfully following the set liturgy; and there is worship which is spontaneous and ecstatic and can be expressed only in song. There is the silent *amidah*, contemplative and thoughtful; and there is the public repetition of the *amidah*, exploding in the communal response of "Holy, Holy, Holy." There is the Talmudic advice (Berakhot 32a) to "set in order" *(yesader)* one's prayers and then to pray. Thus, while the book of prayer articulates the deepest recesses of the heart, the name of the book is *siddur*, which means, "order."

God demands that we offer Him both the heart and the mind: that we sing before Him and think before Him; that we rejoice before Him and stand in awe before Him; that we serve Him through song and dance and that we serve Him through the subtle analysis of His holy texts; that we serve Him in discipline and order, and that we serve Him in the disorder of fervor and ecstasy.

God desires both the sounds of the heart and the silence of the mind, for in truth, His Presence is discerned both in the sound and in the silence. His omnipotence is manifest in the explosion of the thunder and the crackle of the lightning, and we bless Him; we bless Him again in the silent majesty of mountain peaks or rainbows in the heavens. He is heard in the sounds and the lightning of Sinai (Ex. 19:16), and also in the still small voice of I Kings 19:12. He is present in His *gilui shekhinah*, the revelation of His face, and He is present in His *hastarat panim*, the hiding of His face. One sings to Him with flute and cymbals (Ps. 150), but He is also the One to Whom "silence is praise" (Ps. 65:2).

Two paths diverge, and we are bidden to walk on both of them. God does not want us to be either a *hasid* or a *mitnaged*. He wants us to be both *hasid* and *mitnaged*. We will make the effort, but our simultaneous odyssey on two separate paths must await the thaumaturgy of the end of days when, in the words of Zechariah 14:9, "God will be One and His Name One." In that day, all paradoxes and dilemmas will be resolved and become one, and it will be possible to analyze the Rambam and to sing touching melodies at the same time.

I awoke from reverie with a start. *Ma'ariv* had begun. Rambam and Rashba and all their company had departed, and the *Lekha Dodi* melody had faded away. It occurred to me that, until the Great Day of the Lord arrives, it might be prudent to find a seat in Shul that is not near an open window.

The Stranger Among Us

A FEW WEEKS BEFORE ROSH Hashanah I was walking home from morning minyan in Jerusalem when a construction worker came over to me and said: *"Ani lo dati* — I am not religious — but I know that it's not Rosh Hashanah yet. Why do they sound the shofar every morning around here?"

I explained to him that we sound the shofar every day during the month preceding Rosh Hashanah. He had never heard of this practice, he said. He seemed interested, so I told him that this was like a spiritual alarm clock, designed to awaken us from our spiritual slumber in preparation for the great judgment day of Rosh Hashana. He smiled and said he thought this was a splendid idea: *"Metzuyan. Kol hakavod!"* We wished one another a *shanah tovah,* and we each went on our way.

I was touched by this brief colloquy in two distinct ways. Firstly, I was saddened that a Jew in Jerusalem who knew about shofar and Rosh Hashanah knew nothing about the daily Elul shofar; but I was I uplifted by the open and respectful way in which he listened and accepted my explanation.

II

The encounter brought to mind the recent seminal Guttman Institute Report published by the Avi Chai Foundation, "Beliefs, Observances, and Social Interaction Among Israeli Jews." If the study accurately reflects reality — and it has engendered much discussion in Israel and abroad — non-observant Israelis are not as anti-religious or even as non-religious as one might have thought.

Certain traditional observances and beliefs are found among almost all Israelis: some celebration of major Yom Tov festivals; performance of life-cycle mitsvot such as *berit milah;* a commitment to Jewish continuity. Other traditional practices, such as marking the onset of the Shabbat, involve about two-thirds of the population. Only twenty percent of Israelis characterize themselves as "totally non-observant," (remarkably, thirty-nine percent of these marked Shabbat in some way) while fully forty percent say they are "somewhat observant." Fourteen percent call themselves "strictly observant," and twenty-four percent define themselves as "observant to a great extent." Sixty percent believe in the existence of God, and twenty percent of the non-observant hold this belief. Half of Israeli Jews firmly believe in *Torah Min Hashamayim,* in Divine Providence, that the Torah and the mitsvot are God's commands, and that good deeds are rewarded. More than a third believe in a world-to-come and in the coming of the Messiah.

The study suggests that the so-called polarization of Israeli society between religious and secular may be exaggerated; that instead there apparently exists a continuum from the "strictly observant" to the "non-observant"; that the militantly anti-religious attitude that supposedly animates at least half the population may not exist at all; and that Israeli society has a strong and natural traditional bent.

To be sure, there is resentment against some Orthodox ways and habits, but in the great issues of religion and belief, the division seems to be more of a valley than a deep chasm. And apparently this valley is created less by anti-religious attitudes than by religious undernourishment.

All this attests to the amazing staying power and tenacity of the Torah within the Jewish soul. Despite the best efforts of numerous Israeli governments that have been hostile to traditional Judaism, and despite a state-run school system that has systematically denuded the curriculum of major elements of classical Judaism knowledge and values, it is apparent that Jewish observances, mitsvot, and beliefs still have a powerful hold on many Israelis.

Ironically, if the Guttman report is accurate, it is also a source of some remorse and heartache. For it suggests that an erroneous reading of reality has caused Orthodox Jews to dismiss the non-Orthodox out of hand, and that we have lulled ourselves to sleep with the thought that they are in any case beyond the pale — when all along they have been, and still are, emotionally and intellectually open to some overture and some understanding.

III

In my remorse I begin to fantasize: perhaps this is a propitious time for the Orthodox — not only in Israel but everywhere — to open windows, not for the purpose of allowing the outside world in, but, like the windows of the ancient Beit Hamikdash, to allow the values of Torah to radiate outward.

Opening windows means, firstly, the recognition of the essential Jewishness of fellow Jews, even when they are profoundly ignorant and non-observant of their Jewishness.

It means looking directly at others, not as through a glass darkly, and to regard them as you wish to be regarded, accepting them on their own terms, understanding who they are and why they are, realizing that non-observant Jews are not willfully rebelling against God or His Torah.

It means an implementation of the famous dictum of the Hazon Ish and R. Shneyor Zalman of Liadi, which urges us to reach out to the non-observant with *avotot shel ahavah*, "bonds of love."

It also means looking inward and asking ourselves a painful question: are we in our daily conduct a source of pride to that Torah to which we claim allegiance and whose teachings we so energetically try to disseminate?

In my reverie, individual Orthodox Jews everywhere begin to open windows. Instead of shying away from close contact with the non-Orthodox, perhaps from a fear of being religiously diluted, tainted, or even tempted, they gradually realize that in today's climate, when the souls of the non-Orthodox are actually yearning for a touch of sanctity, it might be in the best interests of God, Torah and Israel for at least a few individual Orthodox Jews to break through the isolation which has separated them from the non-observant and to initiate some contact with these our brothers.

Fantasies have a way of running wild, and in this one, Orthodox Jews suddenly ask themselves questions never asked before: Is there any longer a need to be fearful of the stranger who is not exactly like us? Should there be a sense of unease when a non-observant Jew moves into the neighborhood? What would happen if those new Israeli housing developments which advertise that they are "for religious families" were to admit the rare non-observant family that is undaunted by these words and that wants to live in an Orthodox community? Should some Orthodox Jews consider the possibility of living in non-Orthodox neighborhoods? Would not the impact of an understanding, giving, observant family have a salutary effect on that neighborhood which is in any case not as far removed from Judaism as we have been led to believe? And might not the experience also have a beneficial effect on the members of the Orthodox family, causing them to look at themselves anew and to articulate that which had always been taken for granted?

Who knows? If things go well, perhaps those iron barriers that go up every Friday night to keep the traffic out of Orthodox enclaves in Jerusalem and which help ensure that tranquil and other-worldly Jerusalem Shabbat — perhaps those barriers might some day be removed, and with them the state of mind that blocks out the view of all others who are not like us.

IV

But fantasies have a short life-span. Mine ran out of steam when I asked myself a painful question: how can we ever reach out lovingly to a non-Orthodox Jew when our own fully observant Orthodox neighbor — who believes in the same God and the same Torah and observes the same *tefillin* and *kashrut* and *mikveh* and Shabbat and prayer as we do — is nevertheless a stranger to us because he: wears a *shtreimel* or does not; wears a *kippah serugah* or does not: wears a broad-brimmed black hat, or does not; wears a long black coat, or does not; wears a sport jacket, or does not; follows my rebbe, or does not; pronounces Hebrew the way I do, or does not? If we cannot live together even with observant Jews unless they are our identical ideological twins, will we ever be able to touch the souls of non-observant Jews?

Even fantasies have their limits.

Which is too bad. Because without such fantasies all the windows will remain tightly shut, and all the surveys which suggest that there are millions of Jews in Israel — and around the world — waiting to be touched by the magic of Torah will remain lifeless statistics.

And worse still, not only the construction worker but also his children will very likely grow up without ever hearing the shofar that is sounded in Elul, and maybe not even the shofar that is sounded on Rosh Hashanah.

Observant Jews
and Religious Jews

AMERICAN ORTHODOXY'S VIRTUAL RESURRECTION from the dead in this last half of the twentieth century has been marked by impressive achievements in the great battles for Shabbat, kashrut, *mikveh*, synagogue standards, and serious Torah study. But I think it is fair to say that, beyond occasional islands here and there, we are still far short of being a truly spiritual community.

In a word, while we have created many observant Jews, we have not created many religious Jews. Mitsvah observance is clearly the *sine qua non* of Jewish living, but is only the first step towards becoming a religious Jew. For many, however, it has become both the first and last step. When it is possible for a Jew to don tefillin, be rigorous in his kashrut, live a life marked by many *humrot,* and yet be lax in his *bein adam la-havero*, something is clearly not right (or left, or centrist). We tend to emphasize, for example, the *tseni'ut* of the sleeve length, but in our genius for compartmentalization, conveniently overlook the *hatsnea' lekhet* which covers attitudes as well. A vivid example: across the spectrum of American Orthodoxy, things such as piety and materialism, mitsvah observance and consumerism, being *frum* and throwing ostentatious *semahot*, are not seen as contradictions. *Ruhniyut* and *gashmiyut* maintain a peaceful co-existence among us, but wherever this happens, *ruhniyut* always finishes second.

The idea of *mistapek be-mu'at*, of living without luxuries, is non-existent among us, a forgotten casualty of the times, and, save for an esoteric *musar shmuess* in a yeshiva, not even on the Jewish agenda. The very invitations which, amidst a flurry of thanks to God, caution the uninitiated to eschew immodest clothing, beckon us to participate in functions whose profligacy and waste fly in the teeth of Micah's call for restraint, modesty, and understatement. Self-indulgence, even among the *frum*, has been raised to unprecedented levels. (In this regard, see Keli Yaqar to Ex. 13:17: the quality of being satisfied with minimal needs was a prerequisite before Israel could receive the Torah at Sinai, as indicated in Avot VI:4: *Kakh darkah shel Torah....*)

Since even religion often mirrors the society around it, it is little wonder that much of Torah life has been brought down to the level of externals. It is not only that we are content to judge piety on the basis of the color of headgear, the material of *kippot*, the width of hat brims, or the length and color of men's jackets. Even our teaching of Torah is measured by surface standards. Students of Torah are considered to have "succeeded" when they know this or that Gemara and are expert in certain areas of halakhah. But the noblest internal possibilities of the Jew — *bitahon*, awe, humility, courage, loyalty, *hesed, ahavah* — are by and large not an integral part of the learning program — as if *middot* and general spiritual development will somehow take care of themselves. We seem content to stop at the basic level of Torah study and of mitsvah observance, neglecting to push onward to that most challenging and fulfilling of all plateaus in the life of Torah: the inwardness which results from the deep awareness of the author of Torah and mitsvot. Without Torah study and practice, one cannot reach the basic level. But these alone are not the criteria of the religious personality.

There may be good historical reasons for the phenomenon of a resurrection of Orthodoxy that has not been accompanied by a parallel resurrection of genuine piety. Objective observers of the American Jewish scene of fifty years ago knew that Orthodox Judaism was dead, a casualty of the looseness, hedonism and *laissez-faire* of America. A *shomer Shabbat* was a rarity; *taharat hamishpahah* or regular Torah study were curious exotica — especially away from the major cities. As a result, Orthodox rabbinic leadership (those who had not surrendered altogether) stressed the performance of traditional ritual as the minimal first step in a return to Judaism. But people somehow gained the impression that this was the only step. And now, having achieved a modicum of mitsvah observance over the years, we are experiencing difficulty in moving to higher levels. We have been concerned that Jewish men should don *tefillin* and observe Shabbat, but having achieved this, we seem unable to affect their behavior once they remove their *tefillin* and once Shabbat is over. *Mitsvat anashim melumadah*, soulless exercise in rote, is unfortunately not uncommon in contemporary American Orthodoxy. To our chagrin, it is not difficult to find Orthodox synagogues with appropriately high *mehitzot* whose congregants converse more with each other than with God. Somehow, observance has been viewed so narrowly that *bein adam lamakom* has come to mean action and not affect.

Fortunately, we are beginning to hear voices that stress concepts such as *hesed*, generosity of spirit, ethical and moral behavior, and the idea that a Shabbat meal whose main course consists of the denigration of others is not a holy meal. The emphasis on such things — it used to be called *musar* — represents the hope for an authentic Jewish future.

The Orthodox community has achieved a certain maturity. The qualifying "certain" is used advisedly. Full maturity implies self-confidence, serenity, a sense of self-worth and value. Orthodox internecine battles over exclusive turf-rights to piety or tolerance reflect an Orthodoxy still adolescent, unable to exercise civility and self-discipline.

What does it indicate when a worldly, sophisticated, observant Jew (a long time ago he was called "Modern Orthodox" and more recently "Centrist Orthodox") is much more understanding of the non-observing, secularized, bareheaded Jew on his so-called left than of the black-hatted, black-suited Jew on his right? Or when the Jew on the so-called right can find no better target for his vitriol than a fully observant Jew who happens to wear a *kippah serugah*? I am not certain what such hostility means. But one thing it surely does not mean: that *derakheha darkhei no'am* and *kol netivoteha shalom* are being taken seriously, or that *hatsnea' lekhet* applies to anything beyond the material. Certainly, debate on major issues is healthy. But debate which is shrill and *ad hominem* is a reflection neither of genuine piety nor of full maturity.

Orthodoxy in the last decade of the twentieth century in America has demonstrated its ability to touch the minds of its adherents through the emphasis on learning and absorbing the classic religious and intellectual texts. Similarly, it has shown that it can affect the daily behavior of its adherents, as demonstrated in the upsurge of *mitsvot ma'asiot*. But if Orthodoxy is not to harden into a wall of self-congratulation, we must mount a serious assault on the most difficult barricade of all: the character of our people and the nature of our piety, and — if I may be innovative — our awareness of God. Otherwise we will become secular Jews with yarmulkes, de-religionized observant Jews, vacuous embodiments of the *naval bi-reshut ha-Torah* about which Nahmanides warns in Lev. 19:2.

Only if we move beyond our present condition can we speak of providing a serious alternative to the rest of the Jewish world which, in its heart of hearts, bears an inchoate yearning for the transcendental voice of Judaism, but has understandable difficulty hearing it amidst the cacophony which today passes for Orthodox Jewish life — Right, Left, or Center.

A Helicopter Crashes

When there comes a time of affliction, the community must cry out [to God]... and everyone must realize that because of their own misdeeds has this befallen them.... [This] will cause such afflictions to be removed....

But if they do not cry out, but say that what happened to us was simply an ordinary accident, this is the way of callousness; it convinces them to hold fast to their wrongful ways, and leads to further affliction. (MISHNEH TORAH, LAWS OF FASTING 1:2)

THESE WORDS OF MAIMONIDES KEEP throbbing in my mind. Seventy-three young Israeli lives have been snuffed out, seventy-three bodies have been laid to rest. We, the living, mourn, weep, and wonder.

The commission of inquiry will inquire. It will determine that the accident was caused by mechanical failure, or human error, or fatigue, or vertigo. It will make recommendations about changes in procedure, about improving equipment.

The report will be greeted with pain and anguish. There may be resignations, there will certainly be adjustments in flight plans, and there will be debates about Lebanon. But our lives — though not the seventy-three families' lives — will probably go on as before. Accidents, after all, do happen.

On the physical level, commissions of inquiry are relatively easy to convene. Gather respected experts, people whose integrity is beyond reproach, and let them ask the questions, arrive at the conclusions, make the recommendations.

But there is a different kind of commission of inquiry — a personal, spiritual one. This kind of inquiry is much more difficult, but it is no less necessary. For in the spiritual realm we are all fully interconnected, as human beings and as Jews.

"Every man's death diminishes me," said John Donne, "for I am part of mankind." He continues with the words that have become famous: "Ask not for whom the bell tolls/ It tolls for thee."

In our personal, spiritual commission of inquiry, each individual becomes his or her own expert who must conduct a thorough investigation based on honesty and integrity.

Here the questions are far more painful:

If there is an invisible thread connecting my actions with my land, my fellow Jews, and my God, should not something now change in my life as a result of this tragedy? Can my spiritual flight path remain the same?

My goals and the means of achieving them — perhaps these need reevaluating. Perhaps there has been human error in my relationship with my fellow human beings and in my connectedness with my people that requires readjusting.

If I consider myself secular, perhaps I should begin reevaluating my relationship to my heritage. Am I more influenced by the ways of the West than by my own millennial tradition?

If I consider myself religious, does my everyday behavior sanctify the name of God or profane it? Is my service of my Creator full-hearted? And what about my relationship to other Jews? Is it filled with understanding and kindness, or with hostility and contempt?

And if I am neither secular nor religious, not sure who I really am as a Jew, perhaps I could begin thinking seriously about such things.

I am not suggesting that any group blame or accuse any other; only that we look inward, at ourselves.

We keep hearing that the seventy-three shall not have died in vain. In the religious sense, their deaths can have eternal meaning if they become the catalyst for spiritual inquiry.

No one can claim entrée to the mind of God; no one can claim to know why such tragedies occur. But one fact is clear: Life cannot, ought not, to go on as before. We need to ask honest questions of ourselves, and arrive at honest answers.

Maimonides suggests that it would be callous to ignore such events, continuing, once the shock wears off, as if nothing had happened. Dare we be callous after such a tragedy?

One of the boys who died bore my Hebrew name, Menahem Feldman, a fact that continues to burn in my soul. Each of those young men gave his life for all our sakes. Each bears the name of each one of us. This knowledge must surely lead us to better our ways.

Dailyness and the Daily *Ness*

Although this was written right after the Gulf War, the discussion of open and hidden miracles is not limited to that moment in time.

THE INTERVENING MONTHS SINCE THE Gulf War provide a good perspective from which to view the strong God-consciousness, which enveloped Israel during those heady days. People spoke fervently of the Messiah's imminent arrival: of *gimatriot* which equated the numerical equivalent of "Patriot" (314) with that of God's name on the *mezuzah*, which, of course, is an acronym for "*Shomer Delatot Yisroel,* (Protector of the Doorways of Israel)," and other numerical gymnastics which equated Saddam Hussein with Haman or Amalek; of miracles associated with the surprisingly minor damage inflicted by the Scud missiles. Although we had a mixture of the serious and the silly, overall it seemed to be a positive religious development.

Yet I must confess that I was not fully at ease with every aspect of it.

Granted, a crisis should be a catalyst for a return to religious essentials. God occasionally taps us on the collective shoulder to remind us that He and not we are in charge, that there is a One above us Who controls our destiny. This is an authentically Jewish idea. There is nothing like trouble, personal or national, to concentrate — and consecrate — the mind. Sometimes, it is only *mi-ma'amakim* that one hears the clearest *keratikha haShem* (see Ps. 130).

But have we in fact witnessed a return to essentials?

Some of the reactions to the missile attacks on Israel, it seems to me, were a bit demeaning: they tended to reduce *emunah*, which is exalted, personal, and deeply serious, into something simple, glib, public, superficial. The self-assured certainty about God's plans; the daily sightings of the Messiah: the incessant trumpeting of the government's use of the term *ness* or Haim Herzog's use of the term *hashgahah* were so overblown that they threatened to trivialize Jewish belief and to transform profound matters into a shallow pseudo-piety. The essence of belief is *tseniut*, reticence, shyness, modesty; but the *lo bara'ash HaShem* of I Kings 19:11 seems to have been forgotten. It is not in the stormwind or in the raucous or in the shrill, but in the *kol demamah dakah*, the thin voice of silence, that true faith is to be found. The tablets given in silence which were accompanied by thunder and lightning were shattered; those given in silence were eternal (Cf. Rashi on Exodus 34:2 *"ein lekha yafeh min ha-tseniut."*)

An even deeper unease stems from my fear that the recognition of God's hand may once again fall short of a genuine return to Jewish religious consciousness. Messianic awareness and the recounting of Scud stories are perhaps helpful starting points, but no more than that. Genuine return — what we mean by *teshuvah* — is manifested not only on the surface of being, but primarily in the re-thinking of personal priorities, renewed study of Torah, intensified prayer, *hesed*, and serious mitsvah performance.

In the recent past , we have all experienced God's hidden acts. The sudden downfall of Communism, the influx of Russian and Ethiopian Jews to Israel, the hardening of Saddam's heart and the subsequent destruction of Iraq's military capabilities in a war whose victory came on Purim — these are heady, breathtaking things, clearly not in the natural course of events.

Such events cry out not merely for shouts of *ness*, but for profound inner reassessment. The purpose of miracles, after all, is not to demonstrate the heavenly capacity for pyrotechnics, but to encourage the human capacity for change. When God knocks on the door — *kol dodi dofek* — we are expected to respond. It is insufficient to marvel at the sound of the knock and then simply offer praise and thanksgiving. We need to approach the door and open it. We are called upon to look beyond surface things, and to seek out the hiding God Who wants us to focus not merely on the miracles but on their Author.

Specifically, a response to the knock involves a realization that God is always present, not only during Scud attacks. Three times each day we declare our gratitude for "Your miracles, which are with us every day, and for Your wonders and goodness of every moment, evening, morning, and noonday...." Because we all become inured to the miraculous and hardened to the wondrous, we utter prayers, which are designed to penetrate our hard outer shell and make us aware daily of God's presence and His miracles. Daily — not only in times of crisis. (Nahmanides on Exodus 13:16 states that "... from the great and famous miracles a person acknowledges the hidden miracles, which are the foundation of the entire Torah...") A good beginning in the process of responding to God's presence would be to seek out not only that aspect of God which functions in the arenas of crisis, but also to seek Him in arenas of dailyness (daily *ness*) and to look for the miracles of the mundane. The rare dramatic miracle, after all, is only prologue to the daily ones.

In Sanhedrin 93a, the religious leaders of the time of Hannania, Mishael and Azaria were humiliated because the nations said to them, "If you have such a God, why do you worship idols?" They had not responded properly to miracles.

We believe with perfect faith that God performs miracles at every moment, evening, morning, and noon. We do not believe that He is visible only in times of crisis and danger. And we know, with Judah Halevi and others, that Judaism, unlike other faiths, is not based on miracles. (See also Rambam, *Yesodei HaTorah*, 8:1) But when dramatic incursions of God into history do take place, it is imperative to react in authentically Jewish ways.

God is the constant protector of our doors, our homes, and our Land. Every day, not only in crisis.

God exists; He does not require unceasing anecdotal evidence of His presence. The issue is not whether Messiah is or is not around the corner. The issue is whether we are ready and prepared to encounter the One Who sends the Messiah.

A Death in Jerusalem: The Real World

IT WAS PROBABLY THE SINGLE largest assemblage of Jews in Jerusalem since the destruction of the Second Temple nineteen centuries ago.

Even in a city accustomed to extraordinary events it was remarkable; over three hundred thousand people gathered for a funeral — not of a head of state or a famous public figure. They had come to honor the life of Rav Shelomo Zalman Auerbach, who was universally recognized as one of the premier *poskim* of this generation, and who had just died at the age of eighty-five.

For almost two hours they stood silently in the streets and lanes around his home, weeping as they listened over loudspeakers to the eulogies, after which they followed the bier on foot in a three-hour procession to the cemetery. The sight was staggering. Every inch of every street and byway in central Jerusalem was tightly packed with men, women, and children: broad-brimmed black hats and long black coats; white shirts and *kipot serugot*; Sephardim, Ashkenazim, Hasidim, and what seemed like every single student of every yeshiva in Israel — and even many who had apparently never worn a *kipah* on their heads. Balconies were crammed; young boys gazed down from rooftops; traffic was at a standstill for hours; helicopters hovered overhead; police stood at attention at every intersection. One could not help wondering: when a Supreme

Court Justice dies, venerated as he may be, do hundreds of thousands of ordinary people flock to his funeral? When a renowned and popular university teacher dies, do throngs of students weep? Even the state funerals of David Ben-Gurion, Golda Meir, and Menachem Begin did not bring forth nearly such multitudes.

Here was a man who shunned all publicity, had no official titles, never granted media interviews, had no PR office, issued no bulletins or journals, assiduously discouraged any view of himself that might tend to ascribe anything but ordinary human abilities to him, was not even mentioned in Jewish encyclopedias, and had never left the borders of the Holy Land — and yet the myriads of religious Jews around the world felt so intimately connected to him that hundreds of thousands spontaneously flocked to pay him a last tribute on just a few hours' notice.

Clearly, it was more than prodigious scholarship that was being honored here; it was what lay beyond that learning. The people were responding to qualities which have grown increasingly rare; genuineness, wholeness, straightforwardness, impeccable integrity — what our tradition calls an *ish emet*. What touched them was the awareness that not only were his halakhic rulings avidly sought out and followed by believing Jews, but that this quiet, self-effacing man was the embodiment of this *emet*.

That the multitudes identified with an *ish emet* was tribute not only to the man; it was a tribute to the people themselves who, in an age of non-*emet*, demonstrated that the instinctive yearning for this ideal is still inextinquished. And for those who know that one can determine the character of a nation by determining who are the heroes of that nation, and who felt a certain foreboding when fifty thousand young Israelis recently packed a Tel-Aviv park in adulation of Madonna, the fact that more than five times that many paid homage to a rabbinic sage was a healthful restorative.

Born and living all his life in Jerusalem's old and evocative Shaarei Hesed quarter, he took seriously his studies and his responsibilities — but not himself. In an era of faceless bureaucracies, swollen staffs, and self-important officials in chauffeured limousines (one of whom, on trial a few blocks away for inflating his travel and living expenses, claimed as part of his defense that as head of a government agency he was entitled to treatment like a head of state), he, like all great Torah personalities, shunned the pomp and ceremony that adheres to famous men.

It was incongruous — and delicious — to contemplate that this unpretentious man and this aging structure with its unheated and sparsely furnished rooms constituted the veritable nerve-center of halakhah in the modern world.

In him there existed a remarkable fusion of the rigorous intellectual discipline of the *talmid hakham* and the fatherly love for his people. The emotional outpouring of respect and affection for him was an echo of his respect and affection for each of them.

For it was not only halakhah that occupied his days. It was the people to whom it applied. They were instinctively drawn to a man whose primary goal was to understand God's will as reflected in the Torah, whose life was free from the dross of politics, power, and material ambition, who had no personal agenda, who was open and accepting of various points of view within the halakhic framework, and who gave them warmth and attention while asking nothing in return. He was wise and witty, possessed of an incisive mind and an unerring insight into people. Both world-class scholars and ordinary *amkha* felt that few if any were better equipped to guide them both on arcane halakhic matters and on the mundane issues which beset every human being. Inundated with inquiries from everywhere, he was nevertheless accessible to anyone who knocked at his door and needed face-to-face counsel or comfort.

He was, in a word, the embodiment of Torah: majestic yet simple, transcendent yet worldly, old yet profoundly new, rigorous yet compassionate, multi-faceted yet natural and artless. Whatever advice he would offer was inevitably refined through the purifying filter of his learning, piety, love, and halakhic discipline.

They saw in him the ideal of the true *gadol* — one who looms large not only in his learning and his scholarship, but also in his relationship to God, to others, and to the history and destiny of the Jewish people. Perhaps through him they heard resonating the echo of the echo, the *bat kol,* of the will of the Torah and of God Himself. Therefore they sought him out in his life, and therefore they mourned him in their masses in his death.

For this is the definition of a *gadol* and a *posek* — those overtaxed terms — in Judaism. A *gadol* is not elected or appointed; he *becomes.* By virtue of his transcending knowledge, understanding, and sensitivity to God, Torah, and the Jewish people, *klal Yisrael* instinctively responds to this resonating echo within him. He is not a prophet, does not possess *ruah hakodesh,* and is not an other-wordly figure; but he must possess the mind and the heart to carry within his being the Torah of God, and through its teachings to guide the present generation into the future. In every generation such individuals rise to the top, not by virtue of popular acclaim, but because of the sum of all of these qualities. The process is subtle and unstructured, but somehow uncannily accurate. There is no lobbying for specific candidates, no balloting, no headlines, and no white smoke wafting up from the chimneys. Gradually, through a natural process of winnowing and sifting over many years, certain men vault to halakhic and spiritual greatness because their lives are a metaphor for Torah.

Rav Auerbach lived a plain and spartan life, and this is how he wanted his funeral to be conducted. There was no parade of dignitaries, no polished eulogies. The funeral took place not in a synagogue or a mortuary, but out on the front porch of the same apartment in which he had lived for over sixty years.

The most moving aspect of the funeral was the public reading of his last will. In it, Rav Shelomo Zalman requested that, if any words were spoken at his funeral, they be delivered by two of his seven sons (he also had three daughters), that they be brief "in order not to burden those who may be present," and that the speakers endeavor to awaken the religious and spiritual impulses of those in attendance. He emphatically requested that they refrain from words of praise. "I have been greatly pained by such exaggerations during my lifetime, and I request that I be spared them at my departure," he wrote. He added: "I hereby forgive anyone for any offenses committed against me, and I ask anyone who feels that I have deliberately or inadvertently offended him to do *hesed* with me and to forgive me...." And he requested that his tombstone should say nothing more than that he taught Torah at Yeshivat Kol Torah in Jerusalem.

"He lived in the real world," sobbed one of his sons during his eulogy. "The real world is not what we see before us. The real world is the world of holy living, of dedication to God and fellow human beings. The real world, the only world, is the world of Torah." It was too glorious a February day for a funeral. Birds were chirping, the skies were vintage Jerusalem blue, the air was crisp, the winds gentle and sweet, the winding, hilly streets and their buildings of Jerusalem stone shimmered in the noonday sun, the trees lining the lovely old neighborhood were beginning to show their pale green buds. A more appropriate setting would have been the howling winds and drenching rains not uncommon to Jerusalem winters.

But when one considered that hundreds of thousands of Jews had this day caught a glimpse of eternity — in which time itself came to a stop, and terrorists and negotiations and realpolitik ceased to exist — perhaps the glistening skies and the flowering buds were a suitable backdrop for what was, when all is said and done, a fleeting glimpse of the real world.

PART TWO

Living in Jerusalem

Yaakov and Jay:
A Tale of Two Worlds

TWO INVITATIONS ARE IN MY Jerusalem mailbox today, one for Jay's Bar Mitsvah in New York, and one for Yaakov's Bar Mitsvah in Jerusalem.

Jay's invitation is on expensive blue and gold paper, with embossed cover, engraved letters, lined envelopes within lined envelopes, specially chosen postage stamps, all elegantly addressed in professional calligraphy.

Yaakov's invitation is on thin white paper, printed simply in ordinary black and white. It bears no postage stamps; in order to save money, it was hand-delivered to my mailbox, probably by Yaakov himself.

In New York, there will be a Temple service and a dinner-dance the following evening at one of the posh Manhattan hotels.

In Jerusalem there will be a pre-Bar Mitsvah reception in a small room in one of the neighborhood synagogues, at which Yaakov will deliver a complex *pilpul* on the laws of *tefillin*. His *aliyah* to the Torah will take place at the regular minyan on a Monday morning.

Jay in New York attends an exclusive, non-demoninational private high school, with special programs in art, music, science, mathematics. He is very bright, and excels in them all. There are opportunities for extra curricular activities: drama, science, and computer clubs; hiking, track and field, a rich program of intramural and interscholastic sports. Jay can barely read Hebrew, but having been tutored by an expensive private teacher, he will recite his two *berakhot* flawlessly.

Yaakov in Jerusalem attends a small yeshiva. On very cold days, the rooms are inadequately warmed with little heaters, and the children wear coats and scarves indoors. The classrooms are crowded, teachers have no formal degrees in education, and there are no extra-curricular actitivities. Yaakov is studying Talmud, has completed *Bava Kama* and knows it well. He also knows all of Humash and Rashi and much of Nahmanides on the Torah.

By the time Jay is eighteen, he will have forgotten his Bar Mitsvah Hebrew, but having graduated near the top of his class, he will be gladly accepted by Harvard University, where he will encounter some of the brightest secular minds in the world, and where he will fulfill the ambition of his parents for him to become a physician.

By the time Yaakov is eighteen, he will be very skilled in Talmudic dialectic, having then completed *Bava Metsia, Bava Batra, Gittin* and *Kiddushin*. He will have committed to memory much of Mishnayot, and will be very knowledgeable in Shulkhan Arukh. He will be at the top of his class, and will be gladly accepted by Ponevezh Yeshiva, where he will encounter some of the brightest Talmudic minds in the world, and where he will fulfill the ambition of his parents for him to become a *talmid hakham*.

When Jay enters medical school at age twenty-two, he will become engaged to a non-Jewish girl. His parents, both Jewish, will be unhappy that he is marrying out of the faith, but they will be willing to pay the price, especially since Jay has always been such a good boy. The young lady, an honest and believing Christian will refuse to undergo the pro-forma conversion to Judaism, but will consent to have a Reform rabbi co-officiate with her minister at the wedding.

Yaakov and Jay: A Tale of Two Worlds

Yaakov, an acknowledged scholar at age twenty-two, will marry a young lady who has had intensive training in Jewish seminaries, and whose great ideal is to have a genuine Talmud authority as a husband. He will enter a kollel, his wife will work part-time as a kindergartener, and they will manage to live on a monthly income of $600.

Jay will become a physician, and by the time he is thirty-three will have two children, will be earning $300,000 a year, and will heal many people. At forty-three, in addition to owning a splendid practice, he will teach part-time at the local medical school, write for medical journals, and will be a recognized expert in his field. His busy schedule will not permit him to become involved in the Jewish community, but he will sense in himself certain inchoate yearnings for Judaism. He will give generously to the annual UJA appeal, will thrill to the triumphs of the State of Israel, and will support organizations, which fight anti-Semitism. He will spend Yom Kippur day in Temple, recite Yizkor for his deceased mother, listen carefully to the rabbi's sermon, but will wonder why the rabbi deals more with political than with religious issues. From time to time, he will read a Jewish book or attend a lecture on a Jewish theme, but will find in them no great satisfaction. His children will not be raised as Jews, Jay having reluctantly agreed to leave such matters to his wife. His family will observe the annual Pesach seder with Jay's father, and this will deepen Jay's curiosity about his Jewish roots. He will be a proud member of the local country club, which rarely admits Jews, but instead of playing golf on his afternoons off, he will volunteer his services at the local clinic for the indigent, where he will be loved by his patients because of his genuine concern for them. His annual income will be over $500,000 by now, and he will own a three-acre mansion, plus a vacation home by the sea. His children will attend exclusive, non-denominational private schools. His father, though wishing he had Jewish grandchildren, will be very proud of his son.

By the time he is thirty-three, Yaakov will be the father of seven children, and he will barely make ends meet. By forty-three, he will have completed the entire Talmud and Codes several times, and will be teaching in a major yeshiva. He will have many disciples who will admire him for his perception, insight, and his genuine concern for their welfare, and he will give them much time beyond the classroom. Members of the community will consult him about their personal and halakhic problems, and he will be a sought-after teacher of Torah. Although he will think a great deal about the world beyond Jerusalem, he will never leave the borders of Israel. He will sense in himself certain inchoate yearnings for contact with Jews outside his own circle, particularly non-religious Jews. He will be disturbed by the deep abyss which separates the religious and the secular Jewish worlds, will often wonder if he ought to make some efforts to close the gap, but the demands of his own learning and teaching will be so all-consuming that he will have no meaningful discourse with any Jews beyond the immediate world. His annual income will be $12,000. His sons will attend a small yeshiva, poorly heated; his daughters, a girls' yeshiva, very drafty. His father will be very proud of his son, and will take great pleasure in studying Torah with his grandchildren.

At fifty-three, Jay will attend a medical conference in Jerusalem, his first visit to Israel. He will be stirred by the living Jewish state and by the sounds of Hebrew, and will be unnerved by the sight of so many Jews who seem to be so passionately religious. He will be put off by their strange black suits and hats, so evocative of an age that he thought had long ago ceased to exist, but though he will feel like an alien among them, he will be drawn to them and will long for some genuine contact with them.

At fifty-three, Yaakov, now a recognized *posek*, will be a featured panelist at the same medical conference, and will deliver a talk on medical issues in the halakhah. He will be unnerved by the sight of so many Jewish physicians who seem open and curious about Judaism and yet are so unaware of the basic rudiments of Jewish faith and practice. He will be put off by their strange, garish clothes, so evocative of the values of the West, but though he will feel like an alien among them, he will be drawn to them and will long for some genuine contact with them.

In the lobby of the conference hall, the physician and the Rosh Yeshiva will walk out of the same door at the same time. They will nod perfunctorily to one another, and for a fleeting moment their eyes will meet.

As his plane takes off from Tel Aviv, Jay will gaze at the cities and the hills and the sand and the sea. He will think about the pious Jews of Jerusalem; and he will reflect on how it has developed that a Jew can feel so estranged from other Jews in the land of the Jews.

As Yaakov sits on the bus returning him to his yeshiva, he will gaze lovingly at the stone buildings of Jerusalem as they glow in the strange yellow light of the late afternoon. He will think about the physicians he has just seen, and he will reflect on how it has developed that a Jew can feel so estranged from other Jews in the land of the Jews.

A Bar-Mitsvah and a Funeral

ONE WAS A BAR MITSVAH in the morning; the other was a funeral in the afternoon. They occurred on the same day here in Jerusalem, and I was present at each of them. The Bar Mitsvah took place at the *kotel hamaaravi*. The funeral took place on an ordinary Jerusalem street, in front of a synagogue. But something beyond the obvious contrasts of life and death made the one event depressing, and the other uplifting.

As everyone knows, on Monday, Thursday, or Rosh Hodesh mornings, a large number of Bar Mitsvahs, most of them from the Diaspora, can be held simultaneously at any given moment in the huge plaza before the Wall. On a good morning, some thirty Bar Mitsvahs can be processed.

Unfortunately, a Bar Mitsvah at the *kotel* is not always a religious moment. That which should be profound, memorable, and filled with awe is often lost in a maze of chaos. Theoretically, the religious administration of the Wall assigns each family a specific table, at a specific time, at a specific location in the huge plaza. This is to serve as their "synagogue." But in practice, the tables are often appropriated by other Bar Mitsvah families who happen to arrive first and — in the absence of anyone in charge — simply take over the first empty spot.

On the particular morning that I attended, the table reserved for our group had already been commandeered by a young, full-bearded Israeli who informed us that he was holding it for a "Bar Mitsvah from Texas." For a fee, such individuals will handle every detail of a *kotel* Bar Mitsvah, and will even supply Torah readers, *baalei tefillah,* and arrange for a post-Bar Mitsvah breakfast at a nearby hotel. (You have to supply your own Bar Mitsvah boy.)

But the real problems began after we secured a table of our own. Because of the davening taking place at the adjoining synagogue one yard away, we were hard-pressed to follow our own. Melodies and pronunciations and *nuschaot* from around the world vied for our attention; *borekhu, kaddish,* repetition of the *amidah* and Torah reading reverberated from all directions; jostling photographers, anxious to record the memories for the neighbors back in Texas, compounded the cacophony with prowling videos and clicking cameras. (Bar Mitsvahs from America have been known to take place without tefillin, but never without cameras.) *Kavannah* was difficult. Somehow, the Bar Mitsvah boy recited his *berakhot,* the hastily mumbled prayers ended — mercifully — the pictures were taken, and the group went off to its festive breakfast and more pictures. Looming in front of it all almost forgotten in this ingathering of the tourists was the Wall itself, stark, silent, massive, brooding.

The impact of all this babel on the thirteen-year-old himself can only be imagined. For over a year now, he had been looking forward to his Bar Mitsvah at the last earthly vestige of the ancient Holy Temple, but when the big day finally arrived the experience was hardly spiritual. The innocent boy and his family meant well, but they were caught up in a confusion over which they had no control. One can only hope that years later, when the young man looks back at his *kotel* Bar Mitsvah, the memories will not be entirely negative. Perhaps time will dissipate the trivialization of his day. But I wondered if such disarray is found, at the Taj Mahal, or at the Arab holy places such as Mecca and Medina. Do they worship this way in the holiest areas of the Vatican? And Isaiah's acid *mi bikesh zot miyedchem,* "Who asks this of you — to trespass in my precincts," kept crossing my mind. I left the Wall that morning not at all uplifted; depressed would be more accurate.

That very afternoon, my depression evaporated and my spirits were lifted — at a funeral.

In my Jerusalem neighborhood, many of the funerals take place out on the sidewalk in front of the Shul. I was walking down the street when such a funeral was just beginning. Together with many of my neighbors, I stopped to take part in the mitsvah of *halvayat hamet.* The deceased had just been brought by the *chevra kadisha* van to the Shul sidewalk, where family and friends had already gathered. Several simple but genuine eulogies were given, *tehillim* were chanted, the rending of the mourners' garments took place, kaddish was recited. Traffic ground to a halt, buses and taxis waited, neighbors stood respectfully at their windows and porches. Except for the sound of weeping, all was silent and still.

After the service, the van moved slowly down the main street, all of us following on foot. When the cortege passed a synagogue or a yeshiva, the van paused and the mourners once again recited the *kaddish.* Three or four such stops took place. The crowd of about one hundred followed silently for several blocks until the van drove off and the people slowly and quietly dispersed.

As a newcomer to the neighborhood, I did not know who had died, but the honesty and simplicity of the moment affected me. I had the unmistakable sense that I was participating in something authentic, and that this is how mitsvot were meant to be observed: everything was genuine, unvarnished, plain, honest; nothing was out of joint, or phony, or pretentious, or tasteless. The eulogies were simple and plain; the compassion and concern were true and right; the *chevra kadisha* people were obviously pious and learned Jews who performed their duties with dignity. Nothing was on display, nothing was said or done to impress. Even the *chevra kadisha* van was modest and unassuming, unlike the great black hearses which are endemic to so many American funerals. And although I was a total stranger, I did not find it strange at all that tears welled up in my eyes as the van gradually disappeared over the next hill.

Two significant events in the life of a Jew: joy and sadness, life and death, beginnings and ends. One event was off-key and dissonant, while the other struck a true, unerring note. At the holy city's holiest site, a joyous passage into Jewish life was deflated in a mishmash of perfunctory, soulless prayer in which the letter of halakhah was observed but the spirit lost by the intrusion of inauthentic concepts of celebration — and it was depressing. On an ordinary Jerusalem street, a melancholy passage out of life was ennobled by careful adherence to the letter and spirit of the halakhah, and exclusion of inauthentic concepts of mourning — and it was uplifting.

Redeployment & Hare Krishna: Re-engineering the Jewish State

IN RECENT YEARS, ISRAEL HAS redeployed its troops from the Sinai, the Jordan Valley, Lebanon, and — if Assad had been willing to accept our gift — the Golan. (At this writing, Arafat, following Assad's model, has refused to accept Israeli gifts of almost 90% of Judea and Samaria, plus a very generous arrangement over Jerusalem — but we are imploring him to accept our largesse.). Since redeployment, after all, is just another name for retreat, historians will ponder how it came to pass that a strong and intelligent people came begging to its sworn enemies to accept from it land, arms and prestige.

In the beginning, the retreat was a spiritual one: first came secular Zionism's withdrawal from faith in Jewish history and Jewish destiny, from the idea of a unique Jewish peoplehood with a special mission in the world — a mission in which the Land was a major component. Once the spiritual retreat took place, the territorial retreat could not be far behind.

There are many facets to today's physical and spiritual redeployment. The Israeli Supreme Court is a paradigm of Israel's de-Judaization, and offers an insight into the moral and intellectual malaise that affects secular Israeli life today. Legislative and executive bodies come and go, but the impact of Supreme Courts affects the future in ways more lasting than any other branch of government.

Let the obvious be stated: in the scale of important benchmarks of the Israeli Supreme Court, Judaism as a religion, or even the Jewish character of the state, does not hold pride of place. That place is held by "universal democratic values," and wherever such values conflict with Judaic values, it is the latter which must give way. True, this per se does not make Chief Justice Aharon Barak or his court "anti religious," but the overall judicial trend in the court and the legal philosophy of its hyper-active Chief Justice is expressed in his well-known formulation of his judicial philosophy: "the values of the state of Israel are those universal values common to members of democratic society."

Where, one might ask, does the term "Jewish" fit into this schema for the state of Israel? Barak has written that the phrase "Jewish state" should be "given meaning on a high level of abstraction... a level so high that it becomes identical to the democratic nature of the state."

Once the rhetorical fog is pierced, this says that Justice Barak's ideal Jewish democratic state is emptied of anything specifically Jewish, and that its Jewish component is only of value to the extent that it is fully harmonious with, and identical to, "democratic." Plainly stated, the classical and unique Jewish character of the state is of little concern. What is of concern are those values that are common to democracies like the USA, Canada, and England. To be sure, democracies have historically been protective of Jews, and for this, Jews are eternally grateful. But they are not Jewish states. In Justice Barak's view, apparently, Israel need be no more Jewish than the USA, Canada, or England. (For a more detailed discussion, see chapter two of Yoram Hazony's valuable new book, *The Jewish State: The Struggle for Israel's Soul*, which provides the overall historical background for modern Israel's loss of backbone.)

In order to appreciate the fear and trembling with which the traditional religious community views this Court, take this theoretical view of Israel and mix it with Justice Barak's statements about the need to "socially re-engineer" Israeli society. One does not require divine inspiration to predict the direction in which he would like to re-engineer this society (not to mention that the proper role for the judiciary is to dispense justice and not to set out to re-engineer anything).

This is particularly troublesome because in Israel the Chief Justice possesses unusual powers, more so than in the U.S. Supreme Court. Appointments to the Israeli Supreme Court are not made with the advice and consent of the other branches of government. Justices are appointed by a committee dominated by the Court itself. In effect, the Chief Justice appoints those who serve on the Court, with no checks and balances that might affect his choices. Thus we have the following volatile brew: a self perpetuating system; a Court for whom universal democratic values take precedence over Jewish values; a highly activist Court that knows not the meaning of restraint or discretion, and that has taken upon itself the role of shaping the future character of the state.

In sum, this Court considers itself to be the final arbiter of all aspects of Israel — legal, moral, religious, cultural. Its power and self-asserted authority go far beyond that of high courts in the USA or in Europe. It is not only a judiciary; it has also arrogated unto itself the role of a legislature, casting its shadow over every corner of Israeli life.

It is in light of this that one should view the monotonous consistency with which the Court strikes down regulations and rulings designed to maintain the unique Jewish character of the state. Thus the Court, instead of doing what courts should do — attempt to heal the divisions that rend the fabric of society — has become a polarizing influence that rends that fabric even more. And it is against this background that one should view the mass gathering in Jerusalem last year of some 250,000 Orthodox Israelis who protested the Court's rulings. Its purpose was not — despite the railings of the establishment media — to intimidate the Court; rather, it was a *cri de coeur* of a polarized minority whose Jewish sensibilities are regularly ignored by the Court. In the hands of this Court, it was felt, the scales of justice are not balanced, and subjective opinions too often take the place of reasoned legal briefs.

This is not just theory; it has practical implications. Because Jewish ideals take second place to other ideals, a pattern of skewed decisions has emerged in the recent past.

Thus the court has found against the recommendation of the Prison Service and of former President Weizmann to shorten the sentence of Yoram Skolnick, a Jew convicted of murdering an Arab, but has deemed it acceptable to release Arab murderers as part of Israel's democratic obligations under Oslo.

Thus it is legal for teenage homosexuals to be featured on Israeli Educational TV, but it rejects a petition to court-martial a soldier who had delayed entering a firefight because he was ideologically opposed to our presence in Lebanon.

Thus the Jewish Agency was enjoined from using Jewish funds raised worldwide to build exclusively Jewish communities; but in its recent Rehovot ruling, the same Court bucked the Rehovot City Council, the Interior Ministry, and the Attorney General, and created new rules which effectively bar religious Jews from constructing communal buildings beyond their established neighborhoods.

No one was surprised when the Court forced the government to allow the importation of non-kosher meat, something that had always been prohibited by administrative regulation, or when it required rabbis, when dividing property in divorce settlements, to be guided by secular rather than Jewish law.

Further, it was a foregone conclusion that the Court would force area religious councils to seat non-Orthodox members. (That it is ludicrous for non-Orthodox individuals, whose ideological movements are lax about *kashrut* or do not practice *mikveh*, to oversee *kashrut* and *mikvaot* among other communal *mitsvot* did not impress the Court in its relentless drive toward democratic principles; nor did it violate their sacrosanct ideal of "reasonableness.")

And it was obvious that the Court would find it illegal for Jews to pray on the Temple Mount, while permitting women to pray at the Western Wall in a manner unbefitting the traditions of that Wall. (The mere fact that a secular court would involve itself in matters with which it is wholly unfamiliar — such as prayer or the sanctity of the Wall — is itself indicative of its reach for power into areas foreign to its domain.)

Lovely legal packaging wraps each of these decisions in neat designs of juridical logic, but a clear pattern emerges: The "enlightened community's" values invariably override Jewish values — which, in the eyes of the Court, are obviously unenlightened and benighted. Even on matters not involving religion but involving national interests has the Court ruled against the State. For example, certain interrogative methods used by Israel's security forces against terrorists have, predictably, been banned. And Prime Minister Sharon was effectively barred from using his son as a personal emissary to Arafat.

One shudders to think how the Court might rule if some of the current trial balloons being lofted by Israeli secularists — to re-evaluate the Law of Return, or to de-Israelize the flag and *Hatikva* — ever lands on their docket. One can only pray that groups like Hare Krishna or Jews for Jesus will never petition the Court to hold religious services at the Wall. Who can know what the decision will be? The Supreme Court, after all, shares the same secular mindset that sees no problem in an army code of conduct denuded of any reference of loyalty to the Jewish people, Jewish history, or Jewish destiny; and that is quite content with the new textbooks in the nation's schools that "demythologize" the valor and bravery of Israel in its wars against the Arabs. Such a mindset can hardly refuse, in its avid pursuit of humanistic values, to give Jews for Jesus a place of honor at the *Kotel haMa'aravi*.

The ultimate danger to the future of Israel, with fearful ramifications for the Jewish people worldwide, is not the establishment of a Palestinian state, nor the danger posed by the Palestinian 40,000 man "police force," (up from the 7,000 of the Oslo accord), nor the hostility of Israel's peace partners. The ultimate danger, exemplified by its Supreme Court, is the secular rush to abandon Jewish uniqueness, the drive to become *kekhol haGoyim*, "like all the nations."

Whether the Court is or is not anti-religious is not the issue. The real issue is the Court's conscious redeployment from classical Jewishness of any kind. It is this that can lead to the re-engineering of an Israel that everyone will rue.

Violence in Littleton and Jerusalem

THE COLUMBINE HIGH SCHOOL TRAGEDY in Littleton, Colorado will not soon be forgotten by Americans, and Israelis will not soon forget the recent moment when two Israeli teenagers were stabbed to death by other teenagers, and when a gang rumble between some 50 sixth and eighth-graders was narrowly averted.

This is only the tip of the iceberg. Out of 28 countries in a recent study on bullying in schools, Israel ranked worse than Belgium, Switzerland, Austria, France, the USA, Finland, Greece, England, and Slovakia. The head of the Juvenile Department of Israeli police reports that violent crime among Israeli school children has more than doubled in the past five years, and that the level of violence has also intensified.

What are the causes of youth violence? Reacting to the study, The *Jerusalem Post* devoted a full section to the subject under the banner, "Whose fault is it? Maybe yours."

Among the experts interviewed was the chairman of the Behavorial Sciences Department of Israel's Jezreel Valley College, who stated, "Children arrive at pre-school without self-discipline or the ability to control themselves." The key, he claims, is to teach children that there are limits and boundaries. A child has to be made aware from the most tender age that certain things are permitted and others forbidden, to understand restraint and self-control. The professor suggests that when the child wants to watch TV instead of doing homework, the parents have to stand their ground. Further, he advises that "parents have to make sure their kids go to bed on time," and not allow their children to flout the rules.

A second expert was a famous Israeli intellectual, a professor of philosophy at Hebrew University. For him, the reason for youth violence is the switch from a socialist society to a market economy, with its inevitable emphasis on competitiveness and aggressiveness. Because of this, he claims, Israelis do not care about one another as they once did; there is meanness and nastiness everywhere.

Another specialist on youth, from the Hebrew University School of Education, avers that TV might be the culprit, and he advises parents to monitor their children's viewing — although, he adds, it is difficult to ascertain exactly how TV affects behavior. It would not be good scientific method, for example, to compare violence among kids that have TV with those who do not have TV, "because the abstainers would usually be *haredi* families and then the religious elements would be an intervening variable that would distort the results." (In other words, it would distort the sampling if we compared the violence of religious children to the violence of non-religious children — a rather odd logic.)

Rules, authority, obligations, caring about one another, loving one's neighbor: the terms have a familiar ring. Where have we heard them before? One waits for the obvious conclusion from these experts, but there is only silence.

Jewish professors in a Jewish land in a Jewish newspaper call for more discipline, limits and self-control, but have nothing to say about the way Jews have become the most disciplined people in the history of mankind. Are the professors so Jewishly unaware that they fail to know that the Torah offers a way to teach the importance of limits to both young and old? Why does this obvious solution not occur to them, or to the reporter who interviewed them?

The gun is literally pressed against their temples, they recognize that Israeli society lacks self-control and discipline, yet they can only repeat the tired old mantras about going to bed on time and doing homework. The Talmudic dictum (Eruvin 19a) about *pit-ho shel Gehinnom* comes to mind: Those who are mired in their stubborn ways "do not return even when they stand at the brink of Gehinnom."

Littleton, Colorado and the Holy City both have traditions. Littleton takes very seriously the American right to bear arms, and still retains the American frontier tradition that a gun is a man's test of selfhood. Jerusalem also has its traditions. It was meant to be a city of peace, a city of love and kindness and of reaching out to fellow man and to God.

Littleton and Jerusalem are ten thousand miles apart, but in their tragedies they have grown closer together. And yet, in one terrible respect, they are still worlds apart. In Littleton, a wave of religious introspection enveloped the townspeople. Churches were packed, people prayed, and inquiries about religion were made of ministers and priests and religious leaders. Citizens began asking ultimate questions about their values and their behavior: Have we stressed the wrong things? Do we need to reassess, to reevaluate, to reconsider our lives?

One still waits for similar introspection within the secular Israeli community. Its intellectual leaders still utter the same tired banalities, the same generic boilerplate remedies, the same secular mantras. And all the time the remedy they seek stands silently by, waiting to be noticed. But it is not noticed, because religion is an "intervening variable" that "distorts results."

Somewhere there must be a perceptive non-religious Jew who has the courage to say publicly that perhaps Israeli secularists have not been walking on the right path, and that quite possibly that other path — the unmentionable "T" path — has something to offer. No one is suggesting that everyone become Orthodox, but surely the ideology of *kekhol ha-goyim beit Yisrael* ("Let the Jews be a nation like all others") has led us into a dead end. (In this case, it would not hurt to emulate the *kol ha-goyim* of Colorado.)

We keep hearing about the need for Israel to have the courage to make peace with its neighbors. The real issue is whether Israeli secularists have the courage to make peace with their own Jewish heritage.

A Tale of Two Cities

RETURNING FROM JERUSALEM FOR A brief visit to Atlanta in 1996, I discovered that the city had been transmuted into a giant Olympic feeding frenzy. A full year before the beginning of the Event, everything was an official Olympic something or other. On a huge billboard astride the expressway in the midst of the city is a ticking clock which, in a secularized apotheosis of the sacred counting of *sefirat haomer*, counts the days to the Olympics. On the day I arrived it pronounced in bright, digital letters five feet high: "313 days to go."

At the minyan, a congregant approached me with the inevitable joke: "Rabbi, let's designate ourselves as "Beth Jacob, the official synagogue of the 1996 Olympics." There are official everything else. Why not an official synagogue?"

I responded diplomatically that while his idea has a certain cachet to it, I thought I would beg off.

He was perceptive: "Aren't you at all excited that the Olympics are coming to Atlanta?"

"Well, since you ask," I replied, allowing the diplomatic immunity to fall away, "the truth is that the Olympics contain bad memories for me."

He was so shocked by my response that I felt obligated to spell out to him, and to all others who might not understand,

A Tale of Two Cities

why a forty-year resident of Atlanta could be less than enthusiastic about his city's moment in glory.

※※※

Atlanta is my favorite *Galut* city, and I am happy that the delightful town to which I came a generation ago has metamorphosed into a major, but still delightful, international city. But I must shamelessly confess that, having just left Jerusalem a few hours earlier, I found the pervasive Olympomania somewhat unsettling.

Unsettling, because deep within me there was bestirred an ancient spiritual conflict. The Olympics, after all, are not just another sporting event. In every way, they are redolent of Hellenism, which represents an approach to life diametrically opposed to Judaism: paganism, polytheism, the deification of the physical. This Hellenism was a powerful ideological force that posed a major challenge to the integrity of ancient (and, let it be said, modern) Jewry.

When the Greeks captured Jerusalem, the torch-bearing runners brought with them a culture which rocked the classic faith of the Jews to its very foundations. The conquerors attempted to transform Jerusalem into a Greek *polis*. They constructed gymnasia and placed busts of their deities throughout the city. The picture is desolating: the wellspring of pure monotheism, the source of the Invisible God of Israel, the very antithesis of paganism — Jerusalem was now decorated with idolatrous images.

Greek culture was insidiously attractive. Inevitably, many Jews assimilated unto Hellenistic ways. They participated proudly in Greek games, and wrestled naked with the Greeks in amphitheaters built by Herod. The body, which in Judaism was important only as the handmaiden of the soul, was glorified, while the soul itself was relegated to obscurity.

Thus began the classic confrontation between Judaism and Hellenism, the struggle between the historic Jerusalem and the historic Athens. This titanic battle against the great anti-spiritual cultures of the ancient world (see the comments in *Avoda Zara* 18b about stadiums, theaters and circuses) was never finally resolved. It continues to this day.

Granted, today's Olympics no longer represent Greek civilization, nor, for that matter, do they even represent amateur athletics at their best and for their own sake. They have become transmogrified into a professionalized multinational business whose primary purpose is international prestige and pecuniary gain — which are the most hallowed pagan practices of today. Nevertheless, it was disconcerting to leap, in a few hours, from the seat of ancient Jerusalem to a modern town which was buried in the unmistakable detritus of ancient Hellas and all that it represents for Jewish history. Athens is alive and well in our century.

But there was more to my Olympic unease than what occurred twenty centuries ago. It was also what occurred just over twenty years ago.

The Olympic committee would rather not talk about it, and in the eyes of many I will be guilty of unsportsmanlike conduct for bringing it up, but I think a Jew needs to remember it. I refer to the 1972 Munich Olympics, the one in which eleven athletes were murdered by Arab terrorists. They were killed for only one reason: they were Jews.

The civilized world was aggrieved and stunned. There were calls for the Olympics to be cancelled or postponed — some serious gesture to mark the cold-blooded murder of eleven athletes who were participating in the quadrennial symbol of what the Olympics supposedly stand for: decency, sportsmanship, the brotherhood of man.

But the Games (as in God, the "g" is always reverentially capitalized) continued. To be sure, there were expressions of regret by the Olympic committee (chairman Avery Brundage, in an egregiously insensitive memorial statement, equated the murders with a threatened walkout of black athletes because of

A Tale of Two Cities

racist Rhodesia's participation) and there was even a twenty-four hour suspension of the Games. But to cancel them would give a victory to terrorism; the Games must go on. And so forth. (We have since then heard the same justifications many times over, in different circumstances. Substitute "peace process" for "Games" and, in a painful historic irony, the Israeli government now dutifully mumbles the identical mantra after each terrorist atrocity in Israel.)

Thus the decathlons continued, and the 1,000 meter races, and the gymnastics, and the diving events, and the water polo. While eleven Israeli Olympic athletes were buried and eleven families grieved, it all went on, in grotesque fulfillment of the will of the cold-eyed Olympic masterminds whose singular devotion to the Games would not be deterred.

All of which should not have been surprising, for it was the same Olympic steering committee that had caved in to Hitler's racist demands in the 1936 Munich Olympics.

The Games were good for Atlanta, the region's economy, and its international image. It couldn't have happened to a finer town, and certainly I am proud of what Atlanta has achieved.

But the Olympic Committee will have to forgive this one person for not getting overly excited about it. It is not only the fateful ancient visions that the Olympic torch conjures up, but also the depressing twentieth century Olympic memories that it invokes.

It is estimated that throughout the world, some three and one half billion — billion! — people will be watching future Olympic events. The committee will surely not take offense if that number is reduced by one.

Nor will they mind, I am sure, if henceforth I will be spelling Olympic games with a lower case "g."

Why I Miss Yerushalayim

ONE NEEDS A DECOMPRESSION CHAMBER when returning from the highly charged Jewish atmosphere of Jerusalem back to the USA — particularly during the three week mourning period which climaxes with Tish'a B'Av. It is rather ludicrous: I leave Jerusalem for the Galut and then sit in the Galut lamenting for Jerusalem. But perhaps it is best this way: I feel even more keenly the absence of Jerusalem from me — and my absence from her — and isn't this what Tish'a B'Av is all about?

From Israel to the USA, from Yerushalayim to Atlanta. What can compare to the physical conveniences and luxuries of America? Who can match the courtesy and consideration of southerners? And certainly America is much more efficient than Israel, and yes, we have large, well-trimmed lawns and one-family houses and air-conditioning, and at least one car per family.

But I miss Yerushalayim. I miss looking down from the heights of my Bayit Vegan neighborhood to the panorama of the city spread out below, and, on a clear day, the hills rolling down towards Jericho.

I miss the variety of Jews — the Yemenites, the Morrocans, the Kurds, the Bucharians, the dozens of varieties of *hasidim*, the newly arrived Russians and Ethiopians.

I miss sitting in the midst of the congregation instead of on the pulpit, and learning from others instead of having others learn from me. I miss hearing the daily priestly blessings, which in the Galut we can hear only on Yom Tov, but in Israel is available every day, and twice on *Shabbat* and *Rosh Hodesh*.

I miss the undulation of the hills surrounding the city, the city which is so beautiful that even the developers and builders and their un-beautiful apartment buildings have not succeeded in destroying it.

I miss the dark, winding streets of Meah Shearim at dusk, the black-hatted men scurrying to *minhah*, the well-wrapped women hurrying home with *leben* and *felafel* in their shopping bags.

I miss the stone and the sky and the olive trees. I miss the burning noonday heat of summer, and the strange yellow light of late afternoon as the sun begins its rapid descent beneath the hills, the gold turning to orange, to blue, and then the deep purple of nightfall.

I miss the ancient gates: *Sha'ar Shechem, Sha'ar Yaffo, Sha'ar Ha-arayot, Sha'ar Ha-rachamim;* and the *Ir Ha-atiqa,* the Old City, the shuk, the dark, hidden, redolent alleyways meandering and twisting into nowhere.

I miss the clean, crisp night-time air of Yerushalayim, chill even in mid-summer. And I miss the wind that howls through the hills on winter nights, a physical reflection of the spiritual power which hovers over the city.

I miss the Friday afternoon siren, reminding the city that Shabbat is approaching; and the sounds of the city slowing down in honor of the Shabbat, and the magic stillness which envelops everyone as Friday night begins to descend.

I miss the simplicity of life in Yerushalayim, the appreciation of small comforts which here in America we take as our due.

I miss the neighborhood where even old men are students, where every living room wall is lined with holy books, where at any hour of the day or night men and women are scurrying to and from *shiurim* and lectures on the variegated aspects of Torah.

If I miss the Yerushalayim of today, how much more so the Yerushalayim of old whose destruction we mourn on Tish'a B'Av — where God's Presence was manifest and His holiness tangible.

But though I miss the new Yerushalayim and mourn for the old one, I am comforted by the Biblical prophecy that at the end of days, the mourning of Yerushalayim will be transformed into days of joy, for God will have fulfilled His promise to return to His holy city and to restore His dwelling place to His holy mountain.

Mountain Musings

I HAVE A TENDER SPOT in my heart for mountains, and that may explain why two of my favorite places on earth are Jerusalem and Denver.

In Jerusalem, as you walk down certain city streets, you need only lift up your eyes to see some of the rolling mountains which surround this most wondrous of cities. King David refers to the Jerusalem mountains in his Psalm 125: "Jerusalem has mountains roundabout her, (and so) is the Lord roundabout His people..."

In Denver, too, even at a busy intersection in its bustling downtown, you need only lift up your eyes to see, out in the distance, the dramatic peaks of the Front Range. (One can only imagine what David might have written had he seen the Rockies in mid-winter.)

Admittedly, the mountains around Jerusalem are small when compared to those west of Denver. The Rockies are tall, rugged, imperious. Jerusalem's mountains are majestic, and a feast to the eyes, but they are not high or commanding or powerful. The words that come to mind are: undulating, gently curving, even humble — certainly not proud or ostentatious or dazzling.

The Rockies are anything but humble. They point a craggy finger right at heaven; they push right through the clouds, bold, and overpowering. Jerusalem hills are quiet, calm, understated, unpretentious, unassuming. No dominating peaks here, no snowy summits above treelines, no cascading waterfalls or ravines or escarpments.

Jerusalem hills can take your breath away, particularly as they turn golden in the yellow rays of the setting sun, but theirs is a different kind of beauty from that of the Rockies. A deep, profound loveliness envelops these hills and embraces the city. The Rockies are awesome, and hardly lovely. Jerusalem hills, not massive and broad-shouldered, but stooped, brooding, pondering, are both awesome and lovely.

Into the Rockies went miners and pioneers, pushing back frontiers to search for land and gold.

Into the Jerusalem hills went wise men and prophets, pushing back different frontiers in search of God.

God made them both, the Rockies and the Jerusalem hills. You lift up your eyes to each of them, and if you look carefully, you can see the handiwork of the Master: "I lift up my eyes to the hills, from whence cometh my help? My help cometh from the Lord, Maker of heaven and earth." David, in his 121st Psalm, touches on a fundamental truth of nature: we are fascinated by hills and mountains because they are expressions of our need to reach towards something above us.

A mountain is more than its external power and grace. A mountain makes us look up, forces us to lift our earth-bound eyes. It makes us realize that we are human, mortal, un-eternal; that we are not God. It forces us to focus on something larger and greater beyond our small selves. Man climbs mountains not only because they are there, but because they represent man's eternal yearning to move out beyond the self. Perhaps this is why it is that mountains, more than anything else, engender David's sense of dependence on God. (There are in fact almost sixty references to hills and mountains in the Psalms alone, and almost one thousand in the entire Bible.)

Note, however, that while mountains are striking, the really significant historical events in world history, by and large, have

Mountain Musings

not taken place on mountains but in the spaces between the mountains: the plains, the valleys, the flat places. But in Biblical history, the reverse is true: the crucial events take place on the mountains themselves.

In Genesis 22, God commands Abraham to sacrifice his beloved son Isaac on "one of the hills which I will show you." The hill is Mt. Moriah in Jerusalem.

Sinai is a desert, but is famous primarily for the mountain within the desert, which is the scene of the Ten Commandments and of God's revelation to mankind. When Moses enters the thick cloud enveloping this mountain to commune with God for forty days and forty nights, and does not return exactly when the Israelites expect him, the Golden Calf is the tragic result.

Mt. Gerizim and Mt. Eval, just this side of the Jordan River, are the Biblical mountains of blessing and curse.

Aaron is told to climb a mountain where he will die; Moses dies in a similar fashion, also on a mountain.

Mt. Carmel, near today's Haifa, is where Elijah challenges the four hundred heathen prophets. And on, and on.

For the Jews, mountains are not merely places to look at. Mountains are where truly significant things take place: they are drenched with history and reverberate with Biblical echoes.

As one would expect, Jerusalem is not merely a city between the mountains: Jerusalem is part of the mountain. In certain Jerusalem neighborhoods, you have to climb stone staircases of over one hundred steps to go from one street to the next. Spiritually, too, Jerusalem is the mountain, and history is happening here — today as always.

The moral is: lift up your eyes; it is good for the soul.

Jerusalem and Denver are two of the best places I know for lifting up one's eyes.

McDonald's and the Newest Commandment

THERE THEY ARE, JUTTING OUT of the magnificent hills of Jerusalem, casting an odd yellow glow that illuminates the evening sky. They bear the 11th commandment to the children of modern Israel: These shall ye eat, just as your brethren in America eat the selfsame hamburgers. The McDonald's arches.

Did they have to be towering, so domineering of this landscape that they can be seen from miles away? Which bureaucrat sold his soul to grant permission to disfigure those hills of holiness? They are such an intrusion, an offense to good taste. There is an American Gothic. Now there is Israeli Grotesque.

Don't be upset. We wanted to practice our faith in a modern country, a nation like other nations, did we not? We have our armed forces, our universities, our symphonies, our art galleries, and our flag flies at the United Nations. For a fledgling country, this is quite good. Granted, we could live without McDonald's, but you do want to be contemporary, don't you? This is the price of modernity.

If such things are the entrance fees to join the family of nations, then the price is too high. For what do we get in return? The gift of modernity is presented to Israel on a Styrofoam platter: McDonald's hamburgers in the hills of Jerusalem. Is modern Israel now ready to become part of the phony one-size-fits-all McDonald's universe? Somehow I thought the Jew marched to the beat of a different drummer — that instead of walking lock-step with everyone else, we followed our own ideals and norms. Has the stiff-necked Jew now become the pliant, conformist Jew who trades in the authentic for the plastic?

Don't be offended. We are, after all, modern Jews. We do not reject the world around us, for there is godliness in everything that He created. He is to be found in physics, and in biology, and, yes, in music and painting, and indeed in all of culture. Shall we deny that these arches are a potent symbol of twentieth century culture? Surely we who are modern and *au courant* will not turn our backs on contemporary culture but will instead work within it and try to shape it by our values.

Values and culture, you say? Sometimes one thinks that the only values we care for are those of the West. For an appropriate symbol of Israel's fiftieth anniversary, a nationwide search was instituted. Committees, judges, contests. They wasted their time. They need not have gone further than these ugly, convex protrusions.

Ah, but one must examine the arches objectively, with an eye to their full potential, to their hidden value. Do they not bear the configuration of the tablets bearing the Ten Commandments? Look at them: the classic parabolic contour of the holy Decalogue transmogrified into the convex arches of McDonald's.

Don't be swayed by your emotions. Is it really incongruous to look at the hills of Jerusalem and to find an eternal reminder, day and night, of something that calls to mind, albeit remotely, the Ten Commandments? In today's world, can that be a bad thing, to remember the commandments of old? True, the originals were on tablets of stone, and these are golden; and admittedly, there are unfortunate images of idolatrous calves and broken tablets that come to mind when the word "golden" is associated with the Ten Commandments. Still, we must not allow ancient memories to take over. Golden Ten Commandments. From stone to gold: That is true progress. One's feelings should not stand in the way.

You confuse consumer culture with progress. Do we not have our own criteria, our own standards of culture? Is everything Western automatically good, and everything Jewish automatically bad?

Be practical. Let us go, you and I, to the arches spread out against the sky. After all, if we want to understand precisely what it is that the world around us finds so irresistible, a little nibble will do no harm — especially if it has a kosher certification. And if it does not go down easily, we can wash it down with a Coca-Cola endorsed for kashrut by the good rabbis of Bnei Brak, or with a Pepsi certified by the rabbis of Jerusalem.

Look how wondrous is life in modern Israel: Jerusalem and McDonald's: hamburgers and fries; the Ten Commandments; Coke and Pepsi; certified *hekhsherim*. Does it get any better than this? What in the world is bothering you?

The *Shulhan Arukh*, Hidden Verses, and the Israeli Elections

Written after Binyamin Netanyahu's unexpected victory over Shimon Peres, this essay - and the one following it - underscores the fact that history repeats itself. Only the names change.

IT IS USEFUL TO TAKE another look at the Peres-Netanyahu Israeli elections, because its lessons are not limited to one moment in time.

While the morning-after euphoria of the anti-Peres circles has by now dissipated, and while certain problems within the State will not simply evaporate because of governmental changes, it is nevertheless apparent that the elections marked an historical event. The difference in atmosphere was immediately palpable in two areas: the genuflection at the altar of the "peace process," upon which all atrocities against Israel were forgiven; and the coalition's inflammatory rhetoric against Judaism, in which all things religious were ridiculed.

The *Kitsur Shulhan Arukh* (71:5) advises that a person should go to sleep on his left side and awaken on his right side. This is precisely what Israel did on the night after the elections for Prime Minister. It went to sleep on its left side, certain that Peres had won, and awoke on its right side to find that Netanyahu had won.

Careful students of the Psalms did not have to resort to such somnolent signs. The cognoscenti pointed to Psalm 77:11: *"shenot yemin elyon"* is normally translated as an entreaty "for the years of the right hand of the Most High." But the correct reading for Israel's election was that *shenot* contains the letters *tav, shin, nun, vav,* which was the year of the elections, 5756; v. 11 represents the day of the month of the elections, 11 *Sivan*; Ps. 77 is in the section of Psalms read by the pious on Wednesdays, the day of the elections. Thus, the esoteric meaning of the verse is: "in 5756, *yemin* (the right) *elyon* (on top)." Obviously. How could anyone have missed the message deeply embedded in this Psalm?

And how could anyone not have noticed that our forefather Yaakov had sent us a message concealed in *Gen.* 42:36? There he tells his sons: *Yosef einenu veShimon einenu ve-et Binyamin tikahu,"* which only a fool would not recognize as: "Yosef (Beilin or Sarid) is no more; Shimon (Peres) is no more, and Binyamin (Netanyahu) shall you take."

Clearly, the same numerical gymnasts who had displayed their dexterity during the Gulf War (the numerical equivalent of the "Patriot" missile (314), presumably protecting Israel from the Scuds, was the same as that of God's name on the *mezuzah*, which letters also stand for "Protects the Doors of Israel," etc.) were back in full force in this election.

It was an election not only of spiritual signs, but political signs. Perhaps the most damning of all was the series of black and white leaflets that appeared on the streets every few days. Often they were headed with the single word ZOKHERIM, "WE REMEMBER." The message would remind the voters of some egregious anti-religious statement by the Peres government: "WE REMEMBER: what Peres said about King David," (recalling Peres's intemperate comments about displaying a statue of an unclothed King David as part of Jerusalem 3000); or "what Aloni said about *Shema Yisrael*"; or "what Yael Dayan said in defense of abominations." Some were in the form of real estate ads displaying scenes of prime property which was for sale for empty promises: Hebron, Rachel's Tomb, Jerusalem, Joseph's Tomb in Shekhem, the Western Wall. As it turned out, a landslide number of Jewish voters did remember.

When the results became known, the human rights-loving Israeli leftists made it clear that the Orthodox had committed a grave offense by swinging the election. They conjured up the specter of religious coercion and of changes in the religious status quo (they who have been changing the status quo for the past four years). They charged that the election had been won because of amulets distributed by kabbalistic rabbis who threatened curses against anyone who voted for Peres. Their cries, inevitably, were recycled by the Federation/UJA leadership and non-Orthodox congregational bodies in the USA, who led a clucking chorus of fear-mongering about Orthodox ghettoization and polarization — in very undemocratic disregard of a fairly won election. In unconscious but striking symmetry to Arab hints about renewing the intifada, the American Jewish establishment even dropped broad hints about cutting off aid to Israel (just as they threatened to do when things did not go their way during the "Who Is a Jew" imbroglio). Democracy is fine as long as the other side does not win.

Overlooked by them and by the Israeli media was the salient fact that the Israeli electorate, over and above its justified fears about security, was also saying something else: they wanted not only a state for Jews, but a Jewish state. The Peres coalition's hostility to Jewish tradition did not reflect the views of Israelis. They are not all pious or *haredi*, but neither are they ready to abandon their Jewish roots. They did not forget the virulent anti-religious reaction after the Rabin assassination, and they realized that this was but an escalation of the coalition's daily mugging of Israel's Jewish character that long antedated that event.

Somehow, the electorate sensed in this a loss of spiritual compass. Every transitory ideological vogue was embraced. Peres himself envisioned a Jewish-Arab region in which Jewish and Arab national identities would disappear "and our self-identity will be based on this new reality." The Minister of Education announced that he would remove the archaic interest in "Jewish values and culture, love of homeland, loyalty to the Jewish people," and replace it with a "pluralistic concern for the cultures of all the peoples inhabiting the region." It is hardly surprising that the new code of ethics for the Israeli armed forces, "The Spirit of the IDF," contains no reference to the Jewish tradition or to the land of Israel.

The spiritual rootlessness led to daily absurdities that tested one's sanity. Has any sovereign nation ever willingly surrendered contiguous land to a sworn enemy in order to ensure its own security? Or ignored calls from putative peace partners to "liberate Palestine in blood?" Or permitted a sworn enemy on its borders to arm a force of forty thousand men? Or freed imprisoned terrorists who were promptly rewarded with top positions in the enemy's "security forces"? Or blithely ignored the fact that its partners in peace literally danced with joy at the bus bombings?

Nor did anyone trouble to analyze the implications of "land for peace." Is not the concept of surrendering land in order achieve peace an admission that we have no real right to the land we are surrendering, that it is meaningful to us only as a bargaining chip? How is it that Israel does not receive Syrian or Egyptian land in exchange for peace? "Land for peace" pays obeisance to the spurious idea that somehow the Jewish people is committing a crime by living in its ancestral home and must now pay a price if it insists on living in peace in that home.

Israeli leadership had been in a hypnotic trance, numbed by the smiles of an approving world. The Jewish longing for the land, the Jewish attachment to the holy places, were ridiculed by Rabin and Peres. Instead, the most historic portions of the land were promised to Arafat and Assad in exchange for their word that they would be nice to us. It was inevitable that callousness about the Jewish past would lead to callousness about the Jewish present and future.

Beyond the failed peace, the youth's hedonism and its aping of the West demonstrated that secular leadership was incapable of transmitting any ideals — even secular ideals — to the next generation. It was not lost on the public that the only Zionist idealism to be found in Israel was that of the 140,000 Jews — the vast majority of them religious — who had settled Judea and Samaria and whom the government was now demonizing for doing exactly what the early secular Zionist *halutsim*, such as Ben Gurion and his cohorts, had done: settle the land at great personal risk.

The most effective anti-government banner simply said: "You Have Failed: Go Home." It was brutal in its starkness, but it said it all. Failed not only at peace, but failed also in building a society based on Jewish values. It was in the hope that both the peace and the Jewishness could be restored that Israelis did in fact send them home.

※※※

Although it is unlikely that Yaakov was telling us that we should choose Binyamin Netanyahu, or that King David was referring to the election 5756 and the ascendancy of the Right, one thing is clear: new possibilities have been opened up in Israel. There now exists at least the chance for a return — not to the nightmare phantasmagoria imagined by the embittered losers — but to basic things: simple idealism; serious Jewish education and motivation for the young; a modicum of Jewish historical sense and pride.

These elementary goals can be reached if we do not once again fritter away the opportunity that has been offered us. It will require, however, more than amulets and hidden verses.

For starters, it will require that our representatives in the Knesset remember that in the eyes of the wider public they represent such concepts as God, Torah, and classical Judaism. The only Orthodox leadership the Israeli public knows are those who function in the political arena. This public, weary of spiritual emptiness, is ready for a Judaism that is represented with integrity, spirituality, and the best of Jewish ethical behavior.

Orthodoxy now has the opportunity to demonstrate that Torah is not parochial but has a vitality to contribute to our social and intellectual life; that its interests extend beyond kashrut endorsements, funding for pet projects, and the closing of certain streets on Shabbat; that it has something to say about today's cultural degradation and self-indulgence (which has not entirely spared Orthodox life in Israel or the Diaspora); that the Torah as a "tree of life" is not just a pretty slogan.

All this may be only a fond hope — political parties, even religious ones, will probably not hasten the Messiah's arrival — but the glimmer keeps reappearing: perhaps this time we will be wise. So far, with a few shining exceptions, the signs are unpromising.

If we are not wise, and Israelis continue to see only politicians with yarmulkes, the smile from Above which this election represented will have been spurned. In that case, we should not be surprised if other banners soon cry out, "You Have Failed: Go Home," and if Israelis, in contravention of the *Shulhan Arukh's* advice, on the morning after the new elections wake up on their left side. All the hidden *pesukim* in the world will not help us then.

Elections and Pipe Dreams

IT IS MANY MONTHS SINCE the captain and the kings departed, the Israeli elections came and went, and the leavings of the thirty-one parties were cleared from the airwaves and the streets. (Sixteen of them blessedly did not make the cut-off point to enter the Knesset; unblessedly, fifteen did.) Israelis will miss the excited teenagers at crowded intersections holding huge banners for Barak who will change things, or for Netanyahu who will guarantee peace with security, or for the NRP who will give its soul for Israel, or for the *haredi* United Torah Judaism who will preserve the Torah in the state. But no one will miss the detritus of flyers that carpeted the streets for months, reminding one and all of the dire consequences if anyone but their own candidate were elected. Gone are the *Rak Netanyahu* (Only Netanyahu) and the *Rak Lo Netanyahu* (Anyone But Netanyahu) bumper stickers. The American election gurus have floated off to other campaigns, the clamor has subsided, and the media's vitriol and vituperation have been lowered a few notches.

Blessedly behind us also is the post-election campaign, conducted behind the stillness of locked doors: favor-seekers begging Barak for a share of the spoils of victory. Yesterday, Shas warned of the catastrophe that would befall the land if Barak won, and today they beseech Barak for a seat at the table; yesterday, the religious parties warned the faithful of the sacred duty to defeat the Barak who would destroy Shabbat and give away Jerusalem, and today they crowd around him and extend their hand of peace if only they can obtain *shirayim* scraps from their new *rebbe*. Yesterday, the militantly anti-religious secularists bitterly attacked all Torah values and vowed never to sit in a government coalition with representatives of Torah parties, and today they find that perhaps they can sit with them after all if this means that they, too, will get a crumb.

It was an unseemly sight, this spectacle of erstwhile enemies affectionately holding hands. The conclusion is that yesterday they were not really enemies, and today they are not really friends. The one, single-minded goal — to hold on to power at all costs — transcends such naïve things. Much more bracing was the sight of Benny Begin quitting politics, and of Netanyahu saying farewell to his Knesset seat. (One wonders why Peres could not have said farewell after his defeat in 1996.)

At every election, Rabban Gamliel's words in *Pirke Avot* 11:3 resonate with renewed power: "Be careful in your dealings with the ruling powers . . . for they appear as friends when it is to their advantage, but do not stand by a man in the hour of his need."

And at every election, everyone forgets these words.

Although the elections are history, a number of unresolved issues remain in their wake:

- The religious/non-religious hostility that it underscored, and the continued fragmentation of Israeli society.
- The arrogance and venom of the media that makes no pretext of objectivity in their news coverage and that never forgave Netanyahu for the cardinal *hutspah* of winning the election against their wishes in 1996. (After the initial euphoria about the Barak victory, the secular columnists in *Ha-arets* and other such journals are now

Elections and Pipe Dreams 85

> beginning to be critical of him — altogether an encouraging sign.)
> - The American spinmeisters brought in to tell the Israeli candidates how to do their job, and how this is yet another manifestation of how America and the West dominate Israeli life. Through their sound-bite influence, none of the major candidates ever addressed any serious issues, and offered no ideas about peace, or unemployment, or the ideological divide, or the faltering economy.
> - The revolving door of military and politics. The armed forces are viewed as stepping stones into the upper echelons of government. Generals covet cabinet seats, and chiefs of staff covet the Prime Ministership. Do ex-generals make good political leaders? The history of military men in Israeli politics is not a great cause for optimism.

Many issues, but the relative quiet of this post-election period brings certain suppressed pipe-dreams to the surface — which, like all dreams, are only personal and represent no one's views but the writer's.

※❧※

What if Barak had been able to form a government without any religious parties? Would this have been a disaster for Torah? Would *kashrut* and *Shabbat* and all things sacred be tossed overboard by a secular government? Would funding be summarily cut off from religious institutions? If Torah were not part of the massive jockeying at the trough, if it were above the fray and not seen — as it is now seen — as just another political party, would it be held in higher esteem, and would the contempt with which its adherents are held by so many be abated?

One example among many: Although the Deri conviction apparently strengthened the Shas party, did it strengthen

Judaism in the eyes of Israelis, or did it increase contempt for it? Does anyone really think that the courts — which are notoriously anti-religious in Israel — in this case convicted an innocent man? Does anyone really believe, as his defenders like to claim, that Deri is another falsely accused Captain Dreyfus, a victim of a vast conspiratorial frameup of those who hate Sephardim and religious Jews? And is the defense that "they all do it" a legitimate one for those who claim to represent God and Torah? Did l'affaire Deri sanctify the Name of God so that — in the definition of *kiddush haShem* — men will forever say in awed tones, This is how a religious Jew behaves; more glory to the God of Israel and the study of Torah which creates such self-sacrificing Jews; would that my children could be like that? Or will they say with a derisive cantillation, This is how a religious Jew behaves.

And is not the Deri case symbolic of the inevitable fulfillment of Lord Acton's dictum that all power tends to corrupt, and absolute power tends to corrupt absolutely? Is Torah so weak in Israel that it cannot exist and prosper without the degrading wheeling and dealing that is part of the political process? Perhaps withdrawal from politics is an idea whose time has come.

Granted, the thought is naïve, but pipe dreams are permitted a certain innocence. Yes, it would create a financial crunch for many religious institutions. But would Torah and Judaism and the good name of the Jewish religion, now dragged daily through the political mud, lose or gain in the long run? And does not authentic Judaism possess its own persuasive powers, and does not Torah have its own persuasive teachers? And on a practical level, would not the growing electoral strength of the religious community prevent any serious diminution of basic religious principles or a radical slashing of support? For even if they stayed out of the government, religious Jews would still be a sought-after vote in elections.

The erosion of Torah in the community at large — with religion in the government — is slow but steady. The Orthodox grow stronger within, yes, but religion in society grows ever weaker. Would Torah do worse if it were not in government?

The millions of *shekalim* now expended by the government for religious institutions do not come without a price-tag: the good name of religion. Torah's legislative representatives are viewed as just another group of political hacks trying to get a piece of the action — and hacks, furthermore, with an agenda of intolerance and religious coercion. Riding the waves of this sentiment, Lapid's Shinui party, for example, ran a vitriolic anti-*haredi* hate campaign in which the campaign issues were: freedom to marry whomever one pleases, to violate Shabbat, and to eat pork. Instead of being condemned and smothered at the polls as the Israeli counterpart of the Ku Klux Klan, he garnered five seats in the Knesset — as many as did the haredi United Torah Judaism.

The price for being in politics is even steeper than this. It is the complete unawareness by the general population of what the religious community really is. The *hesed* of religious Jews, the *mentschlichkeit*, the exemplary family life, the values, the principles: none of this is known to the general electorate. Nor are they aware of the intellectual rigor of Torah study, the discipline and majesty of Torah life, the profound joy of a Shabbat and Yom Tov, the drama and power of religious life cycle events. It is all obscured by the jostling at the trough. The electorate knows only the terrible clichés that have become part of the daily lexicon of the media: that haredim are all parasites who pay no taxes, share no civic burdens, and have too many children; that religious parents take more money from the government than they should (though the fact is that proportionately they receive no more that the secular community and the secular kibbutzim); that Orthodox Jews want to force Judaism upon an unwilling public; that *gedolei Yisrael* and *hasidic rebbbeim* and the rabbis of Judea/Samaria are all hard-eyed Ayatollahs.

Religious Jewry in Israel has much to offer the country, and has contributed enormously to its spiritual and material fiber. But who outside of the Othodox is aware of this? When the religious parties horse-trade with other politicos, the effect on a marginal Jew who is curious about his Judaism cannot be very positive.

※❦※

It was only a pipe dream, a passing thought. In the cold light of day it is, admittedly, chimeral, for it brings in its wake many realistic problems. But pipe dreams, fantasies and passing thoughts — even if they dissolve like smoke rings — are the essence of a sentient human being. Oscar Wilde once said, "Life is a dream that keeps me from sleeping." This is because dreams are often the seeds of serious questions, such as: In today's world, unlike decades ago, is Torah in politics good for the Jews or bad for the Jews? And: What would God want?

Only God knows. But as the beauty and nobility of Torah is devalued by the dross of Israeli's politics, it is not impolitic to keep in mind the pipe-dream. That there seems to be no satisfactory way out of the present religio-political arrangements is no reason to ignore it.

When all is said and done, it never hurts to ask, "*Vos vill Gott?*" In the dilemmas of life, that is not the last question we should be asking but the first. And that is not a passing thought.

Street Smart
in Jerusalem

A SMALL COMMUNITY ONCE ASKED Rabbi Yehuda HaNasi to provide them with a rabbi. The master dispatched one of him most brilliant disciples. The community erected a great platform in his honor. They came before him to ask questions about halakhah, but he could not answer them.

They inquired about matters of *aggadah*, but he could not answer those either. So they went back and complained to Rabbi Yehuda.

He summoned his disciple and asked him the same question that the community had asked him, and the disciple answered each question clearly and precisely.

"Why, then," asked the Master, "could you not answer these same questions before your community?"

Said the disciple, "They erected a great platform and placed me upon it, and the great pride that welled up within me caused me to forget everything I knew."

A profound story. But just where in the Talmud is it found? Thereby hangs a Jerusalem tale.

I was preparing some notes for a lecture in which I wanted to relate this Talmudic story. I remembered that it was found in the Talmud Yerushalmi, but for the life of me I could recall neither the name of the disciple nor the exact source.

I checked various concordances and CD-ROMs, but to no avail. In desperation, I phoned a good friend, a learned rabbi who lives in our neighborhood of Bayit Vegan.

"Of course," he said. "That's in the Yerushalmi."

"Fine. But where in the Yerushalmi?"

"I think it's in *Yevamot*. Wait a minute and I'll give you the exact page."

He returned to the phone. "I can't put my finger on it right now, but I'll check further and call you back."

One hour later he called me back sheepishly.

"I can't understand it. Such a well-known story, and neither of us can find it. But listen — we live in Jerusalem, a city of scholars. We live in Bayit Vegan, a neighborhood of scholars. Why are we searching computers and concordances? I'm positive that I can walk out on Rehov Hapisga and within two blocks I will find five people who know the source of this Gemara. I'm going right now. I'll call you back."

An hour later he called me, triumph in his voice. "I didn't find five people, but I did find one. It's the story of Levi bar Sissi, and it's in Yerushalmi *Yevamot* 69a in Halakhah 6."

So I had my source. But more important than the discovery of the source was the discovery of an oft-overlooked facet of Jerusalem. This is a dazzling city in many ways. But what is most dazzling is the standard of learning — Torah learning.

This quality is not obvious to the casual visitor, but it pervades Jerusalem. This is where third-graders can discuss Torah and its commentaries in depth, where sixth-graders can discourse about sections of the Talmud, and where thousands of laymen, professionals and merchants attend daily Talmud classes early in the morning before work, after work, late at night, and during work at midday break.

There is nothing extraordinary here — for the enemies of the Jews always burned our books even after they burned our bodies. It was our Torah that they despised, our holy books that they ridiculed. The burning of our Talmud in the city squares of Europe of the Middle Ages and of this century were powerful manifestations of their desire to obliterate the source of Jewishness.

But today, after all that has befallen our people, we have picked ourselves up and become as vital as ever. This manifests itself not only in the establishment of a Jewish state, but even more so in the level of Torah learning within it.

Yes, we live with communal tensions and strains, but underneath it all it is exhilarating to think of the mysterious magic that dwells in this holy land and in this holy city.

The travel ads about Israel do not refer to it, and most tour guides are unaware of it, but the veritable explosion of Torah scholarship — in Jerusalem and in many other places throughout the world — is a phenomenon rarely seen in the last two thousand years.

It is the most compelling response to our enemies then and now. Isaiah's prophecy, "Out of Zion shall go forth the Torah," is as true today as it ever was.

The next time you hear complaints about the proliferation of yeshivot in Israel, keep your eye on Jewish history. And remember what the term "street-smart" means in Jerusalem.

On Rolling Black Hats and Snowmen — Images of Jerusalem

IMAGES OF JERUSALEM? WHAT HAVE chickpeas and snowmen to do with the luminous majestic, mysterious holy city of light and stone and sky? Very much — because in the mystery and the light and the stones there are details, and individuals, and small, mundane events.

... It is a stormy day, with winds of tornado force. In the middle of the street a black hat rolls by on its brim, swiftly propelled by the wind. Its owner, a yeshiva student with *peot* and black *kappotte*, is running hard after it, but, laden down with a suitcase and a heavy Gemara, he will never retrieve it. Sprinting out of nowhere comes a bare-headed teenager. He catches up to it, picks it up, and runs back to the yeshiva *bachur*, and without a word gently places it back on his head...

... Picture cards of great contemporary scholars — the Orthodox answer to American baseball cards — are very popular here with the children. *Gedolim* cards, as they are known, do not come with chewing gum, but the youngsters love them anyway. You can hear the following conversation anytime:

"I'll trade you my Rav Schach for your Rav Ovadia Yosef."

"No, I have two Rav Schachs already. I need a Rav Eliashiv."

The cards are in color, laminated, very attractive. The child with two Rav Schachs has amassed over fifty different cards. (If there are fifty genuine *gedolim* in the world, we are either the most scholarly generation in Jewish history, or inflation has struck the world of Jewish learning.)

. . . Old people are rarely seen on American streets. They stay in their apartments (fearful to leave them) or they are shunted off to old age homes. Not so in the religious sections of Jerusalem. While there are numerous such institutions, old people abound here on the streets. They go to Shul and to classes; they shop, do organizational work, volunteer, and are treated with respect — as befits a city that prides itself on its halakhic scrupulousness and learning. It is good to be old in a truly pious community. In the daily Talmud *shiur* which I attend, one of the students is over eighty. He has never had the opportunity to study in his life, is thus not learned, but he attends faithfully. The teacher of the group is half his age, already renowned as a major scholar (but not yet on *gedolim* cards...). When the elderly man walks in, the teacher stands up out of respect, in literal fulfillment of *mipnei seivah takum*...

... Last winter, Jerusalem absorbed two major snow storms within three weeks. This is a Middle Eastern country, and few know how to deal with snow. Drivers speed, spin their wheels and do all the wrong things when, inevitably, they skid. Across the street from me a man, obviously bereft of a shovel, tries to extricate his car from a snowdrift by using his *sponja* mop. (If you don't know what a *sponja* mop is, you haven't lived in Israel). The neighborhood children, unfamiliar with the niceties of such a winter, throw raw snow at each other. I teach them how to make real snowballs, how to shape them round and how to pack them firm. But since these youngsters do not throw as naturally as American kids do, they take their laboriously made snowballs, place them of the ground and kick them, soccer style. The snowballs don't last long. . . . The snowman out front sports a black frock coat, a black beard, and a black hat; the snowlady has a proper sheitel. In the morning, sabotage: someone has replaced the black hat with a knitted yarmulka complete with bobby-pin, and the sheitel with a *tichel*. In the wars of the Lord, there is no armistice day, even in snowstorms, for in Jewish life, especially in Israel, everything is a religio-political statement: the type of your yarmulke, the color of your hat, the width of your brim — even the snowman you make.

... The Israel Museum mounts a special showing of original manuscripts by the great Sephardi scholars of the Middle Ages. Behind magnificent display cases are original works of Maimonides, Nahmanides, Gersonides, Kimchi. A full pantheon of the *rishonim* – first editions, some in their own handwriting, illuminated manuscripts — is on breathtaking display. Visitors, most of them tourists from American, ooh and ah. The guide is very pleased and very proud. Less than a mile away, at any of the dozens of yeshivot which dot Jerusalem, thousands of young men actually study these same texts. It is even more breathtaking to realize that Maimonides, Nahmanides and the rest are not preserved behind glass, but are discussed, reviewed, analyzed, debated. The tour-guides — for the most part themselves religiously deprived — will not be taking the tourists to see the *rishonim* being studied in the adjacent yeshivot. The tourists will return home duly impressed by the museum. But they will never know that these great figures are not dead museum pieces at all, but are still vibrant a thousand years later. . .

... Jerusalem takes its *hesed* work seriously. The variety of lending societies is dazzling. Here is what you can borrow: tables and chairs for a *simha* in your home, cribs, baby carriages, strollers, high chairs, baby pacifiers, tools, medical equipment, wheel chairs, artificial flowers, wedding gowns, maternity clothes, dishes, silverware, pots and pans, and a Sefer Torah for the *shiva* house. One group will supply you with chickpeas to serve at your *shalom zakhar*. Another will pay a visit to the sick or the house-bound. The poor can obtain good used clothing. If you require medication late at night or on a Shabbat when the neighborhood drugstore is closed, there is a fully stocked unofficial drugstore in someone's home where you can obtain what you need, with only the proviso that you replace it the next day....

...From the windows of the yeshiva on my block comes the sound of many voices on Shabbat afternoon. *Zemirot* are being sung. The voices are lusty, enthusiastic, the sound enveloping the streets below: *HaShem ro'i lo echsar.* "The Lord is my shepherd I shall not want, he maketh me to lie down in green pastures, He restoreth my soul ..." — the traditional words sung at twilight as Shabbat fades into the week. The voices rise up and swell. Other words; *yom ze mekhubad*, "This day is honored from among all the days, for on this day He Who fashioned the universe rested ..."

From below the adjacent hills there rise up other voices. From the distance, as the voices bounce off the canyons and echo upward, they sound like *zemirot*. The voices are lusty, enthusiastic, enveloping the hills and the rocks. But as you approach the sound and look across the hills, you see tens of thousands of people sitting in a stadium watching a soccer game, and you realize that this is not the sound of *zemirot*, but the sound of the crowd cheering their heroes down on the field. The crescendo of voices rises and falls, and they are singing the songs of their team. Jerusalem Betar is playing Netanya for the league championship. As the twilight of Shabbat fades into the night, the voices swell and rise up; "Go Jerusalem, Go Jersualem, Go, Go, Go!"

From the windows of the yeshiva, a hundred voices cry out as one, "*Rahem behasdekha* / Have mercy in Thy compassion upon Thy people, upon Zion the dwelling place of Thy glory." From the grandstand in the stadium, ten thousand voices cry out as one: "Go Jerusalem, Go, Go, Go!"

City of exultation and heartache, of saints and scholars and scoundrels, of light and stone and sky; luminous, majestic, mysterious Jerusalem.

The Scrawl on the Siddur Page

WHEN I OPENED THE SIDDUR in my Jerusalem Shul, I was unprepared for what I saw, but when I opened my Jerusalem newspaper I was startled.

When I opened the siddur, I noticed that across the Prayer for the State of Israel someone had scrawled: *"Hatsionut pashtah regel!"*("Zionism has gone bankrupt.")

I was brought up not to write in *siddurim*; it was enough simply to pray in them. But in Israel there are many passionate opinions, especially about religion and about the State, so what could be more natural than to record one's views about the nature of Zionism and Israel right across the words of a prayer which is a conflation of both?

It was unclear if the writer of the declamation was (*a*) informing God, in the event it had escaped Him, that Zionism had come upon hard times; (*b*) instructing other worshippers not to waste God's time by praying for something that is bankrupt; or (*c*) venting his frustration at a government which seems oblivious to the Jewishness of the Jewish State — and, to make thing more difficult, oblivious to the slipperiness of the peace slope on which it has embarked.

Certain judgments can only be determined by history — although in Israel today the curious truth is that the *tefillah lamedinah* has fallen into some disfavor. A number of settlements in Judea and Samaria, and even some Religious Zionist synagogues in Jerusalem, have ceased reciting the prayer altogether, declaring that they are unwilling to pray for a government whose policies they see as hostile to their religious and national concerns. (Which is a commentary on the ephemeral nature of prayers that are written with one eye on God and the other on current events.)

The scrawl, however, did give me some pause: Has Zionism — by which I presume the scrawler meant secular Zionism — in fact reached a dead end? And, if so, why?

As I was reflecting on this a day later, a news item caught my eye. It stated that some Jordanian teachers, writers and intellectuals are concerned that the new peace with Israel will attract multitudes of Israeli tourists who might bring into Jordan "the worst of Western excesses, and that Arab youths will stream to Israel for whiskey or women." They cite Israeli mores and habits which are inimical to traditional Arab culture, such as immodest dress and behavior, and an inordinate emphasis on material things. In sum, the influx of Israelis is feared as the harbinger of Western, anti-religious values. (I dare say that this is not the kind of fear of the Jews referred to in Deut. 11:25: *Pahd'khem umora-akhem yiten Hashem al p'nei kol ha-arets... .*" the dread of you and the fear of you will God lay upon the land. . . .")

Although a certain anti-Jewish animus clearly pervades the Jordanian comments, and although these Arabs are impervious to the dimensions of piety, Torah study, and authentic idealism which are to be found in Israel, it is nevertheless instructive to see ourselves as others see us.

We cannot gainsay the fact that much of Israeli society today — overwhelmingly the product of secular Zionism — has fallen passionately in love with everything Western: its culture of consumption, its heroes, its physicality and hedonistic indulgence, complete with glitzy shopping malls, degrading videos, a tawdry and sensational media, and all other manner of crassness the world can offer up. (Nor may we delude ourselves into thinking that Israel's *dati* community can completely insulate itself from all of these influences. Glatt Kosher Burger Kings are merely the first herald of things to come.)

Israel can now offer a complete selection of Western goodies in its secular schools: violence, drug abuse, alcohol, plus rowdy rock festivals such as Arad which, like its American progenitors, have already resulted in riots and in deaths of youngsters. That the situation has become precarious is apparent when, reacting to this tragedy, Ezer Weizmann, hardly a paragon of *haredi* rectitude, bemoaned the lack of discipline and the "Americanization" of Israel society. Weizmann warned against the "trend towards copying others. We must beware of Michael Jacksons and Madonnas. We need to return to a culture that is specifically Israeli and Jewish." He decried "the lack of self-discipline and restraint of Israeli society as a whole . . . both in the schools and even in the army."

It is quite unsettling, amidst the lush valleys of the Sharon, the undulating hills of Jerusalem, the winding River Jordan, the still, barren stretches of the Negev, and the brooding *Har haBayit*, to discover that the specter of the *Galut* hovers over this land.

To be sure, the drive for imitation and "normalization" is neither an aberration nor a contemporary phenomenon. It is a natural inclination, which is why the Torah warns us in Lev. 18 — underscored by the Torah reading of Yom Kippur afternoon — that when we enter Canaan we must not emulate the Canaanites. Think about it : If *am Yisrael*, fresh from the numinous desert experience, is tempted to follow the ways of the hostile Canaanites, with their child sacrifices and barbarism and idolatries, how much more so are we tempted to adopt the ways of a friendly, superficially sophisticated, materially successful, and technologically triumphant American civilization.

In fact, the Gaon of Vilna states that the single most difficult temptation (*kasheh neged kulam*) that besets a Jew individually and nationally is expressed in Psalm 26:35: *Vayit'arvu haGoyim vayilmedu ma-aseihem,* "They mixed among the Nations and learned their deeds. . ." (*Birurei Aggadot,* Berakhot 9:1).

Two paths have always been open before us. Either we walk alone on the path of *or Goyim* of Isaiah 42, or we walk with everyone else on the path of *kekhol haGoyim* of Deut. 17 and Ezekiel 20:32.

If secular Zionism shows all the signs of spiritual bankruptcy, the signs are manifest not only in the unseemly haste with which it surrenders so much of the holy land to yesterday's (and probably tomorrow's) terrorists. This is a symptom of a deeper confusion: secular Zionism's attempt to walk both paths simultaneously. It convinced itself that the Jewish people could shed its distinctiveness and still retain its light. Once we create a new kind of un-unique Jew, they claimed, we will be accepted by the family of nations. And if in order to obtain a ticket of admission into this family it is required to renounce the concepts of *va-avdil etkhem min ha-amim* (Lev. 20:24) and of *am segulah* (Ex. 19:55; Deut. 7 & 26) so be it. This is a small price to pay.

Overlooked was a curious fact of life; Jewish uniqueness is not merely a mysterious religious concept, but a practical one as well. The same Bible on which we base our claims to this lovely land also warns us again and again that we will not be able to retain this land unless we retain our holiness and apartness.

Is it a coincidence that the very leaders who represent a rejection of this uniqueness are the same leaders who without any apparent pangs of conscience are preparing to surrender sovereignty over areas redolent with Biblical history: Hebron, Shiloh, Bet-El, Shechem, Bethlehem and its Tomb of Rachel — and even the Old City of Jerusalem? When one abandons Jewish distinctiveness, one abandons not only *Shabbat* and *Yom Tov* and *tefillin* and *kashrut*. Soon enough one surrenders one's pride as a Jew — which is most ironic, since one of the purposes of original Zionist ideology was to restore Jewish pride.

My Siddur and my newspaper have forced me into painful questions. Is Zionism bankrupt? Enough has certainly gone wrong to give that impression. Are Israelis the slavish carriers of the worst excesses of the West? There are certainly enough carriers to give that impression.

Meanwhile, dim glimmers of peace still loom on the horizon. Whether it is a dark and ominous cloud or a bright and warming sun, only God knows. For even if an accommodation with the Arab states somehow guarantees Israel's security through monitors, peace-keepers and electronic surveillance, Israel will still remain at risk, because the risk to Israel and to the Jewish people stems primarily from within.

Perhaps we should append to any peace agreement a private memorandum of understanding with ourselves. Along with the physical monitoring devices, we will establish a spiritual early-warning system that will suppress the overpowering urge to mimetic behavior. The system is readily available today, as it has been for 3,500 years.

Once this is installed, perhaps the day may yet arrive when instead of frightening other countries with our Western baggage, Jewish travelers will be able to demonstrate why the Torah says in Deut. 4:6, *ki hi hokhmatkhem uvinatkhem l'einei haamim*. . . . "for [Torah] is your wisdom and your understanding in the eyes of the Nations. . . ."

In the interim, it would be most helpful if someone would be good enough to inform the Honorable Ezer Weizmann and his friends specifically where they might find some authentic Jewish teachings about discipline, self-restraint, authority, and Jewish uniqueness.

An Unreal Interview: Israel After Fifty

IN HONOR OF ISRAEL'S FIFTIETH anniversary, we interviewed four representative participants: a Jerusalem *haredi*; an Israeli sports fan; a secular Israeli university professor; and the rabbi of a newly built town in Judea-Samaria. The interviews, it should be noted, did not actually take place in the world of reality as we know it, but in another realm entirely: the writer's imagination. Nevertheless, they reflect the currents flowing through Israeli society as she enters the twenty-first century. The mythical interviews took place on *Yom haAtsma'ut*. Below are the questions asked of each participant in these very unusual interviews.

1. What does Israel Independence Day mean to you, and how are you celebrating it?
2. What do you find unique about living in Israel?
3. After fifty years of statehood, what does Zionism mean to you?
4. What do you consider to be (*a*) Israel's greatest achievement in the past fifty years?, and (*b*) its greatest failure?
5. What is the foremost internal challenge facing Israel in the next fifty years?

Haredi

Q1. This is a day like any other day. This morning I will teach in my *heder*, and in the afternoon I will study in my *kollel*. Independence Day? A Jew can never be independent. We are dependent on one another, on our families, and especially on our Creator. I *daven* regularly for His daily miracles, and for His return to Zion and to Jerusalem — but I do not see a need to make a special *yom tov* out of this day. Besides, it was people like these secular Zionists who so despised religion that they took religious immigrant Jewish children from Arab countries, cut off their *peot* and taught them that Torah and *Yahadut* mean nothing. Today all that has been verified. I cannot in good conscience join in with people who could do the things they did to *yaldei* Teheran.

Q2. My family goes back six generations in Jerusalem, through wars and famines, so I am troubled by the incitement against people like me. We are not some dangerous cult. To be publicly ridiculed because one is religious in a Jewish land — this is very hurtful. The media only writes how we refuse to do our part for the country, how we want to force the Torah upon everyone.

Why don't they tell the world that the police in *haredi* neighborhoods are idle because there is so little crime? I don't claim that we are perfect. But why does no one talk about our family life, how we raise our children even though we are poor, how the generations respect and honor each other, how rare divorce is in our community, how widespread is the huge *hesed* and *tsedaka* among us? Are these not contributions to society at large?

Maybe there is prejudice against *haredim* because we are living reminders of what a Jew used to look like — and this makes modern Jews rather uncomfortable. The leftists run to meetings with Arafat and Mubarak and their henchmen. Have they ever sat and talked with a haredi leader? They use language against us that is almost anti-Semitic. They claim to be open and tolerant; where is their tolerance of fellow Jews?

Q3. Secular Zionism is dead, and they know it. Settling the land? The only ones who settle the land these days are people with yarmulkes — and the Zionists call them obstacles to peace. The *kibbutzniks*, the biggest Zionists of all — New York and California are filled with these lovers of Israel. Ninety percent of the *aliyah* from Western countries is Orthodox. Do you find Israeli *haredim* living in the West? Very few. It makes you wonder who the real Zionists are.

I know what really troubles people about us *haredim*: we do not serve in the army. It is a very emotional issue — their sons are protecting us while we seem to be doing nothing to help the land. I understand them, but I think they are not looking deeply enough. Firstly, even in the USA during the worst days of World War II they did not draft students of religion — because religion is crucial for society. Obviously, in times of national emergency we are always ready to do whatever is necessary. But right now we are not living in any national emergency, thank God.

They don't realize that it is not only the army that protects us. Even with the best soldiers and weapons in the world, could we withstand 40 million enemies unless God protected us from them?

Yes, we need the physical soldiers. But we should not forget Who the real Protector of Israel is. The Jewish land is different from all other lands. It also requires spiritual soldiers. And don't think for a moment that it is a life of ease to be a spiritual soldier and to study Torah morning, noon, and night, and to give up many material things. By the way, I do feel that those who are excused from the army because they are studying Torah should be like soldiers; ready to sacrifice everything for the cause of

Torah, dedicated to full-time study and very disciplined. If someone is studying Torah full time and sacrificially the way a soldier does, he should find some way to serve this country.

Q4a. Israel has become a true generator of Torah. Not in 2000 years has there been such widespread Torah study and dedication as there is now in Israel. I don't think Ben Gurion and the founders anticipated this — but it is a fact. We can never be compensated for the destruction of European Jewry, but there is some consolation in the deep level of piety and learning. This is the best answer to our enemies. There is something holy in the atmosphere that makes it all possible.

Q4b. Israel's greatest failure is the coming generation. Too many non-Orthodox youth are empty shells, ignorant of Judaism and of Jewish history. Judaism as a religion, Torah as God's way, is completely foreign to them. Israeli high schools now know violence and drugs and all the good things that we imported from the West — but they don't know who Rashi or Rambam were. Surely we did not wait 2000 years so we could imitate the worst of the world around us! What happened to the light we were supposed to be to the nations?

Q5. The greatest challenge is to fight the overwhelming desire to be like all the nations of the world. Our entire strength is that we are unique and apart — that's what the word *kadosh* means.

That's why the *haredim* make the rest of society nervous, because we stand for this Jewish specialness. Who is ready to give all of *Erets Yisrael* to the Arabs? Jews without Torah. This is no coincidence. They think that if we give everything away to our enemies, then the *Goyim* will pat us on the *keppele* and will love us.

Why do you think I dress in a black hat and long black coat? It's so that I will always remember that I am different, that I am a Jew — and so that others who see me will also remember.

It is decreed from Above that the Jewish people can never be a nation like all other nations. This *ke-khol haGoyim* mentality is our greatest problem. The rest we can handle. I am late for my *kollel*. Excuse me.

Sports Fan

Q1. *Yom haAtsma'ut* means that this day we became a real people like other nations. Up to now we were just wandering from place to place; we were zeroes. Now we have our own land, our own army. We stopped wandering finally and we have a place we call our own. I am celebrating *Yom haAtsma'ut* in the traditional way. The whole family is having a big barbecue — steak, hot dogs and all the trimmings — and I'll be wearing my special chef's outfit — chef's apron, chef's hat, chef's gloves — the works, just like in America.

Q2. I must admit that even though I am proud to be living here, sometimes I am also ashamed. I am proud that we won this year the Eurovision song contest. OK, the Israeli winner was a transvestite, and a lot of people were embarrassed. But I was proud. We are living now, not in the past. We are part of modern society. So he, she, it — whatever — is a transvestite. So what? We shouldn't mix religion into everything. It's enough that the religious keep the buses from running on Shabbat, do they also have to interfere with my song contests?

Don't get me wrong. Even though I go to the football games on Shabbat, my father was a very religious Jew. On Yom Kippur I still go to *bet knesset*. I have nothing against the religious. But they should not try to tell me how to live my life. Like when we won the Eurovision thing, they got very upset. But they are naïve; they don't realize that this put Israel on the map. It proved that we are as good as anyone. Only fifty years of statehood and we won the Eurovision. Who would have dreamed it? The whole world applauded us. Mark my word, some day we will also win the Miss Universe contest and then I will really be proud of us.

But I am also ashamed. You want to know why, I will tell you why. I am ashamed because we are nowhere in soccer. Where is Israel in basketball? Nowhere. Where are we in the Olympics? Nowhere. After fifty years you would think that by now we could compete. No wonder the world has no respect for us. Look at the USA. They are the best in basketball, and that's why they are a superpower and the world respects them. Look at little Mexico. A little country, a poor country — but they are something in soccer. But Israeli sports? Forget it.

Q3. We have developed one of the great armed forces in the world. Without them, do you think we would still be here, with 40 million Arabs wanting to get rid of us? Thank God for them, I say. Without these kids we would all be lost. And another great thing is that in spite of all the problems we have had around here, we have become more and more like the USA — that's one of our great achievements. These days there isn't anything that America has that we don't have. You name it: cable TV, shopping malls, Coca Cola, McDonalds. We even have the golden arches! It's wonderful, I tell you. This is a little country but we have really become something. If only our teams were a little more competitive . . .

Q4. I've already mentioned our failures: our poor record on the playing field. Enough said about that. It only upsets me.

Q5. The challenge for the future is to teach the world that we don't have horns, that we are just like they are. The real problems that Israel has with the world outside is that they think we are different. But we are just the same. They have a land, we have a land. They have a flag, we have a flag. They have their culture, we have our culture. Once we can make the world understand that, then the other problems will be minor. I mean problems like how to make our teams better. But who knows, maybe, with God's help, we can achieve that in the next fifty years. And maybe they go together. I mean, maybe if we can become something in sports, then they will see that we are just like they are. I sure am praying for that. . . .

Professor

Q1. The Jewish nation was asleep for the past 2000 years, and suddenly we awoke and created our own state. It is a veritable resurrection. I am not religious, but to me it is much more important than any other holiday that we have, including Pesah. From slavery and wandering we became sovereign, and we created a democracy. When Israel was established, we declared our independence from the albatross of subservience to the nations of the world. The Jewish nation has always emphasized social justice and we always have stood for universal values, enlightened thinking, and human progress. This is our Jewish heritage and I am proud of that, and that is why I celebrate this day. Now we are subservient to no one.

I don't say special prayers in *beit knesset* today — but then again, the *haredim* don't say special prayers today either. I don't go in to teach today, so I try to read a little, watch the air show, sleep a little later, spend time with my family. And with my family right now I am going to eat hot dogs.

Q2. Here everyone is a Jew and no one points to you like they point at a Jew in the Galut. We have our own land like everyone else, and we are a nation among many nations. I have never understood why Jews like the *haredim* insist on being different. Maybe if we Jews would try harder to blend into civilization, maybe there would be less anti-Semitism.

The *haredim* remind me of a way of life that we should forget. Why do they insist on dressing all in black, and why must their women be all covered up? We are no longer in the Galut. This is Israel, the homeland of the Jew with muscles who rolls up his sleeves and wears shorts and is not ashamed of his body like the *Galut* Jew is.

We are all Jews, but we don't think the same way. It's almost as if we were two different nations. Sometimes I really wonder if they belong here at all.

Don't misunderstand. I believe in pluralism, in live and let live. But why must they hide behind barricades, shut off from the outside world? What are they interested in? Not art, not music, not dance, not culture. Their lives are circumscribed only by the Torah. If they don't enter the modern world soon they will collapse economically from within. And why must they have such large families?

Q3-4. Our greatest achievement is that we became a haven for the oppressed. We rescued millions of Jews from Europe, the Arab world, Ethiopia and Russia. All the disparate cultures have been successfully absorbed within our tiny country. We sacrificed a great deal in order to do this. The Law of Return is the most generous piece of legislation in history. And we have done all this by our own power, by perseverance and sheer guts. This is true Zionism.

Q4b. Our greatest failure is our identity problem. Are we a modern nation in the modern world? Or are we a nation run by medieval clerics? We cannot have it both ways. The ethics of the Torah are fine, but what connection do its other laws have with life in the 21st century? You can't be loyal to an ancient document and at the same time compete in the modern world. Israel was founded to be a modern nation. But we got lost and allowed our thinking to be dominated by outdated standards. Our greatest failure is that we have not resolved this ambivalence about who we are and where we are going. Once and for all we ought to decide that we are part of the world, and if some do not like this, I say let them go live in some fundamentalist state like Iran or Saudi Arabia.

Q5. Unity is the great issue, but we can never achieve it as long as others are forcing their way of life upon us. The Torah is OK, but it should not impinge on my personal autonomy. If I want to marry a non-Jew, or bring in non-kosher meat, I should be permitted to do so. Israel has to be more open, more pluralistic, more democratic. The truth is that if they want to persuade me about the beauties of Torah, they would get better results if they did not appear to be forcing their will upon me. I am willing to learn, but not when it is coerced learning.

Let me make this clear: I am not religious, but I do believe in God in my own way. Even though I do not perform the mitsvot or pray to God, I am a good person and I try to do the right thing. I am tolerant of others. I believe in an open society. This is real Judaism. The Orthodox don't have a monopoly on what Judaism is. And the kind of Judaism they teach is of no relevance to me. If Torah is eternal, why don't I ever hear what it says about unemployment, or the environment, or poverty, or integrity in government and business? All I hear is the sound of stones being thrown at cars on Shabbat.

Besides, I live in Israel and this is enough to be a good Jew. Ben Gurion used to quote the Talmud that living outside of Israel is like having no God — so since I live in Israel that means I am as a good a Jew as anyone, right?

Judea-Samaria Rabbi

Q1. Just because *Yom haAtsma'ut* happened in our lifetime does not mean it lacks historical significance. For me, modern Israel shows the hand of God entering Jewish history in an open way. So today I participated in special *tefillot*. We recited *hallel* — should God not be praised on such a day? I consider it a significant day, so I dress in my *yom tov* clothes.

There are Jews who because of religious reasons feel that they cannot celebrate this day. For them it makes no sense to have special prayers for the modern State, because the State is only important as a means to help them serve God. I don't agree with them. But on the other hand, the opposite point of view — that the state is the end-all and be-all of Jewish life — is not a Jewish concept at all.

Things are not black and white. Some say that to avoid being tainted, and to live a life of unfettered holiness, a religious Jew must separate from non-religious society. If there is a holy community within a not-yet-holy community, everyone will ultimately be sanctified in a subtle way. But others hold that we cannot shape Jewish society unless we are part of it. I myself agree with the second group. I do not think separation is the Jewish way.

How I mark this day is not ordained from Sinai. Others have their own way. I love and respect them. Some go to football games, and some attend the parades, and some learn Torah all day, and some sleep late, and some live in Tel Aviv and some, like me, live out here among the barren and lonely hills in the Judean desert. I do not say that each of these ways has equal weight in the eyes of the Holy One, but it is not for me to judge others.

We are all Jews and we share a common fate and destiny in this land. Every pebble here contains holiness and sanctity, and every Jew is imbued with sanctity — yes, including the soul of the so-called secular Jew. Every Jew in his heart of hearts realizes that there is a God above him Who protects the Jewish people and the Jewish land.

Q2. Moshe Rabbenu was not privileged ever to step foot on this soil — but I not only can walk on it, but can plant on it and build on it, and watch my children grow up speaking our biblical language and living by our Torah. To be living on the land where Joshua walked, and Isaiah and Jeremiah, to breathe the same air, to climb the same hills! I am ecstatic with joy.

Q3. Zionism is only a label. Every Jew is a Zionist, because every Jew has a soul that pulls upwards towards holiness — and in the quest for holiness the Holy Land is indispensable. One can reach great heights of holiness in the *Golah*, but here it has much more resonance and depth. Yes, we should settle the land — but not because it is a tenet of Zionism, and not for military or political reasons. Rather, it is the natural thing for the Jewish soul to want to be in the Land. Yes, we should ingather the exiles from around the world and bring them back to their land — not because it is part of Zionism, but because it is the way we fulfill the biblical prophecies. We must become a true light to the nations by the way we live and conduct ourselves. True, we have a long way to go, but the raw material is right here, within each one.

I think even secular Zionism had a religious dimension to it. The fact that the secular Zionists did not settle for Uganda or some other place — although Herzl probably would have — shows that they had their roots in the Torah, even though they would not admit it. I don't know when the Messiah will come, but he will come.

Deep within even the most secular Zionist there is a hidden strain of the ancient Jewish Messianic belief.

Q4a. Israel's greatest achievement is in its very existence. The very fact that it IS, demonstrates that God is. In all these 2000 years of exile, the Jewish people never gave up on the Torah's promise that some day God would return us to the Land. We kept our faith in Him, and He kept His faith in us and brought us back. And if this impossible dream is beginning to be realized before our very eyes, then it is obvious that everything in the Torah — not just the prophecies about the Land but the laws of the Torah, the ethics, the mitsvot, the warnings, the hope — is all true. They all come from the same God and the same Torah. It is confusion to select from the Torah that which pleases us and discard that which displeases us and makes us uncomfortable.

Q4b. We have become splintered. Right, left, moderate, peaceniks, *haredim*, secularist, South Tel Avivans, North Tel Avivans, development towns, major cities, Sephardim, Ashkenazim, black hats, *kippah serugah*, black *kippah*, *kollelim*, universities, *hasidim*, *mitnagedim*, hawks, doves. Such a small land, such a tiny nation, and so many factions. Even our neighborhoods are carefully delineated. Up to this street is *haredi*, from that point on is *kippah serugah*, and then there begins a secular neighborhood, and after that the Sephardim live, and after that the Hasidim — and so on and on. Few of us look sympathetically at our neighbor unless he is exactly like we are, and every group shouts at every other. At the same time. The din is deafening, the cacophony is maddening. Does any other small country have so many newspapers for so small a population — each with its own agenda? Does any other small country have so many different political parties? Our greatest failure is that we have forgotten that we are one people, coming from one source, that we have one God, one Torah, one destiny.

Q5. The survivalist stage of Israel's existence is, we pray, ending. Now we enter a new stage — not just to survive, but to become a holy people. Each Jew has the challenge of becoming a better Jew, a better person. To study Torah more, to learn about God more, to submit to God's will, to understand that we are not independent creatures, that we have a mission on this earth — not just to eat and sleep. We were put on this earth in order to bring the idea of God to all mankind.

After we begin working on that, the next great challenge is to try to bridge the differences that divide us. True, we cannot compromise on basic beliefs, and I am not prepared to surrender my belief in God, Torah, the Jewish destiny and the sacred character of this Land. But all of us can look more lovingly at those who are different from us. Not at the type of head covering or jacket we wear, but at what we are inside — brothers and sisters. To stop being suspicious of one another and to learn to trust one another. We spend so much energy on peace with the Arabs — what about peace with fellow Jews?

The primary challenge is to become a Jewish Jew. God has given us this land as a vehicle to achieve this. Rescue and immigration are extremely important, but they are the means towards the primary purpose: to reach out and touch God, and to teach the world how to do this. We should grasp at the opportunity. Otherwise we may have to wait another 2000 years before we have this chance again.

Overtaken by History

Once again, only the names have changed.

ABBA EBAN CONCLUDES HIS RECENTLY published memoirs with an exhortation for Israeli youth to adhere to the ideals of the founders of the State.

Prime Minister Rabin eulogizes the victims of an Israeli tragedy at sea by reciting comforting poetry by Natan Alterman and other twentieth century Israeli writers. He also refers to the ideals of the founders.

Minister of Education Shulamit Aloni issues a barrage of anti-religious directives and broadsides to teachers and students in government-sponsored schools, reminding them regularly that they are free to reject any aspect of Jewish tradition which they choose.

Does this mean that Israeli secularism is on the ascendancy? Not necessarily. Israeli secularism's insensitivity to Jewish tradition and its anti-religious posturing barely conceal the serious spiritual bankruptcy of a group that has been overtaken by history.

Granted, this secularism is not going gently into that good night, but going it is nevertheless. To take a twentieth century example, Soviet Communism was dead years before it collapsed, but very few were aware of its actual parlous condition. There was bluff and bluster and sabre-rattling, but as it turned out, there was nothing to fear: it had lost all sense of vision and it was only a matter of time before gravity would exercise its immutable law and pull it down. *Mutatis mutandis* — one is not equating fellow Jews with Soviet Communists — Israeli secularism has degenerated into a rejection of traditional Jewish ideals in favor of a *laissez-faire* quasi-Jewishness without discipline or moorings. And so it drifts, content to flail away at the Orthodox. Were it not for the gaffes and occasionally unspiritual behavior of Orthodox political leaders, the secularists would have little to do.

Yes, there is tumult and shouting: yes, they seem to run the government. But sitting on a cabinet seat doth not an ideology make, and beneath the cant and the sloganeering, the foundations are visibly slipping away. Ms. Aloni and friends may find diversion by inciting the wrath of the religious community, but thoughtful secularist observers acknowledge their own spiritual malaise.

That Israeli secularism — despite its last hurrah in the present government — is in its death throes is evident from the facts on the line: the younger secular generation finds in the ideals and theories of their kibbutz progenitors little meaning for their own lives; hence Eban's anxiety. Zionism per se is dismissed as pie in the sky; secular youngsters often parrot Arab propaganda and wonder aloud why Israelis have taken the land away from the Arabs. They abandon the kibbutz in droves — physically and spiritually — for the less austere city life, and ultimately for the greater comfort and material opportunities of Canada and the USA. That most sacred tenet of the secular Zionist canon — settling in the Land — is utterly ignored. As the secularists painfully know, *yeridah* from Israel is primarily a secular phenomenon, while *aliyah* to Israel from the West is primarily Orthodox. According to conservative estimates, there are close to a half a million Israelis now residing in the West. That is to say — and this is the most painful wound of all — that while those raised on a religion-less diet abandon

Israel for the lure of the West, those raised on Torah and mitsvah observance apparently do not find it as difficult to abandon the luxuries of the West for a less comfortable life in Israel, resulting in the anomaly that finds Hebrew spoken in American electronics stores on 42nd Street and on Pico Boulevard, and English spoken in Israeli yeshivot like *Kerem B'Yavneh and Mir*.

The Orthodox in Israel — the *hasidim, haredim, Sephardim*, or *kippot serugot* — ask a troubling question of the secularists: who today are the real lovers of Zion?

※※※

Israeli secularists would do well to contemplate the strengths of the Orthodox across the board. One should not romanticize — no group is free of problems — but it is clear, for example, that there is little crime among the Orthodox, that its youth is not plagued with drug problems, that so-called alternative lifestyles, supposedly based on genetics, make no inroads upon them, that families are more stable than the norm. When one thinks of concepts like self-sacrifice and idealism in contemporary Israel, what comes to mind — whether or not one agrees with their agenda — are the "Gush-niks" and "Kook-nicks" who found and man new settlements, who love Israel in deed and not only in word, and who have a sense of Jewish vision and Jewish destiny. And certainly the traditional approach to the mysteries of life and death, good and evil, joy and suffering, is far more satisfying than the failed hedonism, positivism and Marxism of the secularists. In addition, the entire spectrum of Israeli Orthodoxy is graced with remarkable leaders whose integrity, scholarship, wisdom, and resultant moral power are undeniable. By every measure, the community which adheres to Torah in Israel has every reason to view the future with confidence and assurance.

There are complex reasons for this strength, but one ingredient which the secularists could with profit emulate is the attribute of pride, the sense of Jewishness uniqueness and distinctiveness. The Orthodox have a sense of past and of respect for sacred history, they know what they are about, and thus do not find it necessary to accommodate themselves to every transitory intellectual or ideological vogue.

One admires the passion and fire which characterized the early founders of the State. But one of the reasons they did not succeed in creating new generations of followers is that, despite their emphasis on the material of Jewish archeology, they closed their eyes to the teleology of Jewish history. The immutable fact is that movements within Jewish life which have lacked the components of spirit, faith and passionate belief in the unique destiny of *am Yisrael* have invariably collapsed under their own weight.

Surely Messrs. Eban, Rabin, and friends do not need to be reminded that there is a Jewish classical tradition of idealism and vision which antedates Weizmann and Ben Gurion, but for some reason they are shy about invoking it. Their religious embarrassment — even the Book of Psalms is apparently deemed inappropriate for comforting bereaved families — is itself embarrassing, and has transformed what once upon a time was movement with a point of view, (a greatly misguided secular one, to be sure, but a point of view nevertheless) into a hollow shell. Face it: if Jewish tradition is only one hundred years old, why should any intelligent individual want to give up anything for it? Why not indeed opt for the easier life of the West?

It would be naïve to urge Israeli secularists to don black hats or *kappottes* or *kipot serugot* and enter yeshivot or *kollelim*. But their ship, having lost its rudder, is slowly sinking (which does not cause one great sorrow), and with it are sinking hundreds of thousands of Jews (which does cause great sorrow). The eroded condition of Jewish secularism — currently in political power but all dressed up with no place to go — should be a catalyst for a radical course adjustment. And in a rapidly changing world, an Israel without spiritual ballast is dangerous to its own health.

Certainly, the Orthodox have enough stock-taking to do to keep occupied for decades. The Orthodox house is far from being in order, but at the very least it has a present and a past, and therefore a future. Those of our Israeli secular brothers and sisters who are concerned about a Jewish future might want to reconsider their relationship to that Jewish past. And pride in the uniqueness of that history would be a small first step.

"Lifnei shever gaon," says King Solomon in Prov. 16:18. "Pride goeth before the fall." In this case, pride might help prevent the fall — and could in time bring the secularists back into the mainstream of Jewish life. For to ignore history — particularly Jewish sacred history — is ultimately to be overtaken by that history.

Strange Bedfellows

THE VITUPERATIVE ANTI-RELIGIOUS MOUTHINGS OF leading Israeli secularists are by now a fact of daily life. When the religious residents of the so-called West Bank are referred to as "gangsters, criminals against humanity, pogromists and murderers" (novelist Amos Oz); or seen to be "exactly like the Hitler Youth"(Prof. Moshe Zimmerman, of the Hebrew University); or *haredim* are habitually called parasites, or a famous Tel Aviv artist refers to the many *haredi* children as insects, one can only feel pity for a Jew who can spew such venom at other Jews. But the fervor of the invective no longer surprises.

What was surprising, however, was the recent call from some leading secularists to fight the Orthodox by joining the Conservative and Reform movements in Israel. This proposed *shidduch* makes no sense, for a secularist by definition has nothing to do with religion; and the Reform and Conservative claim to be religious groups.

There are several ways to approach this conundrum:

- Perhaps the fear of the Orthodox is so great that secularists would even join a religious group just as long as it gives pain to the Orthodox. The enemy of my enemy is my friend.

- Perhaps the secularists, in their heart of hearts, do not really believe that the Reform and Conservative are religious movements. Thus, to become part of them is not really a contradiction. If so, the secular overtures to the non-Orthodox are in fact a great tribute to the Israeli Orthodox.

There is, however, a more likely third option. Israeli secularists and the Reform/Conservative do share one quality in common: the inability to resist the blandishments of the society around them. The Reform movement in the USA provides Exhibit A. There, the left-wing liberal agenda of America sets the Reform agenda: same-sex "marriages" are condoned, homosexual and lesbian rabbis are permitted to lead congregations, abortions are approved, huge rates of intermarriage are tolerated, conversions to Judaism are performed on demand. And whatever American Reform does today is followed by the Conservatives tomorrow.

Exhibit B is the now infamous display by the Reform group in Jerusalem of an educational kit designed by a college student for seventh graders. It describes the Binding of Isaac as an act of molestation by Abraham upon his son Isaac. The accompanying text states that "sexual immorality represents the complete violation of trust between parent and child." The deputy director-general of Reform in Israel, while disagreeing with the interpretation, defended the display as "a bold attempt at explaining the story."

It apparently never occurred to Reform leadership not to show such offensive material. That would be censorship, a naughty word. Besides, child molestation is a very with-it subject today. Why not display the kit as a sign of sophistication and of freedom of expression?

It is perhaps unkind but not untrue to note that the non-Orthodox seem to be more affected by the fashion *du jour* of the world around them than by the thinking of the classical Jewish world. And it is this that binds together Israeli secularists and the Reform/Conservative groups. This, and their common fear of the Orthodox, makes it possible for these strangers to become bedfellows.

The deference to foreign influences is not an intrinsic Jewish trait. What has historically separated the men from the boys in Jewish history has been the biblical concept of *am kadosh*, a holy people.

To be holy means not simply to be very pious; it refers to the ability to be separate and apart, to be unique, and to have standards different from the nations. Most Jews, even non-observant ones, have always been proud to march to the beat of a different drummer. To be distinctively Jewish was a crown they wore with dignity and self-respect.

But a minority was always troubled by this concept. For them, like the early Jewish Hellenists, the very thought of difference was anathema. Instead, it was crucial for the Jews to be accepted by the world, and the only way to be accepted was to become less different.

It is this *Galut* mentality — rather than the proud heritage of Jewish distinctiveness — that is preserved by Israeli secularists and makes it possible for them to consider a liaison with any partner who would dilute the idea of *kadosh*.

Imitation, however, is risky: imitate something long enough and it soon becomes difficult to distinguish between the facsimile and the original. Without the protective hedges of mitsvot and their discipline, one slides down the slippery slope and ends up — in a variation of what psychiatry calls the "Stockholm Syndrome" — as a carbon copy of non-Jewish society.

Amos Oz and his benighted cohorts are vivid examples. Enamored of the world's value system, scornful of Jewish distinctiveness, they hit the bottom of the slope by (*a*) a willingness to jettison their own secularist principles, and (*b*) by engaging in a form of Jewish anti-Semitic rhetoric — what other term can be used for it? — that demonstrates the dangers of becoming what you imitate. And that is not very becoming.

Believers and Unbelievers in the Land that Defies Belief

HAS IT BEEN FIFTY YEARS that Jews have been in our sovereign State of Israel? Founded in the wake of the destruction of European Jewry, immediately attacked by all the Arab armies in the region, did this fractious, contentious, broken people actually maintain a state for fifty whole years — surviving wars in 1948 and 1956 and 1967 and 1973, Scud attacks in 1991, and heightened terrorism in 1997-98 and 2001 — has all this happened to us in just fifty years? It strains one's credulity, and yet here we are, a half century later, looking back in wonder and amazement and in awe.

Awe might be the best word. By all logical standards, this cannot be, this independent Jewish state. But it is.

It is enough to make one a believer in a guiding hand of destiny, to make one a believer in the God of Israel. In the midst of all the hoopla of the fifty-year celebration, above the din of fireworks and patriotic speeches, these are the best words: awe and wonder.

How did this happen? Just the fact that this ungovernable Jewish people has a government; that this sharply divided, opinionated, querulous, stiff-necked people holds peaceful elections; that members of this blend of nations and colors and traditions and languages manage to get on a bus and arrive at a desired destination day in and day out — this is an awesome achievement. Only a loving God could have made it possible for such an open miracle to take place in such a hidden way. It is enough to make a believer out of anyone.

Not that Israel after fifty years does not have its problems, external and internal. As I write these lines, for example, I am trying to find the distribution center for gas masks, just in case our friend Saddam Hussein gets desperate. And internal strife and *kulturkampf* lurk at the doorstep, as religious and secular spokesmen snarl at one another in the news media.

The miracle of Israel should be enough to make believers out of everyone, but one of the great issues that agitates Israel these days — so we are informed — is precisely this matter of believers and unbelievers.

※※※

But who knows what we can believe about believers and unbelievers in this quite unbelievable land? Certainly we cannot believe what we are told by the news media or by politicians — especially since Israel's media is, in the European journalistic tradition, deeply yellow. Such people tend to talk in sound bytes, to employ the catchy phrase designed for the evening news or the morning headlines. The believers among them claim that the unbelievers are ruining the country; and the unbelievers among them say the same about the believers.

On the surface, the contrasts could not be greater. The Orthodox, who like to believe that they are the true believers, find themselves a dynamic and powerful force in the country. Although still a numerical minority, the Orthodox — in which we include observant Jews across the spectrum, from *kipah serugah* to *shtreimel*, from Modern Orthodox to *haredi* — have experienced remarkable physical and spiritual growth. The physical growth is manifested in increasing economic clout and political influence. The spiritual growth is manifested by phenomenal success in retaining their young people through a strong network of schools and yeshivot, and by an increasing intensity in Torah scholarship and in piety. In many quarters it is grudgingly acknowledged that Orthodox young people constitute the last remaining vestige of idealism in the country. *Yeridah* among the Orthodox is very low; Orthodox *aliyah* from the West is the highest of any group.

By contrast, those whom some like to call unbelievers — the non-Orthodox or secular population — seem to be a community without moorings. Zionism is today derided as pie in the sky; even the kibbutzim are losing people in droves to the more alluring and materialistic cities, if not to Canada and the USA. One half million Israelis, most of them non-observant, live in the West. Imitation of the West and particularly of America seems to the leitmotif of non-Orthodox young people. Western dress, music, attitudes and fads are dominant. In the schools, violence and drugs are not the rarity that they should be. Ignorance of Jewishness is endemic. There are secular high school graduates in Israel who have not heard of Mishnah, much less studied it; who know precious little about Jewish history or Jewish heritage; who have never heard of Rashi; who have never entered a synagogue; and for whom Judaism as a religion is completely foreign.

Thus Israel at its fiftieth year seems divided in two camps: believers and unbelievers. Gentlemen, start your engines, we are told: the culture wars are about to commence.

But it is possible that all this is only surface reflection. Somehow, what the media tells us does not seem to square with the reality that we experience daily in Israel. A more careful examination suggests that the religious-secular divide must not be viewed in simplistic black and white terms, and that perhaps the Israeli secularists are not as far removed from religion as seems at first glance.

Firstly, it would be desirable if the term "secularist" were expunged from the Israeli lexicon. The word suggests an anti-religious position that is philosophically and ideologically based. But there is some persuasive evidence that indicates that the use of that term to describe a non-observant Jew is misleading. Not long ago, for example, the report of the Avi Chai Foundation's Guttman Institue suggested that non-observant Israelis are far less anti-religious or even non-religious than is generally assumed. A full forty percent say that they are "somewhat observant," sixty percent believe in the existence of God, and more than a third believe in a world-to-come and the coming of the Messiah.

These rather surprising figures imply that the militantly anti-religious animus that supposedly pervades half of Israeli's citizenry may be highly exaggerated. This is supported by a host of anecdotal evidence: the non-observant person seated next to you on the bus, the non-observant clerk at the supermarket, the non-observant bookdealer, the non-observant taxi driver, do not spout the anti-religious venom that emanates from left-wing politicians or columnists.

On the contrary, it may well be that much of the Israeli population possesses an innate and latent sympathy for traditional Judaism. Many observers have noted, for example, that Labor's defeats in recent national elections were in a large part due to its extreme anti-religious image. In fact, even the secularly oriented Meretz party has been trying to soften its anti-religious dimension in an effort to attract a broader constituency.

To be sure, there is resentment against some Orthodox ways and habits, but in the great religious issues of belief and practice, the division is less an impenetrable abyss than a deep but traversable valley. If this study at all reflects reality, then it is a testimony to the staying power of Torah and Jewish heritage among all strata of Israeli society.

At the same time, this would indicate that the Israeli Orthodox, with all their fine work in *kiruv* and outreach, are still reaching only the fringes of the non-Orthodox community. Faced with a non-observant population that is open to Jewish tradition, Israeli Orthodoxy has been unable to step effectively into the breach. Whether because of a lack of tools, or a misreading of reality, or an innate hostility to those who are non-observant, or a confusion between that which is non-observant and that which is anti-religious, the fact is that the Israeli Orthodox have not been able to make meaningful inroads into the lives and habits of the non-observant. They have been very successful with their inreach, but much less so in their outreach. (The same can be said for the American Orthodox, but that is a separate discussion.)

A religious-secular *kulturkampf* may not be imminent, but neither is a major religious revival imminent. Further, it is questionable whether the residue of positive feelings about the tradition will on its own continue into the future. Good feelings, sentiment, memories and general beliefs can only stretch so far. Without solid knowledge reinforcing its base, even sympathetic attitudes can dissipate within a generation. The heterodox movements, donning a traditional yarmulke for Israeli consumption, are trying to fill this gap. But they are doomed to failure: Israelis by and large do not take seriously religious movements that sanction intermarriage, look askance at homosexuality, ordain female rabbis, and that have presided over a 70% rate of intermarriage in America.

One wonders, at this juncture in the history of the Jewish state, about some new approaches. For example:

Has the time come for the Orthodox to recognize the essential Jewishness of fellow Jews even when they are profoundly ignorant and non-observant of their Torah? This involves looking directly at them, not suspiciously as through a glass darkly. It involves accepting them on their own terms, understanding who they are and why they are as they are. It means recognizing that non-observant Jews are not the enemy, that they are not willfully rebelling against God and his Torah. It means walking in the ways of Aharon haKohen: *ohev et habriot um'karvan laTorah*, that we must "love fellow human beings and bring them close to Torah" (Avot I: 12). Note that the text does not say that we are to love them *in order* to bring them closer to Torah, but that we are to love them *and* bring them close to Torah. Our love for others is not to be a love that is focused on bringing them close to Torah; our love is to be unconditional, with no ulterior purpose in mind. Only such genuine concern will be *m'karvan laTorah*.

It means looking inward and asking ourselves a difficult question: does our daily conduct inspire love of Torah or disdain for it? Do the ways we talk, shop, drive, interact with others, bring honor to that Torah which we represent and whose teachings we so devoutly wish were widely accepted? One Orthodox Jew displaying elementary *hesed* can do more to build love for Torah than can a hundred classes, discussion groups, and textbooks. Conversely, one Orthodox Jew can undo hundreds of texts. One is known as *kiddush haShem;* the other, *hillul haShem*.

Most importantly, opening windows means dealing with our collective xenophobia — the fear of the stranger who is unlike us. Why do we shy away from close contact with the non-observant? Should there, for example, be a sense of unease when a non-observant Jew moves into my Orthodox Israeli neighborhood? Am I fearful of being religiously diluted, tainted, or tempted? Why all those real-estate ads in Israel which announce that this newly built area, or that apartment, is "For Religious"? That is to say, if a non-religious couple wants to live in a neighborhood of *shomrei Shabbat*, they would not be welcome. Here we have, writ in concrete, a message of exclusion. We want no part of you. Your presence contaminates. You are not welcome among us.

Opening windows means that perhaps in today's climate, when the souls of all Jews are yearning for a touch of sanctity, it might be in the best interests of God, Torah and Israel for at least a few Jews to attempt to break through the isolating walls that separate us from the non-observant and to initiate some contact with them.

Would the sky fall if, here and there, a handful of Orthodox Jews considered the possibility of living in non-Orthodox neighborhoods? Who can measure the effect on a community of understanding, giving, observant families? And might not the experience also have a beneficial effect on members of the Orthodox families themselves, causing them to look at themselves anew and to articulate the religious ways that they had always taken for granted?

What catastrophe might ensue if articulate Orthodox youngsters met with their non-Orthodox counterparts? Need we fear that our point of view will not hold its own? And if Orthodox adults — merchants, professionals, housewives, thinkers, teachers — were to meet for regular conversations with their non-Orthodox counterparts, would not Torah be the gainer in the long run?

Certainly Orthodox Jews can afford to shed some of the religious fears that have marked our lives for the past generation. Orthodoxy is no longer on the defensive, no longer in danger of extinction. Israeli Orthodoxy — even the *haredi* variety — can afford to emulate American Orthodoxy and to enter the arena and take some minor risks in the hope of demonstrating to others the spiritual and physical joys of living by Torah norms. The fear of dilution from those not as observant as we claim to be is today — with non-Orthodox ideology in disrepair and non-Orthodox Jews in search of meaning and purpose — an anachronism. The insecurities of the past can now give way to the self-confidence of a movement that, despite all odds, has shown its mettle and its staying power.

Perhaps such contacts with those unlike us would have an ancillary benefit as well. Once we learn to look beneath the surface at those who differ from us, we might also learn how to get along better with our own Orthodox brethren — who may have a different order of prayers, or wear a different head covering, or a different kind of suit or dress, or speak with a different accent, but who believes in the same God and follow the same Torah and halakhah. If we can learn to get along with those who are not observant, we might along the way gain the salutary benefit of even learning to get along with the Orthodox.

It has been fifty years of tension and stress, internal and external. Somehow with the help of a merciful Creator, we have made it through so far. One can be permitted some daydreams. Impractical, unworkable, naïve they may be, but what is life without an occasional dream? And dream we must if we are to move forward as a caring and growing community of Jews.

A Jerusalem Lament

WE SHOULD HAVE KNOWN IT would come to this. Now, with hindsight it is all so obvious.

For a long time we did not take it seriously. Well, we said, even if secular Israelis do not observe, even if they do not believe, they do at least identify with the Land and the history of *am Yisrael*; they continue to live here despite all difficulties, they are willing to give up their lives for it, they identify with the Jewish people.

What we did not realize was that, when you lose contact with the Jewish past, sooner or later you lose contact with the Jewish present and the Jewish future; that inevitably, when you stop thinking like a Jew and praying like a Jew and practicing like a Jew, you lose your identification with the Jewish people, and even your identification with the Jewish Land becomes skewed, and it becomes like any other — Greece, Spain, Turkey: un-special, ordinary, just another homeland, another refuge to which Jews can escape when they need a place to take them in.

We did not realize that when God becomes dispensable, His Land also becomes dispensable. The signs were clear; we should have seen them coming, but we were blinded.

When Israel's Declaration of Independence contained no mention of the God of Israel except for an oblique reference to the "Rock of Israel," we swallowed hard but accepted it. Time will change these things, we said; they mean well; let us be patient.

When through the years, official statements at significant occasions — even eulogies for Israel's leaders — rarely referred to a Creator, and when Prime Ministers, offering condolences to familes of the war dead, preferred to quote contemporary secular poets instead of quoting Psalms, we took no offense, ascribing it not to hostility to Torah but to self-consciousness about religion.

When, after the Six-Day War, the Israeli Chief of Staff declared that the startling victory was not a result of any help from above but was the result of superior planning and tactics, we were hurt, but we kept silent. They are religiously unlettered, we said, they mean well, and in time they will learn.

We knew the secularist leaders considered God, Torah and mitsvot to be albatrosses around the neck of the Jewish body politic, designed for the *Galut* Jew but no longer necessary in a Jewish land, but we were confident that if we were patient, they would ultimately see the error of their ways.

When in their schools the Bible was taught as secular literature and not as a holy book; when their primary fantasy to be accepted *kechal hagoyim* resulted in a secular generation which, like the nations they wanted so desperately to emulate, had little commitment to anything beyond their immediate needs, and for whom even concepts like Zionism became epithets and terms of derision; when much of their youth abandoned the kibbutz for the less austere city life where they worshipped Michael Jackson and the idols of the West, and then joined the hundreds of thousands of *yordim* who had already gone down to live in Montreal and Los Angeles where the cars are bigger and the living easier, and where, if they happened to wander into a synagogue in the land of their dispersion, they embarrassed themselves and us by their sheer ignorance of the rudimentary aspects of Judaism — when we witnessed these things, we were saddened, but we maintained our silence, not wanting to drive them further away.

Yes, we were impatient and angry, but these were directed at the Orthodox Jews who refused the secularists any respect or honor; and we, the tolerant ones, painted the other Orthodox Jews in the black colors of the fanatic, the benighted, and the extreme. Patience, we counseled, all is not lost. The secularists mean well.

And if now the secular leaders shake the hands of murderers and grant them international honor and prestige; and if these same leaders can now benignly transmogrify yesterday's terrorist into today's protector of Jewish settlements; and if they willingly and without pressure surrender territories which place the Arab enemy within minutes of Jerusalem; and if they now explain away the daily atrocities as attacks not on Jews but on the peace process, and the murderers as mere fanatics but not members of the suddenly peace-loving PLO, and maintain that we — but not the Arabs — must take risks for peace; and if they look with scorn at settlers who risk their lives to establish a Jewish presence in the face of mortal enemies and who are the only remaining Zionists in Israel; and if, from their affluent apartments in Tel Aviv and Jerusalem, they are now ready to write off Judea and Samaria, and inform the settlers that if they don't like it they can "go back to America," should we really be surprised?

It is all so clear now in retrospect, and we should have seen it all along. Once the anchor disappears, once heritage, Torah, and God, are abandoned, it follows like the night the day that one becomes so empty of Jewish ideals, so devoid of commitment to any Jewish guiding principles, that one willingly gives up all that is precious in exchange for a smile, a handshake, a pat on the back: Jericho today, the Golan tomorrow, Jerusalem the day after that — and then, certainly, the Peace Prize.

It should have come as no surprise, because once you cast overboard the truths of Torah, what enters the heart instead are absurd delusions which insist that savage murderers can become trusted partners in peace.

From Herzl's willingness to settle for Uganda to Rabin's and Peres's eagerness to give away Jericho, there runs — with the happy aberration of Menachem Begin — a straight, inexorable line.

We should have known it would come to this. Now, with hindsight, it is all so obvious.

PART THREE

Observing Jews

Tefillin in a Brown Paper Bag

THE IDEA FIRST STRUCK ME on a recent trans-Atlantic flight. On my seat I found a copy of the London *Economist.* Though not a devotee of the dismal science, I am a hopelessly compulsive reader and so I browsed through it. I soon found myself reveling in its felicitous style, its elegant phrasing, its precision, its supple prose and keen sense of language. Here, as we say in the South, is English as she is truly spoke — or writ.

And then I picked up the Orthodox Jewish periodical which I had brought with me (whether it was a daily, weekly, monthly, or quarterly shall not be revealed in order to protect the innocent) and the sudden change in atmosphere gave me the literary bends. The alphabet and the words were English, but the sentence structure, the rhythm, the syntax, the tone, were of another language altogether. It dawned on me that what I was reading was not language at all but a jargon.

This is not an isolated case. With some admirable exceptions — such as many of the translations and compilations of classic Jewish texts which clearly are significant contributions to the understanding of major Jewish sources — the lamentable fact is that in much of today's American Torah Judaica in English, be they periodicals or books, one experiences that same bends-inducing jargon that, like some sleight of hand, appears to be English but is not.

You may ask: so what? If it informs and occasionally even uplifts, then who cares if the phrasing is inelegant or the words inappropriate? What difference does it make as long as it does the job?

The point is, however, that poor language cannot do the job, cannot inform or uplift in any lasting way. When language is inadequate, simplistic and one-dimensional, then ideas that are potentially sophisticated, profound, and subtle will, in the reader's mind, be reduced to simplistic and one-dimensional proportions. Impoverished language cannot accurately reflect the wealth of great concepts. Furthermore, since language is the handmaiden of thought, careless thinking results in careless expression, and careless expression has a deleterious effect on thinking. A chronic inability to express ideas ultimately results in a chronic dearth of ideas. When language is inappropriate, thought is stillborn.

Beyond theory, the use of deficient language has practical negative consequences as well, for it prevents us from preaching to anyone but the Orthodox choir. Intelligent, educated non-Orthodox Jews will surely be put off by the argot which passes for much of Torah Judaica today. By and large, we do not, quite literally (or illiterally), write or speak their language. For jargon by definition is a simple, elemental form of communication which includes only the initiated and eliminates everyone else from the discussion. It is hard to imagine that any thinking individual can be persuaded of the depths of Torah when — quite beyond grating misusages such as "being that" instead of "since"; "comes to tell us" instead of "informs us"; "brings down" instead of "cites" — the ideas of Torah are presented in jejune and puerile language. This is a pity, for Torah is precious enough to deserve elegance, grace, sophistication, and precision. After all, we don't wrap our tefillin in brown paper bags, or bind our *sifrei Torah* with coarse, ugly ropes. A world-view which is inadequately articulated not only fails to communicate, but repels those whom it would reach.

The dolorous condition of Orthodox writing may not have come about by design, but it was certainly predictable. It is the price we are paying for the benign (sometimes not so benign) neglect with which non-sacred studies have been treated in Jewish schools. It is a price paid in a lack of communication skills, and inability to articulate ideas, and the resultant unwitting conspiracy of illiteracy between writer, reader, editor, and publisher. For if writers cannot write and readers cannot read, can editors and publishers be far behind? It is no wonder that we are today confronted with a plethora of biographies and histories of great thinkers and important epochs which are nothing more than loosely strung together anecdotes, mostly hagiographic and interchangeable.

In this inability to write in English we are, of course, not alone. It is a phenomenon we share with the wider American community, the result, among other things, of inadequate education and mass addiction to sources of entertainment which have stupefied the American mind. What is curious is the fact that the Orthodox community produces fine *talmidei hakhamim* who have first-class minds, who are at home in the profound and labyrinthine subtleties of Talmudic dialectic, and who surely can think quite well. Clearly, the difficulties they find in expression are more a failure of writing skills than a failure of mind.

The fact is that yeshivot rarely force students to articulate ideas and to express them in writing. This need not be a permanent condition. Our contemporary Torah *she-b'al peh* needs to become more of a *bi-khetav*. It should be possible — even in the context of the most intensive Torah study — to develop at least basic English writing skills. Advanced yeshivot — even those which in principle reject any studies which are not sacred — could require more written work; e.g., research papers on issues of halakhah or Jewish thought; examinations which include written essay questions; written *haburot* in addition to the oral *haburot* on halakhic themes which are now required in many advanced yeshivot; in-house scholarly publications — now occasionally found in Hebrew in some yeshivot — expanded into English when possible. Granted, the limited stress on writing will not create poets, but it does have the potential of identifying and drawing out individuals who have the minimal tools with which to write lucidly in English. And, not incidentally, a new emphasis on the written word can only enhance Torah study, for writing crystallizes thinking and transforms amorphous concepts into order and logic.

We have made real progress in outreach and *kiruv*. But if we wish to reach the mind of the secularly educated Jew — that Jew who is most alienated from tradition — we will have to work towards developing at least a small group of learned, committed Jews who can write English. Speeches, lectures, weekend retreats all play vital and significant roles in introducing Torah to the wider community. But in the long-term struggle to establish Torah values within American Jewry — a struggle in which Orthodoxy has made remarkable strides — we are neglecting the potent weapon of the effective written word.

When the Midrash informs us that "the scroll and the sword descended intertwined from heaven" (Lev. R. 35:5), we are perhaps being reminded that the written word is a powerful instrument of battle, for it has a staying power and an impact which cannot be matched. As Maimonides writes in his *Iggeret Ha-Shemad*, a person should review "two or three or four times that which he desires to say, and should learn it exceeding well" before he speaks in public. However, when it comes to writing, "it would be proper for the writer to go over his words one thousand times if at all possible." According to many scholars, Rambam's influence was in no small measure a result of his "golden pen," his crystalline, pellucid style, and his appreciation of written language. He fully understood the lasting significance of the written word, which does not evaporate and disappear like the spoken word, but remains forever on the page where it can be read and reread.

There are no easy answers — not even difficult ones — to the questions raised here, but some attention needs to be paid to this matter. Otherwise, we will continue to be locked in a macabre dance with ourselves alone, encapsuled by a choreography which, instead of including others, creates walls which exclude, isolate, and turn away.

Jewish Continuity:
More and Less

"FAMILIES WHO EMBRACE BOTH CHRISTIAN and Jewish holidays will find this a welcome addition to the bookshelf," says Publisher's Weekly of a new children's book, *Light the Lights: A Story About Celebrating Hanukah and Christmas*, which has just come across my desk.

The publisher's own blurb, claiming that this is a "perfect holiday story for the many families who observe both Hanukah and Christmas," informs us that the author was "surprised to find that she couldn't find a children's book that reflected the holiday traditions of interfaith families (such as her own)," so she decided to write one herself. This book, we are assured, "will be enjoyed by the growing number of families who celebrate both Hanukah and Christmas."

A minor cavil before the major one: This little volume underestimates the intelligence even of the 3 to 7 year olds for whom it was written, but it provides a valuable insight into what passes for religious observance within intermarried families. Hanukah is nothing more than dreidels, latkes, and colorful candles in the menorah. As for the defilement and purification of the Temple, the rebellion against Hellenistic ways, the miracle of the oil, the intervention of God, the need to thank God — *lehodot ulehallel leshimcha hagadol* — these are apparently superfluous addenda to the main theme, which is the fun that Hanukah is.

Christmas fares no better: it is sugar cookies to eat, carols to sing, a shining tree under which to place gifts, and Santa Claus. Nothing about anyone's birth or about the fact that this is a sacred moment in the life of a Christian. If I were a Christian, I would be offended by a story that deals with my major religious festival and mentions nothing about why the festival is celebrated.

But I am a Jew. I am not offended; I am depressed. Not because this book reduces Hanukah to nothingness — this in itself is not a shock to anyone living in America — but because the "growing number" of intermarried families has become so integral a part of American landscape that book publishers now target the children of such families with attractive little volumes that legitimate their condition.

The major American Jewish organizations are of course concerned by this turn of events. Shocked by a 1990 population study that shows that because of intermarriage and assimilation we are faced with the looming specter of a dwindling Jewish community, they are mobilizing their considerable organizational prowess to guarantee Jewish continuity.

Which hardly alleviates one's depression. These are, after all, the same organizations with the same kind of leadership and agenda that for a generation have set the skewed priorities and forged the wrong alliances which helped steer us to the edge of this black abyss. Instead of pouring millions into Jewish day schools, they poured millions into Jewish gymnasiums; instead of giving precedence to basic Jewish values, they genuflected to the failed gods of liberal secularism; instead of developing a leadership which was Jewishly knowledgeable, they sold the reins of leadership to those who were by and large Jewishly illiterate.

History has a disconcerting way of slapping in the face those who ignore her. That those who contributed to Jewish discontinuity should now be in charge of Jewish continuity, and that the Jewish future is in the hands of those who have little understanding of its past or present, is enough to dishearten even the most optimistic among us.

To be sure, priorities have now shifted somewhat. The Jewish establishment today is a bit more sensitive to traditional Jewish norms, and Jewish education has moved up from the bottom of the list, and here and there one detects a glimmer of understanding of what Judaism is all about.

But one still wonders about the Jewish knowledge and awareness of these well-meaning custodians of the Jewish future. How, for example, would they respond to basic questions such as these:

- What is Jewish continuity, and why is it important?
- What is unique about Jewish history and the Jewish people?
- Is our miraculous survival attributable to our sameness or our distinctiveness?
- What roles do God and the supernatural play in Jewish history?
- Should Jews remain a distinctive, separate people? Why?
- What is wrong with intermarriage? Why not assimilate?
- What beliefs and practices should a Jew follow today?
- Are you disturbed by books that depict families celebrating both Hanukah and Christmas? Why?

And one further question:

- Do you comprehend the Jewish fact of life that no Jewish community in history has ever endured without three essential elements: (1) a sense of transcendence and spirituality; (2) emphasis on religious learning; and (3) the implementation of these concepts in daily life. Those communities for whom these were first principles became viable communities; those who ignored them quickly disappeared.

It is not happenstance that the one segment of American Jewry not suffering a continuity crisis is the one segment which has given these principles top priority. Deriving them from a belief in God, study of Torah, and practice of the mitsvot, Orthodox Jewry, historically dismissed by the major organizations, quietly went about ensuring a Jewish future. A generation ago they began building day schools, yeshivot and *kollelim* despite the opposition of the Jewish establishment that viewed such things as un-American; they stressed belief, spirituality, religious study, observance, and strong family life; they developed a vigorous community structure based on commitment and discipline.

Now, a generation later, they have virtually no intermarriage or assimilation; a birth rate far above replacement level; a community which is singularly devoted to Judaism and to the Jewish people; and, not incidentally, the highest proportion of Western *aliyah* to Israel.

That the Orthodox across the board are far from perfect and that many painful issues require resolution is an open secret. But no one can gainsay the fact that this is the only Jewish American group that is vital and dynamic. Surely they must be doing something right. It is hard to understand, therefore, why it is that in the whirlwind of conferences and the blizzards of papers and proposals that deal with Jewish continuity, the establishment does not consider utilizing the Orthodox community as a model.

To suggest this is not to suggest that everyone should become Orthodox. It is to suggest that at the brink of the yawning chasm it is wise to consider rescue techniques that have worked for others.

What has not worked — the discontinuity model of the secular organizations — is clear. What is now required is the courage to turn back and set out on a new trail. Specifically, it is time to reject glib solutions and to mobilize all the energies of the organized Jewish community in an emergency crash program 1) to educate Jewishly all of our people by funding, building, and upgrading day schools, yeshivot and community programs; 2) to raise teachers' salaries in order to retain talented teachers and to attract new ones to enter this calling; 3) to set as a goal the enrollment in intensive Jewish day schools of the over 90% of American Jewish youngsters who today receive no exposure to classical Judaism — even if this entails communal funding to subsidize tuition; 4) to pioneer innovative programs to deepen the Jewish knowledge and spirituality of single adults and Jewish families. If such a crash program means that pet projects will be curtailed, so be it. There will be no projects, pet or otherwise, if we disappear.

The question, in a word, is: do we have the mettle to move away from the dead end of a failed secularism and to make some tentative steps towards a religious world-view?

Despite all the noble intentions, all signs point to business-as-usual. Assemblies convene, resolutions are passed, committees are formed — and the same failed formulas are decked out in new costumes: take young people on visits to Israel or to Eastern Europe; increase allocations to Jewish education by a few percent; establish new programs for college youth; fund another Holocaust memorial; and — surprise! — reach out to the intermarried.

And while the establishment chews its cud, more and more books will be targeted to the growing number of families who embrace both Christian and Jewish holidays, and more and more once-Jewish children will kindle their lovely menorahs under sparkling Christmas trees, and more and more expensive studies will be commissioned, and more and more cries of alarm will be sounded.

And fewer Jews will be around to listen.

"Buddha Is Not As Bad ...": The Floundering of American Jewry

> *"Do not go gently into that good night... Rage, rage, against the dying of the light ..."*
>   DYLAN THOMAS

NON-ORTHODOX AMERICAN JEWRY — the numerical majority of America's Jews, as we are tirelessly reminded — takes itself very seriously. Toting their impressive membership numbers, its leaders make regular pilgrimages to Israel to rail about *mi hu Yehudi* or to mount demonstrative prayer protests at the Wall. They promote the accepted buzzwords of the moment — pluralism, egalitarianism, feminism, inclusiveness. They behave as if they were vital and dynamic. "If only Israelis would look at the prospering American Jewish community," say the non-Orthodox, "if only they would adopt our ideas of tolerance and diversity, all would be well."

The sub-surface facts point in a different direction. Ravaged by defections and intermarriage, they face, tragically, a very unhappy prognosis. Even wholesale conversions and recognition of patrilineal descent have failed to stem the internal hemorrhaging.

Worse, they are going gently into that good night. Instead of raging about the dying of their own light, they rage only against others. The frustrations about their non-acceptance in Israel have resulted in charges of clerical domination, politics, and obscurantism, and in America their rabbis rarely miss a pulpit opportunity to excoriate the Orthodox. They become particularly vexed at those who dare suggest that they have no future unless they prescribe for their people serious and massive doses of Torah and halakhah.

Here and there, however, there are hints of fresh breezes. Certain Conservative and Reform rabbis, aware of the realities, are heroically trying to introduce reforms into their communities — reforms that include mitsvot and classic textual study. Even more significantly, several frank self-assessments, written by prominent non-Orthodox Jews, have recently appeared in widely read national journals. Perhaps this is the vanguard of a new trend: an honest, unvarnished look at the American Jewish condition.

Writing in *Commentary* of July 1997, Jack Wertheimer, provost and professor of history at the Jewish Theological Seminary, suggests that "far from flourishing, the American Jewish community is in crisis." American Jewry faces a number of serious problems: the huge numbers of contemporary American Jews who have abandoned all Jewish identity; the several hundred thousand who have converted to other faiths; the astonishing rate of intermarriage; the wholesale neglect of Jewish education. In addition, the acceptance by Reform of patrilineal descent poses grave consequences. Wertheimer writes that "we are rapidly approaching the time when there will be rabbis who are themselves offspring of interfaith families, and who will not be recognized by their colleagues *as Jews*."

Despite the vaunted pluralism of American Jewry, says Wertheimer, its religious movements do not accept each other's definitions of who is a Jew, nor do they accept each other's converts. Moreover, within American Jewry there is virtually no agreement on what Jews should minimally practice or believe. Anything goes. Native American rites, Eastern religions, actual idolatry — all can fall under the rubric of America's loosely identified Judaism. The only thing all Jews agree on is what they do *not* accept: they do not accept Jesus as the Messiah. Not a few Jews have been known to experiment with Buddhism (which, according to many halakhic authorities, is out-and-out *avoda zara*), but in the eyes of masses of wavering American Jews, Buddha somehow seems not as bad as Jesus.

To further complicate matters, mantras like "inclusiveness" are invoked to welcome even non-Jews into policy-making councils of American synagogues and Jewish communal agencies. A Reform temple in Wisconsin boasts of a religious school in which a large part of the faculty, including the chairman of the school, is gentile.

The boundaries between Judaism and other religions have become fuzzy, but according to some influential American Jews, such as Alan Dershowitz, this is a good thing. "Instead of working to clarify what Judaism requires, " writes Wertheimer, "they counsel religious dilution. Instead of setting clear lines, they enjoin Jews to lower the barriers between Jewish and non-Jewish religion still further." Concludes Wertheimer: "this way lies not pluralism, but anarchy and self-extinction."

Another remarkable article is in the May 19 *National Review*, in which Elliot Abrams, Undersecretary of State in the Reagan administration, also sees a community in decline, facing "a demographic disaster. Jews, who once made up 3.7% of the U.S. population, have fallen to about 2 percent. . . ." Judaism *per se* is not being observed by most American Jews, and "the substitute faiths, which were devised in an effort to stay Jewish, are failing." And as the mortal danger to Israel seems to recede, even the State of Israel is failing as a substitute faith. Abrams declares that the only place one can find Jews who are committed to Israel these days is in a synagogue on Shabbat. "The faith of religious Jews, of whatever denomination, holds them in permanent covenant with God and with the land of Israel and its people. Their commitment will not weaken if the Israeli government pursues unpopular policies. . . ." Before very long, "what will be left is the covenant with God that created the Jewish people and ties them to the land of Israel — or nothing."

Similarly, the banner of so-called "prophetic Judaism," which was translated as support for American liberalism and a rejection of halakhah and Jewish practice, has also reached a dead end. The same is true of that other substitute for faith, the Holocaust. "Commemorating the Holocaust is for many Jews quite convenient . . . . It is neither a significant commitment of time nor a life-changing passion." The Holocaust revival has taken place "precisely during the years when intermarriage has spread, and ritual observance and synagogue affiliation have declined." Awareness of the Holocaust, important as it is, has not had much effect on the actual behavior of American Jews.

Abrams notes that "Jewish life that is not centered on Judaism is disappearing in America, while traditional Judaism — above all, Orthodoxy, which we expected to disappear — is stubbornly holding on." In a peroration worthy of an Orthodox rabbi, he concludes: "Jews are a people by virtue only of their Torah. They will decline if they are driven by fear of their neighbors, fear of their own traditions, and fear of the distinct identity that their covenant imposes upon them. They will survive if they cling to their Torah. It, and it alone, is for the Jews... a tree of life.

Israeli Jews are fully aware of the failure of non-Orthodox Judaism in the Diaspora, its quickie conversions, its appalling rate of intermarriage, and its defections. They know that the preponderance of American *aliyah* to Israel is Orthodox, and that the non-Orthodox, by and large, do not settle here. This is why even secular Israelis still identify Judaism with the Orthodox. They may not be willing to follow it in their own lives, and may even occasionally resent it, but for them this is still the authentic faith of their fathers.

Israelis do not read *Commentary* or *National Review,* but they sense instinctively what Wertheimer and Abrams have identified so perceptively: Reform and Conservative Judaism in America have led to a dead end — the natural consequence of too little attention to one's own values and too much attention to the values of the world around us. And Israelis are too level-headed to import a form of Judaism that has demonstratively failed to create or sustain Jewish Jews in America.

Rather than expend resources in exporting the dying embers to Israel, would it not be more beneficial to put these resources to work in America, to help revive what can be revived and restore what can be restored? The non-Orthodox observers who are pointing to the dire facts on the ground, and those non-Orthodox rabbis who are working to stem the tide, should not casually be dismissed. And instead of raging against the Orthodox, the non-Orthodox leadership might take to heart the salutary lesson that the best way to create a learned, devoted and passionate following is to expose people to the basics: study of Torah, practice of *mitsvot,* and faith in the God of Israel. These are not slogans or gimmicks or PR stunts. These are the real things, the things that work.

The loss of huge numbers of Conservative and Reform Jews is an unfolding tragedy within American Jewry. Intelligent, caring and serious Jews will rage against the dying of the light; they surely will not go gently in that good night.

A Ten Coarse Affair

THE WEDDING INVITATION IS EMBELLISHED with endless declarations of *baruch haShems, im yirtze haShems* and acknowledgments of God's goodness. The first page of the invitation is in Hebrew, and only on the second page is there an English translation, together with the admonition to ladies that they must dress modestly. It will take place at a luxurious wedding emporium, with the best caterer and the strictest possible *hechsher*. It is going to be the very model of a modern *frum* wedding.

The hour for the *hupah* comes and goes, but time is irrelevant when the smorgasbord tables are piled shoulder high in meats, fish, chopped liver sculpture, and a variety of drinks soft and hard. Waiters hover nearby, offering more drinks and more delicacies. The wedding is running very late; one might as well fill the time by filling the stomach. If this is merely the smorgasbord, can the dinner be far behind?

The *hupah*, two hours late, finally begins. As the principals gather on the platform, the din of chatter does not abate. There is a momentary hush when the bride glides down the center aisle, but as soon as the ceremony begins, the interrupted conversations carry on. Beyond the first row of guests, neither the *ketuba* nor the *berakhot* can be heard above the talk. The ceremony, clearly, is only an unavoidable interlude before the main meal.

The tables are laden with a riot of sumptuous flowers, and the dinner itself is an endless affair, with different types of precious breads, entrees, soups, varieties of chicken and meat, several desserts, and a Viennese table that out-Viennizes the Viennese: a ten-coarse dinner. Since this is a very *frum* wedding, men and women do not sit together. And it is all glatt, perilously close to glatt gluttony.

The music provides an appropriate ambience for the food. Loud and pulsating, the noises emanating from the bandstand are to good music what this food is to fine dining: a grossly exaggerated caricature. The jungle beat of percussion and drums dominates. One must shout in order to be heard. But with so much food, there is no time to converse about anything.

The music is set to Hebrew words and Biblical phrases, but there is no connection between word and melody, only a confusion of noises and a harsh jangling of sounds. In these holy words set to the profane rhythms of the street, there is no relationship between form and function. The words are the words of Jacob, but the beat is the beat of Esau, a transmogrification of the sounds that Moshe Rabbeinu must have heard when Israel danced around the calf: *kol 'anot*, the wild sound of tumult (Exodus 32:18).

Even when they play what had once been sweet and affecting Jewish melodies, the music is distorted by the raucous tempo and the insistent, strident rhythm of the jungle. One does not have to be a musicologist to detect the unmistakable echoes of rock, reggae, hip-hop, western, and even rap. The very people who so zealously strive to hermetically seal off their homes and lives from outside influences, and who are so vigilant about the prohibition of *behukoteihem lo telekhu*, are somehow oblivious to the depraved echoes of the street that seep into one of the sacred moments of Jewish life. If, as R. Shneor Zalman of Liady once said, "melody is the pen of the soul," what does this musical penmanship reveal about our souls?

One should not, by the way, assume that even the playing of tasteful music is without its halakhic questions. Following the dissolution of the Sanhedrin, all instrumental music was banned as a sign of national mourning. (Talmud Sota 48a, Gittin 7a, among other sources) This is codified by Rambam (Hil. Taanit 5:14) and R. Yosef Caro in O.C. 560:3. It is only R. Moshe Isserles (*ad loc*) who permits instrumental music when it involves a mitsvah such as at a wedding, in order to enhance the joy of the bride and groom. One wonders how R. Isserles would react at the kind of instrumental music one hears at today's weddings. He might be reminded of the comment of the Sages that he who makes a secular song out of verses in Shir Hashirim causes the Torah to wrap itself in sackcloth and to say before the Holy One, "Your children have made me as a harp upon which the frivolous (*letsim*) play their songs." (Sanhedrin 101a)

In connection with this, a *humra* observed by many residents of the Old City of Jerusalem is worthy of note. As a *zecher l'hurban* and a sign of mourning for the destruction of the Temple, they play no musical instruments whatsoever at their weddings in the Old City — only drums and vocal music. Since we live in a time in which people take a certain delight in new *humrot*, perhaps this is a *humra* whose time has come.

A non-Jewish friend recently married off his daughter in a church wedding. He described it to me. It was called for two p.m. on a Sunday afternoon. It began promptly. The reception consisted of tea, coffee, soft drinks, and pretty cakes and cookies. There was no dinner. The music, mostly Bach, Mozart and Mendelssohn, was provided by a string quartet. There was total stillness during the ceremony. My friend told me that not only was the occasion joyous, but it was also uplifting and inspiring.

This is a *behukoteihem* that we might want to emulate. When was the last wedding we attended that was religiously inspiring? Perhaps we should be concerned not only with the platitudes of our invitations and the glatt-ness of our food and dress, but also with Ramban's warnings about *naval bireshut haTorah*.

A wedding, as rabbis never cease to remind us is *kiddushin*/sanctification. To be charitable, there surely is a spark of holiness that is hidden under the excessive food, the raucous noise, the endless talk, and the bacchanalian music that are the hallmark of our very *frum* weddings. But one has to be very charitable — and very diligent — to find it.

Abbreviations

AS I WALK THROUGH THE lobby of the European hotel where I am staying, I pause before the large TV screen to watch the English news. But instead of news, an American baseball game is about to begin. A closer look shows that the two teams are the Atlanta Braves and the Chicago Cubs.

The infections of one's childhood do not entirely disappear from the bloodstream; like measles and the mumps, a tiny residue remains. And so, when home-town baseball is available to a recovering baseball addict in the middle of Italy, who needs news? Yes, a session of the rabbinic conference is about to begin in the hall downstairs, but no harm would be done if I watched for a few moments. Atlanta baseball in Milan; what could be more piquant?

The first Cub batter swings at the very first pitch and grounds out to short. Second batter: three quick strikes and he is gone. Third batter: on the second pitch, a screaming liner off the left field wall. Fourth batter: a sharp grounder, but the Atlanta shortstop makes a great save and from a kneeling position throws him out at first. Inning over. The juices of my youth are flowing freely.

Before Atlanta comes to bat I go to the desk to inquire if the session has begun. It has not; I return to the game. It is already two outs. Two outs? I didn't realize I had been gone that long.

The next batter grounds out on the first pitch. Score at the end of the first inning: nothing to nothing.

I glance at my watch. One full inning has consumed a total of five minutes. Something must be wrong. Obviously, this cannot be a live broadcast. Have they speeded up the film? It doesn't look like it.

I pay closer attention now, and soon I somehow realize what is happening. They have not speeded up the film; they have speeded up the game. Batters are not really swinging at the first pitch; the producer has simply eliminated what he considers to be irrelevant. Rarely does he show ball one, ball two, or ball three. These are just a waste of time. Only strikes are shown, and precious few of those. Wood striking the ball, runners rounding third and scoring in a cloud of dust — this is what we are shown. Action and excitement: a runner sliding into second on a steal, or being thrown out at home in a collision with the catcher, a home run, a great outfield catch — only these are significant. The rest are just frills, distractions from the essence of the game.

The technique is obvious. The third base coach does not rub his chest, stroke his arm, spit in the dust, clap his hands, hitch up his pants, touch the beak of his cap in the frenzied symphony of signals that marks his august office; there are no conferences on the mound between catcher and pitcher, their spikes scratching the ground; no big-bellied manager strolls out to the mound to slap his pitcher in the hind quarters, take the ball from him, and signal to the bullpen for a left-hander; relievers do not toss warm-up pitches: they simply appear on the mound and begin throwing. The titanic struggle between lonely pitcher on the mound and lonely batter in the box — the pitcher rubbing the ball insouciantly, peering in to see the catcher's signals; the batter twitching his bat and rhythmically rocking to and fro as he concentrates on the pitcher's every move; the hush of the spectators as the ball speeds towards the plate — all this is irrelevant and unsuited to people who are ignorant of the subtle nuances of the game, who demand action, are quickly bored, and who with a flick of the finger can eliminate you from their screen. And so the irrelevancies are pruned and excised in the interests of time and of holding the audience's attention.

I am probably missing an inspiring *devar Torah*, but I am transfixed by this tasteless, tawdry parody of a classic sport. I should not have been surprised. After all, in our souped up generation, a Beethoven symphony can be reduced from forty minutes to ten, a Bach symphony can be trimmed from one hour to twenty minutes, CDs feature the essence of the "Ten World's Greatest Symphonies" in less than ninety minutes, and likewise *War and Peace* can be obtained in a special, scaled down edition.

Our time has no time. We live in a fast-forward age. We expend millions of man hours to speed up our computers by microseconds so that we have more leisure time to listen to Diet Beethoven and read Tolstoy Lite.

So if the classics can be refurbished, why not a mere boys' game that in the ultimate scheme of things has no meaning or purpose?

But what about the more serious things in life? What about Torah and mitsvot? Have not these also been subject throughout our history to similar attempts at improvement and transfiguring — to make them "more appealing" — and have these not also been the victim of similar parodies?

How many times, then and now, have Jews heard the chiding voices of those who disparaged the need for the myriad details of Jewish life and exhorted us to streamline and modernize lest we drive people away?

Was it not Korah who sought to undermine the authority of Moshe and the significance of mitsvot? Humanize the Torah, he cried, give it a kinder, less authoritarian face. The goal is to be holy, so let us remove the impediments to holiness which are the commandments. Abbreviate, democratize, bring the Torah up to date lest the people abandon it.

A thousand years after Korah, Jewish sectarians railed against the Torah's details and rituals — the entire mitsvah system of do's and don't's — as irrelevant and unnecessary. The goal was to be spiritual, and the details stood in the way of the higher goal. The Torah was a "law of sin and death," while the newer teachings contained the "spirit of life." Modern man requires a higher, more relevant form of religion. To save Judaism we must eliminate the mitsvot and delete the frills; what goes into the mouth is not as important as what comes out.

Things have not been very different in our own century. Synagogue *mehitsot* were dropped because they would drive people away; the repetition of the *amidah* eliminated because it was a waste of time; *birkat kohanim* deleted because it was an anachronism; *Shabbat* services abbreviated and Hebrew changed to English lest we lose the audience; mitsvot made optional because we are all autonomous; references to the sacrificial system excised from the *siddur*; rabbis urged to wear a clerical robe instead of a wool *tallit* in order to appeal to the youth; mitsvot like *sukkah* and *lulav* and *etrog* and *tefillin* and *mezuzah* and *tsitsit* and *shatnez* and *mikveh* ignored in order to bring Torah up to date; conversion procedures streamlined to make Judaism more accessible; *gittin* discarded because they were outdated; same-sex marriages condoned because the spirit of the times demanded it.

The producers of CNN Sports have concocted a game that utilizes baseball uniforms and bats and gloves, but anyone who knows the game and its nuances and rhythms will find both risible and appalling these attempts to update it, as will anyone who appreciates Torah and mitsvot find appalling the contemporary parodies of Judaism.

Only a game, this baseball, and not to be taken seriously. But what I was seeing here was a metaphor for other, more significant aspects of human life which are in constant risk of being distorted by producers who couple their own hubris with ignorance and insensitivity.

When I finally walked into the rabbinic session, some of my colleagues asked me why I was so late. I replied cryptically that I was watching *divrei Torah* on Italian television. They thought I was joking.

Not a Jewish Princess

THE OUTPOURING OF GENUINE GRIEF for the dead Princess Diana; the unending rows of flowers in London; the tributes from statesmen; the media adulation throughout the world; the editorials and columns in the world's major newspapers — all this should not blind us to one essential fact: Princess Diana was not a Jewish princess.

Note the words of David's Psalm 45 about the Jewish princess: *kol kevudah bat melekh penimah* / "The entire glory of the princess is within." The Jewish reading of this is that the classic Jewish woman is a private person who is comfortable with her self, and has no need to strut and fret her part upon the public stage. She knows that what really matters are not her clothes but her character; not her make-up but what she is made of; not her valuable jewels but her inner values. She is the symbol of that which is internal, not that which is external. Her glory is within her, not outside her.

This is the origin of the Jewish concept of *tseniut*: modesty, reticence, quiet, reserve. Among the qualities that God desires in His creatures, says the prophet Micah in chapter 6, is that we do justice, love kindness and (that word again) *hatsnea lechet im elohecha* / and walk quietly with thy God." The key word there is *tsanua* — quiet, humble, self-effacing — self-confident but private.

As sad as her death is, one could hardly refer to Princess Diana as the embodiment of the classical Jewish *tseniut*. This princess was not familiar with that which is internal — or eternal. For the past two decades she lived the life of the external. She would profess the desire to be left alone, but even when she had the choice she opted for the glitter, for the flamboyantly rich, for high style, café society, fast cars and fast boy friends, exotic trips, photographers, press releases, provocative behavior, and notoriety — tragically climaxed by a very public death and a very public funeral.

The eulogies speak of her sympathy for ordinary people, her interest in children, her compassion, her good works. No doubt. But her concern for others apparently did not extend beneath the surface. She clearly enjoyed the fact that the public was exhilarated and titillated by her non-conventional escapades, and the fact that her destructive behavior was destructively mimicked by an entire generation of young people did not seem to disturb her.

The sadness and the accompanying media hype about her life and death should not obscure the essential fact that the greatest interest of this princess was in her princess-hood and its accompanying glamour and luxury. A model for young people she certainly was not. Nor can her self-indulgence and her disdain for traditional values all be blamed on her cad of an ex-husband. She was the very model of a modern princess: she was pre-occupied with her self and her image and her titles and her chauffeurs and her riding instructors. Yes, she was beautiful; yes, she was vulnerable; yes, she had personal problems; yes, she was fascinating. But at bottom she was the quintessential contemporary person: synthetic, plastic, skin deep, living primarily for the present moment.

During the week after Diana's death, another famous woman died: Mother Theresa. Her passing did not evoke the profound universal grief that Diana engendered, but her death served as a remarkable benchmark against which to test the kind of life that really matters. It was as if we were being reminded, in the midst of our adulation for the dead princess, what the true touchstones are by which one should measure the ultimate value of a life.

The contrast between the two could not have been greater. The one lived primarily for herself, the other, for those outside her self. The one dedicated her life to ornamentation and gloss, the other devoted her life full time to helping the sick and the infirm. The one led a life of raucousness and headlines, the other a life of quiet and prayer.

The world offered Theresa its admiration, but it showered Diana with its love. This speaks eloquently about the values of the world. Mother Theresa was not hounded by the *paparazzi*, because an old woman feeding the hungry is not something we really care about.

But the world also instinctively knows the answers to these questions: whose life was the more meaningful? And whose life, in the end, was more happy and gave its bearer more genuine joy?

The glory of Princess Diana was not within; it was all without. Although she has been idolized and transformed into a myth, it would be wise to look at her life candidly and to ask ourselves, after the tumult and the shouting have faded away, if this is how we would want our daughters to turn out.

The tragedy and the sadness of her life and brutal death are enough to give one pause. Maybe King David knew something 3000 years ago that we still do not know.

The Hebron Murders: Enemies and Friends

LEST IT BE MISUNDERSTOOD, LET the obvious be said at once: the murder of Arab worshippers at Hebron brought no honor to *am Yisrael*. Whatever pain and frustration Dr. Goldstein may have suffered over the murder of his friends and neighbors, individuals may not decide on their own to take human life. Killing them while they are at prayer only compounds the anguish.

Having said this, it must also be said that the Israel government's reaction to the tragedy was as unsettling as the tragedy itself. The servile genuflection towards world sensibilities, the obsequious *mea culpas*, the closing of the *kotel hamaaravi* to Jewish worshippers, the daily concessions and gestures to coax Arafat back to the peace negations, the public self-flagellation, the increase in numbers of the new "Palestinian Police Force," the agreement to permit an international presence in Hebron — all because of a solitary act which had already met with national revulsion — were more than demeaning. They reflected instead a sense of uncertainty about Israel's place in the world.

Of course, it is beside the point that one looks in vain for even a mild Arab expression of sorrow at the thousands of terrorist acts they have committed against Jews. It is beside the point because we are an *am kadosh*, and we do not imitate our enemies lest we become like them. Therefore, heartfelt regret and remorse by the government were surely in order (as is soul-searching among the Orthodox as to how such an act can meet with the approval of even a tiny minority of observant Jews.) But the abject groveling was unseemly, and hardly a sign of physical or moral strength. At the very least, some Begin-esque tough-mindedness or Golda-esque sense of balance would have been useful.

Why this daily drenching in bathos? Was the government so eager to demonstrate the inherent morality of the Jewish people that in a sudden religious apotheosis, Rabin, Peres, and Ezer Weizman, whose roots into Jewish tradition normally reach no farther back than Herzl and Ben Gurion, unabashedly found themselves awash in religious, halakhic, and traditional Judaic categories? "Sensible Judaism spits you out," they shouted. "You are outside the wall of Jewish law . . . as a Jew I am ashamed . . . an embarrassment to Judaism . . . ." — rather hollow sentiments from people not previously renowned for their sensitivity to Judaism or to Jewish law.

It's not that there are not things to be embarrassed about in contemporary Israel, even as we are justifiably proud of her stupendous achievements. It would be salutary, for example, if the Prime Minister would confess that as a Jew he is embarrassed that fifty-thousand young Israelis who were raised in this holy land ecstatically worshipped Michael Jackson in his Tel Aviv performance in Ellul, and that another fifty-thousand paid obeisance to Madonna in Tel Aviv on Hoshanah Rabbah, or if Ms. Aloni were to admit that as a former Education Minister she is embarrassed that tens of thousands of Israeli youngsters graduate high school without ever having been exposed to concepts — even in the abstract — like halakhah or mitsvah or Mishnah, and who consider Zionism a silly notion whose time has passed.

But this is what happens when people lose their authentic Jewish moorings. Their perspective becomes distorted and the lines between shame and pride become blurred. Thus, Israeli secularists, having lost their inner vision, are able to see themselves only through the prism of the outside world. Their view of who they are, their sense of Jewish self, is solely rooted in what they think others think of them. As one watches them perform, a variant of a familiar verse keeps intruding on my mind: "for out of Zion shall come forth a *Galut* mentality."

※✡※

Worse than the face Israel showed to the outside world was the face it showed to a significant section of its own citizens. Just a few years ago the settlers of Judea and Samaria were heroes for risking their lives to go into hostile — but traditionally Jewish — areas to establish communities. The country hailed them as courageous and idealistic Zionists, ready to face danger and physical hardship to maintain a Jewish presence in the Land.

But even before Hebron it was apparent that in the eyes of the present Israeli leadership they had become an inconvenience, a thorn in the side which they would willingly abandon at the first opportunity. Now, in the aftermath of Hebron, the Jewish residents of Judea, Samaria, and Gaza are vilified. There are calls to "disarm" them, to mete out prison sentences, to dismantle settlements, to evacuate residents forcibly from Hebron, Shiloh, Bet-El and other front-line places. They are viewed as if they were the terrorists, some Knesset members actually referring to them as "Hamas with kippot." And at the very moment that voices in the Knesset were demonizing these Jewish citizens — the overwhelming majority of whom are ordinary, loyal tax-paying citizens who love Eretz Yisroel — the government approved the release of convicted Arab terrorists from prison as a peace offering to a pouting Arafat.

The contrast is stark: the constant, well-planned terrorist bus bombings, stabbings, and brutalities are all greeted by the government with a certain equanimity, a let's-not-interrupt-the-peace-process rhetoric, and a renewed begging for a condemnation or at least an apology from Arafat. But Dr. Goldstein's solitary act unleashed the entire fury of the government against him and "those like him."

"Those like him" means those who wear *kippot*. The anti-settler diatribes emerging from the Knesset revealed greater hostility towards religion than towards the murderers of Maalot, Munich, and TWA. The paranoia reached a crescendo when a leftist member of Knesset, unwittingly mouthing both the ancient blood libels and the anti-Semitic canard that the Torah teaches strict justice while the New Testament teaches love, averred that religious Jews learn vengeance and hatred from their Torah studies. As proof, he pontificated that it was Megillat Esther, with its "message of vengeance against the Goyim," which was directly responsible for the Purim tragedy.

This ludicrous insight was picked up with delight by secularist Israeli journalists and was quickly echoed by parroting pundits around the world — none of whom had troubled to actually read the Megillah and to learn that the Persian Jews were acting in self-defense against raging mobs who had been unleashed by governmental authority (Esther 9:16; 9:22); that the Jews did not pillage the non-Jews (9:10; 9:15); and that, far from teaching vengeance and killing, Purim was established as a time of "feasting and sending food portions to one another and gifts to the needy" (9:22). Nor did the chorusing columnists stop to wonder how it is that in nineteen-hundred years of Megillah reading, Jews, unlike their counterparts in churches and mosques, never were so inflamed by this or any other reading that they spilled out of their synagogues to kill non-Jews.

Thank heaven for religion's best friends in the Knesset, the extreme left-wingers (best friends because their anti-religious fanaticism is so crude as to make religion's own zealots look civil by comparison) who introduced a touch of comedy with their grotesque statements that Hebron was never a sacred city for the Jews anyway. What transformed it into tragicomedy was the fact that they were serious.

But the secular leftists play only a bit part. The full drama unfolding before our eyes is much more riveting: yesterday's idealists are metamorphosed into today's villains, and yesterday's terrorists into today's policemen; enemies are treated like friends, and friends like enemies — and it is all done with a straight face. One can only pray that the God of Israel will send down from on high His own *deus ex machina* which will bring this dark entertainment to a merciful and peaceful end.

Into the Looking Glass: The Rabin Assasination

THE MURDER OF PRIME MINISTER Yitshak Rabin reminds us once again that it is possible to wear a *kippah* and observe sacred mitsvot like *tsitsit* and *tefillin; daven shaharit, minhah,* and *ma'ariv;* recite *berakhot* before and after every meal — and still act in ways that bear the unmistakable imprint of the profane.

For murder is not only a cardinal violation of the Torah; it is also the ultimate capitulation to the unholy. To express one's rage in fist, sword or bullet is to surrender the voice of Jacob into the hands of Esau.

The confessed assassin was surely concerned about the *kashrut* of his food, the reliability of his *eruv,* and the quality of his *lulav*. How can it be that the taking of a life or the desecration of the name of God apparently did not concern him?

Who can know the answer? Only God knows the intricate machinations of the human heart, says Jeremiah (17:9-10). But that human beings can rationalize any act is evident from the incident of the strange *ish* with whom Jacob wrestled through the night. Who was he? One Talmudic view (Hullin 91a) holds that he appeared to Jacob as a heathen (*ke-akum nidmeh lo*); the other, that he appeared as a Torah scholar (*ke-talmid ha-kham nidmeh lo).* On which the Avnei Nezer (R. Avraham Borenstein, known as the Sochatchover Rebbe, d. 1910) famously suggests that within each person there reside two types of temptation: one persuades the sinner to transgress even if it is wrong (*ke-akum*); the other persuades the sinner that the transgression is not wrong but is in fact a mitsvah (*ke-talmid hakham*).

In our day we have moved beyond this: not only do transgressions become mitsvot, but the transgressors convince themselves that they are reincarnations of Pinhas, pure and untarnished zealots acting on behalf of God. But those who realize that they are not pure or untarnished will take this opportunity to look unflinchingly in the mirror.

We Orthodox of the contemporary West have been rather sanguine about our involvement in the secular society around us. We were confident that we could resist the strains of spiritual diminution which inevitably emanate from the unholy elements within that society. Not only were we certain of our immunity; we would even help repair and sanctify this society through *tikkum ha-olam*, while all the time the purity of Torah would remain inviolate within us — nay, would even be enhanced.

But to our chagrin we in this generation must now ask if this confidence has been justified. How deeply have the profane elements of the surrounding culture penetrated even the camps of the Orthodox? Have we sanctified this culture in the process, or have we been desanctified? In sum, has our foray into the world stopped at the borders of Greece and Rome, or have we lost our way, crossed the border, and permitted the values of that world — including the use of violence as a means of negotiation — to insinuate themselves into our beings?

Consider the creeping little profanations that have wormed their way under our *kippot* and black hats into our heads and hearts:

Popular Jewish music with primitive jungle beats masquerading as Biblical lyrics (can Jewish religious "gangsta rap" be far behind?); Orthodox weddings that are *glatt* kosher exercises in conspicuous waste (why do we not in this regard ape our non-Jewish neighbors and their dignified and restrained weddings?); night-clubs which feature kosher food (the *Yoreh De'ah* is strictly observed, but the *Even haEzer* is hidden in a corner); the vulgar entertainments which we welcome into our Orthodox homes (we are, after all, open to the surrounding culture).

These are the lighter profanations, adumbrations of the darker ones yet to emerge: imitating the nations around us, thinking and reacting like them, marrying and assimilating with them, and soon enough becoming them.

It comes as a disorienting jolt that the ultimate profanation — murder — should now have become the expression of choice by a product of Orthodox schools and an Orthodox community. But upon reflection, was not this ultimate profanation drawn upon the silhouettes of the petty ones that foreshadowed it?

This is not to suggest that gluttony or vulgar entertainment or involvement in the affairs of society inevitably lead to the willingness to murder. Nor is it even to suggest that contact with the cultures around us is to be shunned. But it is to suggest that we become newly aware of an old axiom: that unholiness has a way of insinuating itself into our existence in a variety of ways, and that murder, no less than kosher night-clubs, is a paradigm of the ways these values can effect even observant Jewish lives.

Although many Orthodox Jews remain committed to the concept that openness can be a helpful handmaiden to the affirmation of God in the universe, it should be conceded that those of us who wrestle with the Prince of Esau, even if we emerge victorious, do not always emerge entirely unscathed. Like Jacob, the encounter can culminate in a limp in our thigh.

We who have learned to tolerate and even cherish the co-existence we have negotiated with various profanations must not turn aside from painful soul-searching. This in no way condones the reaction of the Israeli media and of people in high places who instigated a witch-hunt against the observant community; who, in a text-book display of *dati*-phobia, encouraged the demonization of hundreds of thousands of *kippah*-wearing Israelis; who paraded respected rabbis into police stations for interrogation as if they were common criminals; who instead of healing wounds, inflamed anti-religious prejudices and succeeded in casting a pall of suspicion and mistrust over the land. (No one was really surprised that the instigators were advocates of "human rights" who preach constantly about democracy and freedom of conscience.)

Despite such behavior and the concomitant temptation to lash back — and despite the temptation to claim that the assassin was only an individual and we should not overreact — it is appropriate for us to look inward and ask ourselves some troubling questions.

Have we successfully explored the culture of the Nations without being affected by their values? Have the Torah's values been accorded the same gravity in our time as have the various handmaidens with which it has been allied? Or have the handmaidens been given the keys to the treasures of the house and become co-equal with the mistress? In sum, must we, in these difficult days, "to the marriage of true minds admit impediments"?

The answers may not be easily formulated, but it would be unhealthful for the questions to be suppressed.

Nor should such probing be limited to those who are involved in the surrounding culture. A careful look in the mirror would be salutary for every single group and every single Jew, including those who reject such involvement. For example, can a lack of social consciousness also serve as a precursor of unholiness? Is the impulse for personal autonomy, as opposed to recognized authority, limited to those who wear colorful *kippot*? Does encapsulated self-absorption pose risks of spiritual diminution that parallel those of complete openness?

The fact is that desecration of the name of God is not the monopoly of any one group. It appears in many disguises and in many head-dresses. If we truly believe that all Israel are *avevim*/responsible for one another, no camp will self-righteously stand aside and say, "*Yadeinu lo shafkhu et ha-dam ha-zeh* ('our hands have not shed this blood')" (Dt. 21:7). The Jewish land and the Jewish people are enveloped in several layers of crisis. The sound of the distant *shofar* should cause us to tremble.

May it come to pass speedily in our day that we who pray regularly, observe mitsvot, and are engaged in God's world will also come to engage ourselves in *tikkun atsmi*/repairing of the self — and by so doing will learn to distinguish the handmaiden from the mistress, and to recognize the borders that separate that which is profane from that which is sacred.

The Old Man and the Secularists

In the early nineties, politics – always fascinating – took an intriguing turn. All eyes were on a venerated sage from Bene Beraq.

IT HAD ALL THE INGREDIENTS of a great news story: take a Likud government which has just fallen, add efforts to form a new government which end in a sixty-sixty Likud/Labor deadlock; mix in a dose of Degel Hatorah, the *haredi* religious political party which, as yet uncommitted, now holds the balance of power; stir in Degel Hatorah's spiritual mentor, ninety-five year old Rabbi Eliezer Schach, world-class Talmudic scholar and dean of the prestigious Ponovez Yeshiva in Bene Beraq, where he lives a spartan, scholarly life; pour in genuflecting visits by leaders of Likud and Labor to the venerated rabbi, who listens respectfully but commits himself to no one; stir in the mixture of awe, curiosity and dislike which secular Israelis hold for the *haredi* Orthodox; and as a final touch, toss into the pot the fortuitous date of Degel Hatorah's first annual convention, planned long before the government crisis, which will take place at the height of the deadlocked negotiations, with Rabbi Schach as a keynote speaker — and you have a sure-fire media dream recipe.

The media plays it to the hilt: front page headlines each day ask what Rabbi Schach will say. Analysts speculate, editors

The Old Man and the Secularists

hedge their bets, politicians hope. Upon a signal from him, his followers will join a Labor/Peres coalition; another signal, and it is Likud/Shamir; the *Jerusalem Post* headlines: "Tel Aviv stock market awaits Schach speech."

The event had originally been planned for Jerusalem's convention hall, with a capacity of five thousand. But as the date approached, it became apparent that this would be too small, so the site was moved to the Yad Eliahu sports arena in Tel Aviv, (Hebrew, *heichal ha-sport*, literally, in a typical modern Israeli juxtaposition of sacred and profane, "Sanctuary of Sport") with a ten thousand-plus capacity.

Demand for seats is intense. Priced officially at five dollars, ubiquitous entrepreneurs are scalping them at fifty dollars.

On the night of the convention, the arena neighborhood teems with traffic police, security personnel, soldiers. There is a crush at the gates; thousands of yeshiva students who cannot obtain tickets wait outside to catch a glimpse of famous scholars and yeshiva deans. It is as if a religious World Series is being played, a Super Bowl — or, since this is Israel — the finals of the World Soccer Cup.

Inside the arena, a capacity crowd waits expectantly. The press gallery is packed; photographers roam about; a large battery of TV cameras is poised at the center of the floor.

But the atmosphere is hardly like a sporting event. For one thing, all ten thousand spectators are dressed alike: black hat, black suit, black shoes, white shirt, dark tie. Many wear *kapottes* down to their knees. Most have full beards and are young, in their twenties and thirties. The tiered seats rise up into the rafters, but many of the "fans," while they wait, are studying not line-ups but *Humashim, Mishnayos,* and *Shulhan Arukh,* in odd counterpoint to the scoreboards and huge advertisements for blue jeans. A reserved section holds specially invited guests, renowned Talmudic scholars, religious thinkers and writers, venerable yeshiva heads.

The proceedings begin with *Maariv,* the regular evening service. It is a remarkable sight: ten thousand black-clad, swaying bodies calling out the *Shema Yisrael* together, "Hear O Israel, the Lord Who is our God, the Lord is One." This is not the cool, automatic, laid back *Shema* which is read in monotonic singsong in antiseptic American synagogues, but a Jewish *halakhic Shema*: passionate, loud, intense, unself-conscious; an oceanic roar cascading through the arena, echoing off the roof, reverberating across the vaulted seats. It is difficult not to listen to this *Hear O Israel* as its waves come rolling through the vast space of the arena. Equally striking, by contrast, is the silent *Amidah*: for seven full minutes, ten thousand whispers envelope the arena.

As the crowd sits down, the chairman announces the entry of Rabbi Schach, who is walking down the aisle from the far end of the arena. The crowd jumps to its feet and begins to clap in unison and to sing the words from Psalms 61:7: *Yamin al yemei melech tosif, shnosav kemo dor vador*, "prolong the king's life, may his years be as many generations." Rav Schach, about five feet two, can hardly be seen behind the security men and students who form a protective phalanx around him as he makes his way to the podium. The crowd, eager to catch a glimpse, surges towards him. The phalanx is muscular and holds them at bay. The self-effacing Rosh Yeshiva, a classic Lithuanian opponent of *Hasidism* which tends to deify its Rebbe, is clearly embarrassed by the adulation. Finally he arrives at his place on the podium, and the people get a good look at the short, cherubic-looking man with the white beard who is about to deliver the address so crucial to the future of the nation. The audience hangs on every word. It is being carried to the rest of the country by live TV and radio.

Anywhere else, a speech whose every nuance and gesture might determine the composition of a new government would have been prepared by a swarm of speechwriters and consultants, and would have been reviewed, revised and rehearsed dozens of times. But Rabbi Schach speaks off the cuff, perfectly at ease, as if he were in a lecture hall talking to his students. His language is a mix of modern Hebrew and

Yiddish, sprinkled with Biblical allusions and phrases. He decries the secularism of certain groups in the State of Israel; the State is not a land like any other, but has its roots in sanctity and in the ways of Torah. To live in a Jewish State and not to behave as a Jew is ludicrous. The spectacle of certain secular kibbutzim who do not even recognize Yom Kippur is painful, for they have cut themselves off from their roots, from the tradition which has sustained the Jewish people through the millennia. They are dead to religious values. Rav Schach begins to sob: How has it come to pass that some Jews in this Holy Land do not even know the basic statement of faith of the Jew, the *Shema Yisrael*? What good is a Land when all the holiness is removed from its inhabitants? We were not placed here by God in order to imitate the ways of the nations of the world, their crime, their drugs, their cynicism, their essential emptiness. His voice is soft, conversational, intimate. The crowd is mesmerized.

He continues: Both major parties have represented the worst aspects of secularism. They have both disregarded basic Jewish religious values. The Labor Party was in power during most of the existence of the State, and it was precisely during their reign that tens of thousands of youngsters were deliberately alienated from Judaism. The crowd is tense: is a political statement being made? We will not be drawn to people who have no links with Judaism or with our past, he declares.

Having disposed of one side, he takes on the other: nor must we think that more territory, more land, is the solution. (Cognoscenti have long known that Rabbi Schach is hardly a Khoumeni, and that his territorial views are even more dovish than that of Shimon Peres). What good is a land without religious content in that land? Not territory or land makes us a people, but the Torah. Without Torah we are lost, even if we possess all the land in the world. Neither of the leading parties is truly worthy of the support of a religious Jew, he declares. And, exhorting the assemblage to deepen their knowledge of Torah and to hone their ethical behavior towards God and fellow man, he blesses the audience and sits down. The entire talk runs less than twenty minutes.

Instant analysis on TV and radio: What did he mean, what did he say, what did he not say? Is Labor the loser? Shimon Peres take comfort in the vagueness of the talk, Shamir is confident of Rabbi Schach's blessing. Rabbi Schach's lieutenants give strong indications that their old man favors Likud over Labor as the lesser of the two evils. The commentators comment, the pundits pontificate, the jokers joke and the next day the country begins to examine the implications of the speech.

The implications turn out to be more religious than political, which is clearly what Rav Schach intended. And since this is religion *and* Israel, the reaction is emotional, passionate, pure Jewish *kishkes*. TV and radio talk shows and call-in programs — and the daily press — reveal how sensitive the issue is. Secular kibbutzniks fiercely defend their Jewishness, saying that it is not true that Yom Kippur is cavalierly disregarded today as it may have been in past; they declare that certain secular kibbutzim even have synagogues — something unheard of thirty years ago. President Chaim Herzog adds much to the heat and contributes little to the light by suggesting that those who "have not heard the roar of battle (a plain reference to those who are deferred from army duty for religious reasons) should ask forgiveness of those who died in Israel's wars." *Haredim* retort that Rabbi Schach's theme was neither patriotism nor heroism, but that he was pointing to the lack of Jewish content in secular Israeli life. He called their behavior *un-Jewish*, but did not say they were *non-Jewish*. The Rebbe of Lubavitch, in an apparent change of tone from his hard-line position on last year's "Who Is a Jew" controversy, weighs in with the statement that those who would divide the Jewish people must repent. The media lap it up, and feature huge pictures of the Lithuanian Rav Schach and the *Hasidic* Lubavitcher Rebbe in front page face-offs which, to the history-conscious reader, has the *deja-vu* quality not only of

The Old Man and the Secularists 179

recent Rav Schach-Lubavitch disagreements concerning the Messiah (Rabbi Schach is unhappy with Lubavitch *Hasidim* because they tend to ascribe messianic attributes to their Rebbe) but is redolent of the classic *Mitnagdic-Hasidic* disputes of the eighteenth century.

※※※

Through it all, however, one odd fact emerges. Secular Israelis are wounded and are clearly on the defensive. Their responses have one common element: we are Jews, we want to remain Jews. Many thoughtful Israelis find the secular response, vehement as it is, quite revealing. A generation ago, no self-respecting secular kibbutznik would have paid the slightest attention to the opinions of a *haredi* Rosh Yeshiva. The Rosh Yeshiva of Ponovez says I am not Jewish enough? So what? The fact that an aged Yeshiva dean today can capture the country and can open up such a national debate is a sign of the increasing numbers, power, discipline, and sophistication of the *haredi* community. The very heat of the present response is a major indicator that times have changed. The militantly anti-religious thrust of the older secularists — on and off the kibbutz — has changed to a more benign view of Judaism. To be sure, secularists are not about to don black hats or grow *peot*, but the fact is that secular Zionists have been seriously reevaluating themselves, and are wondering if secularism has not run its course. They are faced with a growing secular emigration from the country, and to add pain to their wounds, the only *aliyah* to the country that does exist from the West is overwhelmingly Orthodox. Further, they know that secular *yeridah* often results in assimilation to the culture of the West, with a concomitant weakening of attachment to Israel. Increasing drug and crime is evident in the Holy Land. Zionism itself is not popular among the youth, and while Arab students militantly claim the Land as their own, secular Israeli students are apologetic and unsure about Jewish rights to Israel. Is this wavering due to the fact that Israeli secularists do not take the

Bible seriously, including its claims to the Land? The more thoughtful among the secular Zionist leadership have been asking quiet, painful questions. Rav Schach's pointed remarks have opened the wounds and touched a nerve.

Throughout the month that follows, the matter of the deadlocked Knesset is overshadowed by a new media question. Before the speech, it was: What will he say? Now, after the speech it is: What did he say?

The old man, who nurtures no political or personal ambitions, and who grants no interviews, has — by his brief religious message — engendered a curious national debate in Israel. In the best Talmudic tradition, commentators and interpreters engage in close textual analysis, looking for nuances and hidden meanings. And in Bene Beraq, the aged Rosh Yeshiva remains silent, engaged only in his favorite activity: poring over his Talmud, looking for nuances and hidden meanings of a more ancient and lasting kind.

Melanie, Not Moses

LET US PUT ASIDE THE slogans and the public relations spins. Entering the covenant of Abraham — what we call conversion — is not a matter of TV sound bites or buzz words like "pluralism" and "Jewish unity."

Current attempts to pressure Israel's government into accepting non-Orthodox conversions across the board only obfuscate the religious facts of life.

As an Orthodox rabbi who served an American pulpit for forty years, I can testify that the overwhelming majority of conversions in America are motivated not by love for Judaism but the desire to marry a Jew.

Non-Orthodox conversions are by and large transparent covers for such intermarriages. Parents who are embarrassed that their child is marrying a non-Jew can have him or her quickly and painlessly converted — often without the requirement of a minimal knowledge of or commitment to Judaism. The primary interest in such conversion is usually not Moses, but Melanie or Michael.

(When would-be converts came to see me, trying to weed out the frivolous from the serious I would ask: "Why do you want to become Jewish?" More often than not the question would stump them. I often found myself having to explain — to their dismay — that Jews do not believe in Jesus or celebrate Christmas.)

Not bound by halakhah, each non-Orthodox rabbi sets his own conversion standards and guidelines. As a result and under pressure from the congregants, few of their conversion procedures follow traditional Jewish norms for entry into the Jewish people. A commitment to practice Judaism is not required, nor a minimal standard of Jewish knowledge. Mikveh immersion, the classical *sine qua non* for conversion, is frequently bypassed.

Sometimes the entire conversion procedure is omitted. In many Reform temples the rabbi will officiate at an intermarriage between one of his members and a non-Jew if they promise to attend conversion classes *after* marriage.

Beyond this, it is not unusual for the procedures to be supervised by non-Orthodox rabbis who themselves co-officiate with Christian clergy at inter-religious weddings. Cliches like "religious coercion," "discrimination" and "tolerance" cannot obscure the fact that conversions under such conditions are largely meaningless.

Whether one does or does not recognize the rabbinic credentials of the rabbis involved is beside the point. What is at stake is the wholesale and corner-cutting acceptance of converts who have no interest in being Jews. This is why no self-respecting halakhic community anywhere in the world recognizes such conversions.

Becoming a member of the Jewish people involves hallowed procedures followed by our people since the conversion of Ruth the Moabitess. To say, as she said, "Your people is my people, and your God my God. . . and only death shall separate us" is serious business; it involves more commitment than buying a new outfit.

Conversion should not be subject to limp sentimentality or silly threats from abroad about cutoffs in funding. Every nation and every people has the right to set its own entrance requirements.

Judaism has always welcomed genuine converts. Our people has been enriched by those prepared to accept the yolk and privilege of Torah. My Atlanta congregation included a number of converts who were models of Jewish commitment and practice. And of course, Ruth herself was the great-great-grandmother of King David.

To demand that the Jewish state recognize questionable conversions because of formulaic mantras like the Israel-Diaspora partnership, or because the majority of world Jewry is not Orthodox, may play well in the media, but it is fatuous and disingenuous. We are, after all, a people by virtue of our Torah and its guidelines, not by virtue of frivolous bromides.

A Talmud by Any Other Name

THE LATE TWENTIETH-CENTURY EXPLOSION OF English-language Judaica has reached its inevitable climax in the ongoing publications — from two separate sources — of translations of the Babylonian Talmud. There have been Talmuds in English before, most notably the Soncino translation which, despite its many shortcomings, was a staple for generations. But never before have there been such bold and ambitious translation and commentary projects, with Artscroll/Mesorah having so far published more than thirty tractates in fifty-five volumes, and the Steinsaltz, which is based on its own popular Hebrew translation of the Talmud, over ten tractates in twenty-two volumes. Apparently, each volume sells several thousand copies — a remarkable apotheosis for the world's most monumental work of law and learning which until recently was monumentally neglected.

More remarkable is the fact that all this is taking place at a time when Jewish rate of intermarriage is as high as seventy percent in some US cities, and even higher in Europe — and from devastating assimilation and ignorance. One would have thought that at such a time all interest in classical Jewish literature had long disappeared. On the contrary, it has increased. As the periphery of Jewish life drops off the edges into tragic oblivion, the core apparently grows stronger and more intense.

That these immense Talmud projects should be simultaneously undertaken by two separate groups of scholars poses a typical Talmudic question: Why do we need two when one would have sufficed?

The answer is also Talmudic: one might have sufficed if both were the same, but these two works are very different from each other — both in their approach to the Talmud itself and to their present-day readership.

Space does not permit an examination of the translations themselves. Suffice it to say that the language in each is eminently readable and elegant, that each makes a serious effort, through explanatory notes and commentary, to make the Talmud text more accessible. But an analysis of certain externals does reveal internal contrasts which are intriguing.

You cannot judge a book by its cover — but a cover makes a clear statement. The Steinsaltz displays a striking dust jacket of blue, orange, maroon, white, black, cream and gold, and its pages are gold-edged. There is no Hebrew on the dust jacket, which simply reads, "The Talmud, The Steinsaltz Edition." It has the appearance and feel of a luxuriously produced volume of contemporary art or photography. It opens from left to right, as does any English volume.

The Artscroll/Mesorah Talmud has no dust jacket at all. It successfully replicates the classic, dark brown Gemara "look," displays the famous Holy Ark of the Vilna Shas, and features on its cover the engraved Hebrew words, "Talmud Bavli," and the following statement: "The Gemara: the classic Vilna edition, with an annotative, interpretive elucidation as an aid to Talmud study." It looks and feels like the Gemara one would find on the shelves of a yeshiva. Unlike the Steinsaltz, its first pages contain letters of approbation from Talmudic authorities around the world who applaud the concept of an English translation. It opens from right to left, as does any Hebrew volume.

These surface differences are reflected in the page layouts. The Artscroll page is identical in every respect to the structure of the classic Talmud page — with the same pagination scheme, the unvocalized Talmud text in its original typeface in the center, surrounded by the commentaries of Tosafot on the outside border of the text, and that of Rashi on the inside border. The translation appears on facing pages, ingeniously arranged so that the more expansive English constantly faces the more compact Hebrew/Aramaic. The transliterations are the Ashkenazi and not the Sephardi pronunciation.

The respective Introductions to tractate *Bava Metsia* are also instructive. The Artscroll stresses the divine origin of the Written and Oral Torah, and states that the purpose of the translation "is to help the student understand the Gemara and improve his ability to learn from the original, under the guidance of a *rebbe*. The Talmud must be *learned*, not merely read." It expresses the hope that this edition will help people appreciate "the overriding importance of seeking a *rebbe* to provide guidance in plumbing the Divine wisdom." The word *rebbe* — and not "teacher" — is mentioned six times in the Introduction.

The Steinsaltz Introduction is less hortatory and more academic. It does not deal with divine origins, does not use the term *rebbe*, and simply explains the special features of the ensuing pages, noting that "the best way of studying the Talmud is... a combination of frontal teaching and continuous interaction between teacher and pupil and between pupils themselves."

These divergent approaches were reflected in the respective publicity campaigns. The Steinsaltz, published by a major secular publisher, was massively advertised in the Jewish and general American media. Rabbi Steinsaltz was a guest on a number of network TV programs, and conducted a publicized Talmud class for secular Jewish intellectuals in New York. The Artscroll, in contrast, limited its advertisements to the Jewish media.

Clearly, all these differences reflect conscious editorial decisions. The Steinsaltz appears to be aiming primarily at those who are far removed from Jewish tradition and from classical Jewish learning, and to be offering them a volume whose subliminal message is that the Talmud is really not as forbidding as they might have feared.

The Artscroll, on the other hand, appears to be making a conscious effort to demonstrate that, other than its English translation and commentary, its Talmud is not different from the classic Gemaras of old, and that it has not moved out of the ambit of traditional Talmud learning. Like the Steinsaltz, it is "user-friendly," but it does not emphasize its modernity.

The Steinsaltz attempts to pull the classic Talmud into today's world, dressing it up in contemporary clothing; the Artscroll attempts to pull today's world into the classic world of the Talmud, retaining its classic dress. One is evocative of the university library; the other, of the yeshiva *beit midrash*. This may explain why so many *daf-yomi* ("daily folio") groups and yeshivot around the world seem to be more comfortable with the Artscroll than the Steinsaltz: the ambience it presents is more conducive to traditional Jewish "learning."

It is significant that recently, in an apparent bow to the power of the *daf-yomi*, the Steinsaltz volumes have begun to appear in a less academic format. Now available is a Steinsaltz with a muted brown cover that, although original in its design, is reminiscent of traditional Talmud volumes, and which offers a page layout that reflects the old-fashioned "blatt Gemara."

But in either case, *caveat emptor:* let the reader beware that no matter how expert the translation, Talmud is like no other study. It demands discipline, rigor, and serious intellectual labor. It cannot be "read," or even "studied." It must be "learned," and learning demands total immersion and concentration. It requires the hard chair and table of the study hall and not the soft contours of an easy-chair beside the coffee table on which rests an English Talmud which is occasionally picked up and perused while listening to the radio. There is no quick road to genuine Talmud scholarship. And a translation doth not a scholar make.

And yet, the Talmud was never meant for specialists only, and works such as these, if approached with appropriate caution, can give the reader a taste of Talmudic logic and discourse. In practical terms, these are certainly valuable as an aid in reviewing material that has been previously studied with a teacher/*rebbe*.

Whether it is successful marketing or the staying power of the Oral Torah — or a bit of both — these two historic undertakings reflect the Jewish community's abiding curiosity about its origins; its lack of real literacy (a literate community can study its classics in the original); and, in their striking differences, two divergent approaches to Jewish life today and to the Jewish learning of the past.

And — who knows? — perhaps works such as these will provide the stimulus towards that ideal world where the masses of Jews are literate enough to study Talmud in the original.

Talmud Happily Ever After

Although for centuries the Talmud could be read only by those steeped in Jewish learning now you can read it, study it, treasure it, as you could before.

Our new translation "removes the language barrier and makes the classic Jewish learning experience available to everyone."

Our Talmud edition is now "in a form that is easy to understand...."
              ADS FOR SEVERAL RECENT TALMUD TRANSLATIONS

The proliferation of Judaica in English translation has been, on balance, a positive development, a manifestation of the renewed interest in classical Jewish sources, and an opportunity that has enabled tens of thousands to explore aspects of Torah which might otherwise have remained hermetically sealed to them.

While there is an ongoing debate as to whether the Talmud in particular, because of its special nature, can ever be successfully translated, and whether it even should be attempted (the classic "can/should" dilemma), there is a less complicated matter which has yet to be resolved. We refer to the kind of public relations blitz which has accompanied the new Talmud translations, the garbled signals which are imparted, and above all, the unintended mischief done to the good name and integrity of the study of Talmud.

Although the publishers and translators of the various Talmud editions have by and large done excellent and in some cases impeccable work, they have apparently been less than attentive to the advertising being disseminated in their names.

The hard sell and hyperbole which sells autos, toothpaste and deodorants by persuading us that without them we can never live happily ever after have become staples of our existence. We should have become inured to them by now. Nevertheless, one finds himself a bit discomfited by the breathless, quick-fix tone of the Talmud ads and their implicit promises — so reminiscent of the classic encyclopedia salesman's assurances that with the purchase of the twenty-volume set on easy terms, you and your children will place "the world's knowledge at your fingertips" and will be magically transformed into educated and cultured people.

In an amusing juxtaposition which reveals volumes, one of the Talmud advertisements features a color picture of Tractate *Bava Metsia* on a bookshelf shoulder to shoulder with the Encyclopedia Brittanica. This makes several not so subtle points: (*a*) an apotheosis has taken place, and it is now respectable in polite society to own and display a set of Talmud; (*b*) just as the Brittanica on your bookshelf says something about your general intellectual pretensions, so now does the new Talmud say something about your Jewish intellectual pretensions; and, unwittingly, (*c*) this new Talmud will be promoted in the time-honored encyclopedia manner.

It is not that the claims present half-truths; it is that they suggest complete untruths: that Talmud can be absorbed in a relatively painless way; that it is no longer necessary to "devote years to mastering its language and logic"; that it need no longer be exclusive province of those "steeped in Jewish learning"; that anyone — "you and your children" — can now become Talmud scholars simply by "reading" and "studying" the new translations; that just as you can read an encyclopedia and learn new facts almost effortlessly, without bothering to understand Kant or Milton or Wittgenstein, so can you now read and study the new translations and learn new facts about Judaism almost effortlessly, without bothering to understand, *lehavdil,* Rashi, Rambam, or the Gaon of Vilna.

All this, of course, is no revelation to the translators and publishers. In fact, the Introduction to one of the translations explicitly states that it is not a substitute for serious "learning." But apparently the publishers have allowed the salesmen free rein, who in turn have skewed the real meaning of Talmud study.

What the salesmen do not realize is that the barriers to knowing Talmud are not those of ordinary language which can be overcome by lucid translations. The language barriers to Talmud study are of a different dimension altogether, because this language contains words and concepts which contemporary society simply does not fathom: discipline, concentration, sacrifice, toil. These are untranslatable in a society which demands that the most complex matters be mastered in six easy lessons and that the profoundest ideas be reduced to the ten-second sound-bite (reminiscent of the perhaps apocryphal comment of the great rabbi who complained that *"Yeder Yid vill verren a talmid hakham in ein nakht – abber die nakht vill er zich gut ois-schlaffen* ("Every Jew would like to become a Talmud scholar overnight — but during that night he would like to have a good night's sleep"). These are concepts which emanate from another time and another place, and they are not found in any modern dictionary. These are the real barriers.

The Talmud is not for dabblers. The concept of *'amelim ba-Torah* and of *yegi'a;* and Joshua's *vehagita bo yomam valayla;* and Perek Kinyan Torah; and Rambam on Torah study — all make it clear that Torah is not acquired from a lounge chair. It demands dedication by day and by night, through heat and cold, in youth and in old age, in sickness and in health. It is not something you glance at occasionally and then return to the coffee table. To know it truly, to comprehend it, requires endless hours bent over a Gemara trying to coax the proper logic and meaning out of an argumentation which, despite the toil you have devoted to it, refuses to reveal its inner self, its subtle, hidden logic. In a couch potato society whose major expenditure of energy consists of pressing the button on the remote-control switch, such concepts are beyond translation.

Beyond all this, what the translators know but neglected to tell the salesmen is that successful Talmud study requires not only a disciplined mind, total intellectual focus, precise thinking, and constancy, but that primarily it requires faith in God and in Revelation, plus belief in the intellectual and religious integrity of the Talmudic sages, plus the conviction that by studying Torah and Talmud one is fulfilling a religious obligation which outweighs all other mitsvot. That's why study of the Torah and Talmud requires a prior *berakhah*.

And since they don't mention such things, an even more vexing problem emerges: that of the dilettante's half-knowledge. Having been assured that the new English text makes Talmud "crystal clear," he becomes an overnight *mayvin*, and in short order he notes what to him are strained analogies and obvious inconsistencies, and ascribes them to the credulity of the ancients. Why, he inevitably wonders, all this fuss about the brilliance of Talmud? He has, after all, read it, and parts of it make no sense at all, and in fact appear trivial and completely irrelevant.

Sadly for him and for the reputation of the Talmud, he will never perceive the eddies and currents which flow beneath the surface — he will not even be aware that there are levels deeper than his own — and he will never realize that beneath that surface, waiting to be discovered, lie the elegant, stately, and harmonious resolutions of the *rishonim* and *aharonim*.

If a little learning is a dangerous thing, superficial Torah study can be downright perilous.

That the translators have translated skillfully and that the publishers have published expertly and that their work has the great potential of broadening the exposure of masses of Jews to

Talmud Happily Ever After

the influence of Talmud study — all this is self-evident. Similarly, it is axiomatic that Talmud study should be open to all and not become an exclusive club for a small coterie of aristocrats. Torah is given to all Jews — *morashah kehillat Yaakov* - and its study is the privilege, right, and duty of us all.

This, rather, is a plea to control rhetoric, to limit claims, and to review advertising copy as meticulously as if it were textual material. Once this is done, then in my fantasy future ads will read:

> This translation will not make you a Talmud scholar. For that you will require years of intensive study. But this Talmud edition can assist you with difficult terms in the original Aramaic, can be an aid in preparing and reviewing the Talmud class you will attend, will give you some insight into the Talmudic method of thinking, will serve as an introduction carefully, patiently, and humbly, and if you work with a competent teacher regularly, you will gradually become aware of the subtleties of the text, you will begin to appreciate some of the majesty of the Oral Torah, and your mind will be stretched as it is exposed to the depths of the Talmudic process, to new ways of thinking and to the precise analysis and insights of our sages — and you will begin to understand why Jews believe that not only the Written Torah but the Oral Torah stems from Sinai.

Admittedly, such ad copy would probably not sell many volumes, but it would help preserve the integrity of Talmudic learning and the good name of the Talmud and its true and faithful disciples. In the interim, we can be grateful for small things — among them that Ravina and Rav Ashi did not have to depend on PR people to disseminate their redaction of the Talmud.

Cellular Kavannah

TO WHOM EXACTLY IS HE talking, this man with the cellular phone? Standing next to the Western Wall, is he talking to God? He doesn't need a cellular phone for that. He is standing within earshot of God at the Wall, for heaven's sake. To a friend or a business associate? To his wife? None of these can wait? He needs to talk on a cellular phone while he is standing at the Kotel?

Is it so urgent, this conversation? It can't wait, this communication? This black-hatted man talking into his cellular phone at the Kotel, telling someone at the other end that he will be a half hour late because there is much traffic around the Kotel — what would he have done last year before he owned this cellular phone? He would have been a half hour late because there was so much traffic around the Kotel, and neither his life nor the affairs of mankind would have been affected.

This bearded, black-suited man at the Kotel talking earnestly into his cellular phone: why does he not daven, or recite *tehillim*, or just contemplate the Wall, or just think about where he is and let the place quietly penetrate his being? Why must he talk to his friend or his associate or his wife for so long a time, why must he pace back and forth before the Wall, apologizing for being late, reminding his listener to meet him on the corner of Yaffo and Strauss near the camera shop at 4:30 instead of 4:00

and to remember to bring the package — all the time oblivious to the reality of where he is now standing?

This man at the Kotel informs his listener that right now he cannot talk any more, he is joining a minyan for *Minhah*. He folds up his cellular phone, slips it into his pocket, and begins *Ashrei*. He sways powerfully to and fro, back and forth, opens his palms outward as he recites *poteach et yadecha*, bows deeply as he recites the *amidah*, answers *amen* earnestly during the repetition, closes his eyes as he recites the *kedushah*, recites "who hast not made us like the nations of the earth" with fervor, and responds *yehei shmei rabba* with passion.

As *Minhah* comes to an end and the last *kaddish* is recited, he slips his hand into his pocket. At the final *amen* he pulls out his phone and dials his friend or associate or wife and tells him/her that he has just finished *Minhah* and will be leaving the Kotel in a few moments and please remember to bring the package.

As he prepares to leave, he glances at his watch, swiftly approaches the Wall, leans forward, lowers his head, places his hand on the stones and kisses the Wall fervently. Out of respect to the Wall he does not turn his back to it as he leaves. He makes his exit from the immediate Kotel area, pulls the phone out of his pocket and dials. "I am leaving now. See you in a few minutes."

The bus fills up and winds its way into town. At 4:31 the bus arrives at the corner of Yaffo and Strauss. He alights from the bus and walks briskly to the camera shop. It is 4:35. No one is there waiting for him. He pulls out his phone and dials. "You're coming? Oh yes, I see you now."

The person approaches. "I see you didn't forget the package. Thank you very much. How much is it?"

"Right now we won't talk money. I want you should try it out for a few days, then we'll talk money. I tell you, you will love this one. First of all, it has a very strong reception. You can send and receive calls even from New York. And clear? Clear like a bell. Better yet, it also has a fax on it, to send and to receive. You can also send and receive e-mail, and it connects to your computer. And it has an address book and a reminder notebook — the absolute latest thing on the market. Top of the top of the top of the line. And you can do all that with just one finger, so no matter what you are doing, no matter where you are, you can be in touch with the whole world, and the whole world can be in touch with you."

"Sounds wonderful. Fine. I will talk to you in a few days. Thank you."

He presses one button on the new phone. "Hello? I am using the new phone. It is great. With one finger I can be in touch with the whole world. And clear like a bell. I am on the way home and will be there in a few minutes. But first I want to grab in a *Maariv*."

In the little Shul on Yaffo he recites *borekhu* with zeal, sways powerfully back and forth, to and fro, bows deeply as he recites the *amidah*, answers *amen* earnestly during the *kaddish*, recites "who hast not made us like the nations of the earth" with fervor, and responds *yehei shmei rabbah* with passion.

As *Maariv* comes to an end and the last kaddish is recited, he slips his hand into his pocket and fingers the phone. At the final *amen* he pulls it out and looks at it admiringly. He can think of no one to call. He heads for home.

The German Soldier

SNOW IS FALLING AS OUR El-Al jet lands in Munich for a brief stopover. Munich: so much Jewish pain revolves around this city. Hitler; Nazis; appeasement; Jewish athletes murdered at this very airfield. I do not want to be a part of Munich, do not even want to breathe its air, and I will not get off the plane. Just a few days ago I walked on the sacred soil around the Western Wall in Jerusalem. Shall I now defile myself by touching the land and breathing the air of those who attempted to destroy the people of that Wall and that City? So I sit now in my place, gazing out the window at the airstrip and the desolate wintry weather which today envelops Munich.

The plane is far from the terminal, in a remote and lonely corner of the field. Out on the tarmac beside me a German soldier in the green uniform of the Wehrmacht, machine-gun in hand, paces back and forth. He stamps his feet for warmth on the frozen German earth. It is ten degrees outside, and a strong wind tears across the open field. But in the snow and wind the German soldier does his duty. His gun in hand, the heavy trench coat falling imperially below his knees, the peaked officer's cap forward on his head, this German soldier is protecting me, the Jew who sits comfortably in the warm, enclosed Jewish airplane.

He is young, perhaps twenty-five. His hair is blond, and though I cannot see them I know his eyes are blue. He is tall, erect, a very proper model of a very proper Aryan. He is ready to use his weapon in my behalf should anyone try to harm me or my plane. Ready, even to give his life for me. Those are his orders, and Germans follow orders and do their duty.

Here and there are signs on the field: *kein rollweg: bundesgrenitzchutz: flughafen* — the harsh Teutonic gutturals which in this place at another time formed words like *judenfrei, vernichtung, verbotten, gauleiter, enderserlosserung* in the mouths of other German soldiers with machine-guns and other Wehrmacht uniforms and trench coats and peaked caps who played pretty Bach and tended gentle pink roses just outside the walls of the crematoria while above them the choking chimneys belched black smoke. And in the fields not far from the crematoria young German soldiers — blond, blue-eyed and Aryan, guns in hand, alert and at the ready — did their duty to the Fatherland by forcing naked Jews to stand at attention for hours on end in the bitter cold of German winters as the winds tore at the emaciated bodies, and the soldiers in the green uniforms paced back and forth and shouted orders in harsh German gutturals and then shot the Jews down in clean bursts of fire.

Brave young German soldier, protecting me so diligently out there in the snow and wind, forgive me. I acknowledge what you are doing for me at this moment and I am glad that you are so alert — but my mind wanders. I know that you were not there in 1944 in the fields of Matthausen and Buchenwald and Bergen-Belsen not very far from here. And I know that on your uniform there is no swastika, and that you no longer murder Jews, and that you are not responsible for what took place in the days of your father and grandfather fifty years ago. You are innocent and I thank you for watching over me so well. But forgive me my hallucinations, you who are my present guardian and protector.

The seat-belt sign flashes on and we are about to take off. I will be glad to leave all this behind and fly to warmer places in Jerusalem. For even when the sun shines, it is always desolate in Munich; and when the skies are blue and clear it is still gray and cloudy there; even when in the springtime petals form on the roses, there is always a bitter snowstorm; and in the middle of the hottest summer it is icy cold in Munich, and smokestacks and chimneys belch out smoke, but even they cannot blot out what I see; and winds howl, but even they cannot quite drown out what I hear.

PART FOUR
Thinking About Judaism

HaMakom, the Place of the World

WHEN AHARON HAKOHEN'S TWO SONS died at the dedication of the *Mishkan* (Lev. 10:3), the Torah recounts his reaction in two stark words: *va-yidom Aharon/* "Aaron was silent."

There is majesty and holiness in silence. Granted, the power of words is truly miraculous — *mavet ve-hayyim be-yad lashon* — "Death and life are controlled by the tongue" (Prov. 18:21). But when all is said and done, one often finds that words, because they are finite and mortal, are not up to the task, and frequently useless. Particularly is one struck dumb when one is caught in the whirlwind between the mysterious force of life and the awesome counterforce of death. It is in this state of dumbness, this awe-filled silence, that one can sense the Presence of the One. The Psalmist's "to Thee, silence is praise" (65:2) takes on new life, and one begins to understand the *kol demamah dakah*, the voice of stillness of I Kings 19:12. The din and cacophony of daily discourse can drown out His Presence.

There are, however, certain words which bear within them the power of healing. Such healing is found in the key phrase of the *shivah* period, recited by each comforter before he takes his leave of the mourners: *HaMakom ye-nahem et'hem be-tokh she'ar aveilei Tsiyyon viYerushalayyim*. This can be translated either as a prayer ("May God comfort you among the mourners of Zion and Jerusalem") or as a reassurance ("God will surely comfort you...."). In either case, it suggests that true and lasting comfort is beyond the power of mortals to provide and can emanate only from the Source of all being.

To be sure, the presence of others does offer some measure of comfort. A terrifying sense of isolation and aloneness encompasses a survivor when death strikes. He is isolated even from God during the *aninut* period between death and burial, when no positive *mitsvot* may be performed: no *tefillin*, no *berakhot*, no formal prayer. All his energies are to be focused on the needs of the burial, yes; but symbolically, the survivor is cut off from everyone — even, temporarily, from God. The nerves of the soul seem to have been severed from the rest of mankind.

But with each *HaMakom* sincerely uttered, it is as if a nerve were reconnected. Each *HaMakom* is a verbal caress that soothes and heals, and step by halting step one is brought back into the society of man. By the end of the *shivah* period, guided by the halakhah and its prescriptions, one's connections are somewhat restored, and the mourning soul can now attempt to rejoin the company of mankind.

It is a powerful and moving statement, *HaMakom*... . But it engenders some questions. Why is this term — which is not listed among those holy Names of God that may not be erased or destroyed (*Shevuot* 35a-b) — used for God? Why not Hashem or the Holy One, or the Master, or one of His many other Names? And what is meant by "the mourners of Zion and Jerusalem"? Of these questions, we will address here only the major one: what is the significance of the term *HaMakom*?

❊

At the beginning of his wanderings, our father Ya'akov approaches a certain field where he will spend the night (Gen. 28:11). The Torah describes his arrival with the words, *Va-yifga ba-makom*, "And he alighted onto the *makom* / place." It is curious: no less than three times in that single verse — and two more times, in verses 16 and 19 — is that spot referred to as *makom*. Earlier, in 22:4, when Avraham sees this same place from afar, *ha-makom* is once again the key word: *Va-yar et ha-makom me-rahok*, "And he saw the place from afar."

Why the insistent repetition of this one term? Clearly, the text wishes to stress that this is no ordinary geographical location. Something wondrous lies beneath the surface of these words and beneath the surface of this place.

Truly, this is no ordinary place. This is the place which would ultimately be the location of the Jerusalem Temple (see *Hullin* 91b): it was this spot that supplied the dust for the creation of Man; it was here that the *akedah* took place; this was to be the site of Ya'akov's dream of the ladder connecting heaven and earth; and this is where God grants to Yaakov the promise of the Land.

This is not a common field. This is the Place of the World. Here Yaakov encounters the bedrock of all creation, the genesis from which all else emanates: the creation of Adam, the interrelationship between man and God. The matrix and the mystery of all creation converge and are concentrated into this one space. (Note *Keli Yakar's* commentary at *Gen.* 28:11.)

When applied to God, the term *HaMakom* has a similar connotation: God as Source and fount of all. (See Esther 4:14, where Mordekhai informs Esther that the salvation of the Jews will come from "another place," an allusion, according to the Sages, to God. The term used is, once again, *makom*.) As Bereshit Rabbah 68 says:

> R. Huna said in the name of R. Ami: Why do we use a euphemism (*kinuy*) for the Name of the Holy One, Blessed Be He, and call Him *makom* / "Place"? *She-hu mekomo shel olam, ve-ein ha-olam mekomo* / "Because He is the place of the world, and the world is not His place."

The world does not contain God; rather, God contains the world, and is Himself The Place of the world. A place encloses all that is within it; similarly, *makom* refers to God's capacity to contain and sustain everything within His universe. (For a seminal discussion of this subject, see R. Haim of Volozhin, *Nefesh haHayyim*, *Sha'ar* III.)

It can even enclose apparent opposites and contradictions. Just as a physical place is all-inclusive and can contain opposites, so does this appellation for God encompass apparent contradictions: the ultimate goodness and joy which is in the original design of the universe, as well as that which appears evil and causes suffering and pain. *HaMakom* is both Mercy and Justice; it denotes Sovereign Power, and also *avi yetomim vedayan almanot* / "Father of orphans and Spokesman for widows" (Ps. 68:6); it refers both to the Creator of light and Creator of darkness, Creator of good and also Creator of evil (Is. 45:7). God as *HaMakom* is the Source of all, subsuming everything within its limitless matrix-space.

Perhaps the designation *HaMakom* also contains within it all the various manifestations of God. Unlike the other Names of God, each of which represent only a single aspect of His Being (Hashem: the Merciful One; *Elo-him*: the bearer of strict justice; *Ado-nai*: God as the Master; *Melekh*: God as Supreme Sovereign), *HaMakom* includes in it every aspect of God.

※※※

The bereaved individual is struck dumb. He or she does not comprehend why life has come to an end. In the midst of pain and suffering, it seems folly to hope for the ultimate wiping away of tears and the full restoration of the laughter of *sehok pinu* (Ps. 126:2). To sow in tears and reap in joy is a paradox beyond his present comprehension. More than anything else the mourner requires complete and unconditional solace, reassurance, and the ability to understand — something which no mortal can provide. This can emanate only from Above, the ultimate Keeper of the mysteries. And only that attribute of God which encompasses within it both light and darkness, and both laughter and tears, can grant that ultimate solace and understanding. That all-embracing attribute is referred to as *HaMakom* / The Place.

For at the end of days, the confusion created by opposing forces — the white of limitless joy and purity and the black of limitless sadness and defilement — will clearly be seen as integral elements of the multi-hued fabric whose threads connect God to man; and that which today appears as a torn and chaotic universe will in that great moment be recognized as only an illusion. Through the all-embracing prism of *HaMakom*, reality will finally be perceived as it is: not torn at all, but whole, complete, and, finally, *ehad*/ One.

✺

There is majesty and holiness in silence. But there are certain spoken words which contain their own majesty and holiness.

Life's Second Chances: The Second Passover

> *And they made the Pesah [offering] in the first month, on the fourteenth day, at dusk, in the wilderness of Sinai. According to all that the Lord commanded Moses so did the children of Israel do. But there were certain men (anashim) who were unclean by [contact with] the dead body of a man, so that they could not make the Pesah [offering] on that day; and these men came before Moses and Aaron on that day. And these men said to him; we are unclean by [contact with] the dead body of a man; why should we become diminished [lamah nigara'] not to bring the offering of God at its appointed season in the midst of the children of Israel? And Moses said to them: Wait, that I may hear what God will command with regard to you.* NUMBERS 9:5-8

A strange complaint. These complainers obviously recognized and comprehended the inner meaning of a Divine commandment. They clearly sensed that doing God's sacred deed creates infinite echoes, that fulfillment of His will is a fulfillment of the self, a climbing upward, a heightening of the one who is commanded, another step toward the completion of the unfinished image of God in man; so that if the commandment is not done, the sacred deed not performed, the individual is somehow diminished, less complete. Thus, *lamah nigara*, "why should we become diminished?"

In the wilderness sojourn, beset by dreams of fleshpots, and distrust of Moses, and idolatrous calves of gold, and fantasies about the melons of Egypt, and envy and fear and rebellion and resentment, this extraordinary complaint is a reminder that the wilderness generation, despite everything, deeply understood that a sacred deed unperformed, a *mitsvah* unfulfilled, diminishes the person.

Some questions: (*a*) Who were these *anashim* who came to Moses, and how had they become ritually defiled? (*b*) Why does Moses seek an immediate audience with God; why does he not simply inform these men that nothing can be done now that the time for the *mitsvah* has passed?

As to who these *anashim* were and how they become defiled, the Talmud cites several traditions:

> R. Ishmael says: They were the carriers of the bier of Joseph [and had thus become defiled]. R. Akiva says: They were Mishael and Eltsaphan who became defiled by touching Nadav and Avihu [whom they carried from the Tabernacle after they had been struck dead; Leviticus 10:1-5]. R.Yitshak says: if they were the carriers of Joseph's bier, there was sufficient time for them to have become purified. And if they were the carriers of Nadav and Avihu, there was sufficient time for them to have become purified. Who were they? They were individuals who had become defiled because they were involved with the burial of a *met mitsvah* [an unattended corpse found in the field]. (*Succah* 25a; cf. also *Sifri* 19.)

That is to say, were there sufficient time for these men to have become purified and they chose not to, there would have been no need for Moses to approach God for special instructions. By remaining defiled, they chose not to become eligible for the *Pesah* offering.

But those involved with a *met mitsvah* have no choice. Even if an individual were on his way to perform the *Pesah* offering and suddenly confronted a *met mitsvah*, he would have to tend to the *met mitsvah* in full knowledge that by so doing he would become ritually defiled, and thus disqualified from participating in the *Pesah*. Even a *kohen*, a priest, whose attendance to the dead is carefully circumscribed and limited, is released from all restrictions when he is confronted by a *met mitsvah*.

Thus R. Yitshak argues: Is it just that a person who fulfills God's commandment to bury the unattended dead, and in so doing becomes ritually defiled, be rendered ineligible to fulfill God's commandment of the Pesah sacrifice? How does one respond to this individual's plaint when he says: my defilement was placed upon me, forced upon me, by God Himself? It is a holy defilement, contracted during the performance of a holy act, which, because it is God's will, enhances, expands, and magnifies him, and brings him closer to the perfection and completion for which his soul yearns. Having been defiled by God's fiat in the performance of a holy commandment, shall he now be diminished, denied the privilege to perform this *Pesah* commandment?

Perhaps it is because Moses sees the pristine logic of the argument of these *anashim* and senses the pain of their diminution that he brings their complaint before God — Who responds immediately, as if He had been waiting for someone to ask the question:

> If any man of you or of your generations shall be unclean by reason of [contact with] the dead, or be on a distant path, he shall keep the Pesah unto the Lord; in the second month on the fourteenth day at dusk they shall keep it.
> ....But the man who is clean and is not on a journey and neglects to bring the Pesah, that soul shall be cut off from his people because he brought not the offering of God in its appointed season, that man shall bear his sin. (NUMBERS 9:10-13)

God's words here (not only here) require careful scrutiny. God does not say that he who missed the first Pesah because he was involved with a *mitsvah* is given the opportunity of a second *Pesah*; nor does He say that anyone who missed the first Pesah because he was occupied with the performance of an act of

Life's Second Chances: The Second Passover 211

mercy is given a second chance. The laws of the Second *Pesah* — the *Pesah Sheni* — are formulated in much broader fashion: Anyone who does not deliberately absent himself, anyone whose heart was willing and who sincerely desired to bring the first *Pesah* offering, but was somehow prevented from so doing, is given a *Pesah Sheni*, a second chance. And, astonishingly, even he who deliberately did not bring the first Pesah offering is granted a second Pesah. (See details in Rambam, *Korban Pesah* 5:1-2 ff.)

II

Further questions: a) Surely there were those who, because of circumstances, were occasionally prevented from hearing the shofar on Rosh Hashanah, from fasting on the holy days of Yom Kippur, or from taking the lulav on Sukkot, all of which are also commandments of God. Why did they not approach God with similar complaints about their personal diminution? b) Had they done so, would there have been a *Shofar Sheni*, a *Yom Kippur Sheni*, a *Sukkot Sheni*? c) Had these men not approached Moshe but simply accepted their situation, would the Torah ever have contained the laws of *Pesah Sheni*? In other words, d) why were the laws of *Pesah Sheni* not given at Sinai? And the fundamental question: e) what is it about the Pesah offering that, alone among all the commandments of the Torah, it is the only one for which, if the opportunity to perform the deed is missed, a second chance is given?

The Pesah offering (*korban Pesah*), more than an ordinary sacrifice, demands more than ordinary thought. The words of *Meshech Hokhmah* by Rabbi Meir Simcha ha-Kohen of Dvinsk (1843-1925) illuminate:

> ....We find that wherever it was necessary to separate Israel from the worship of idols and bring them back to the worship of God, it was done through the Pesah offering. In Hezekiah's time (Chronicles 11:29-30), after idolatrous defilement and impurity

was rooted out from the Jews, they offered a Pesah sacrifice to God....

Further, the Pesah offering teaches Divine providence, for it was on Passover that God distinguished and separated the Israelite first-born from the Egyptian first-born. Beyond this, the Pesah sacrifice teaches that God Himself is the Prime Cause and Mover, without any intermediaries, and does not act through the stars or the planets, on which is based all idolatrous worship....

Further, the Pesah sacrifice instills in the heart of the Children of Israel the idea that they are all equal, that they are a holy nation unto God, and that each individual is able to come under God's personal protection....

It also teaches God's desire that no individual shall dominate another, in keeping with God's words, "They are my servants, and not servants to servants. . . ." (Kiddushin 15b). And it is God's will that no man should be subservient to a heavenly body or a force of nature, for each of these is in itself subservient to the Holy One....

All (four points) are taught by the Pesah offering.

This is why Pesah occurs in the springtime when, after the dormant winter, the forces of the natural universe return to their full vigor and strength, and one is tempted to ascribe great powers to them. Pesah occurs in this season so that mankind will be reminded that all of nature is really a tool in the hands of God, as He demonstrated in Egypt. It is for this reason that the Torah calls it "a Pesah to God" (Exodus 12:11-27).

There are further reasons, profound and hidden, behind the powers of the Pesah sacrifice to purify us from idolatry. Thus, when Josiah (Kings 11:23) cleansed Judea and Jerusalem from the idols, he offered up a Pesah offering (v. 21; see also Chronicles 2:35:18). The Pesah sacrifice contains an essential ingredient: it is an antidote to idolatry. This can be seen from the commandment given to Israel while in Egypt: "*Mishchu*, withdraw [from idolatry; *Mechilta*, Bo, 84] and take unto yourself a lamb...." For this same reason, after Israel sinned with the Golden Calf, it was commanded to make the Pesah, so that there would be created a separation between them and the emptiness of the idols, in order that Israel might be purified. Therefore, in the fortieth year, when Israel fell under the temptation of the idol *Be'al Pe'or*, it was once again commanded to make the Pesah in *Gilgal* (Joshua 5:10)...."

Thus, according to Rabbi Meir Simcha, it is apparent that the commandment of the Pesah offering is preeminent among all other commandments because it brings in its wake (*a*) purification from idolatry; (*b*) divine concern and protection of His people; (*c*) freedom to be subservient to God alone; and (*d*) the concept that there is no other power or force in the universe save the power of the Holy One.

Other considerations may be added to these. It must not be forgotten that the lamb of the first Pesah sacrifice in Egypt is the deity worshipped by Israel's taskmakers. The Pesah is thus the commandment that marks Israel's rebellion against, and revulsion from, the natural temptations of the dominant culture. Of all commandments, Pesah is primary and transcendent, for this is the transforming commandment: with it, the disparate children of Jacob become the children of God.

Pesah, in the biblical first month of Nisan, is also primary in the chronology of the Jews. It is the first *mitsvah* that Israel performs as a people, the *mitsvah* with which Israel celebrates her emergence into nationhood, the *mitsvah* which transforms Israel from a people subservient to another into a people subservient only to the Other.

A *mitsvah* as comprehensive as the Pesah is a transcending imperative for the Jew. The Pesah offering is only one of two positive commandments whose violation carries with it the penalty of *karet* / excision (the other being *berit milah* / covenantal circumcision). As the commandment which purifies from idolatry, stresses God's concern for mankind, and epitomizes Israel's becoming a people; as that which symbolizes Israel's rebellion against the merely natural and marks entrance into the supernatural, and which represents Israel's leap from the merely historic into the meta-historic, the Pesah is the embodiment of all mitsvot, and no Jew should ever be forced to set it aside. Therefore, if the Jew, having yearned for this commandment, somehow finds himself on a *derekh rehokah*, a distant path, unable to reach Jerusalem at the appointed time, or if he becomes ritually defiled, or other circumstances prevent him from taking part in this commandment, he need not become diminished. One month later, on the same day and the same time, at the exact position of the mid-month moon, he can again offer up the Pesah. He is given a second chance.

For no other commandment is there a second chance; because of no other commandment can it be said that it embodies all that is embodied in this first and primary commandment, the commandment which represents all the others.

III

But the first and primary commandment is even more. The second chance that it offers is more than a second chance.

Deeply imbedded in *Pesah Sheni*, hidden from view, is a gift from God to His finite and mortal creatures, a gift without which there can be no lasting connection with the Creator. For the *Pesah Sheni* is more than opportunity to compensate for a neglected Pesah offering. It is in fact *a regel bifnei atsmah*, "an independent festival" (*Mishneh Torah, Korban Pesah,* 5; cf. *Pesahim* 92b). This may explain why God's response to Moses expands the question, and includes in the privilege of *Pesah Sheni* not only those who were, at the first Pesah, involved in a *mitsvah*, but anyone who did not deliberately absent himself.

We may suggest that overarching the *Pesah Sheni*, flowing from it, is an intimation of *teshuvah*, the possibility for errant and restless man to reach and touch the outstretched hand of his Creator. This primary mitsvah can be viewed as a paradigm: buried deep within it lies the adumbration of the idea of repentance, the foreshadowing of *teshuvah*. For repentance is the assurance that despite man's frequent failure to discover God — despite his moving forward and his falling backward, his holiness and his profaneness, his vision and his blindness —

his longing for God can yet be fulfilled. If he veers away today, there lies the possibility of correcting the course tomorrow. The Pesah is in this regard Every mitsva, containing within it the essence of man's connectedness to God, of which repentance is the primary element.

"And the men came before Moses and Aaron and said. . . .Why should we become diminished not to bring the offering of God. . . .?" Significant is not only their complaint and their wisdom, but their coming before Moses. Had they not come, there may never have been a *Pesah Sheni*. Yes, it was in God's design to bring a *Pesah Sheni* to His world, but He was, as it were, waiting for someone to ask the questions. *The design required that finite man, not the infinite God, take the first step*. Note the comment of the *Sifri* that the law of *Pesah Sheni* was worthy to have been presented at Sinai, but that Mishael and Eltzaphan were given the merit to have it enacted because of them. *Teshuvah* is God's gift to mankind, but it is man who must seek it and initiate it. If there is no human yearning, if there is a deliberate turning aside from God, there can be no *Pesah Sheni*, no second chance: "If a man is clean, and not on a journey, and neglects the *Pesah*, he shall be cut off from his people. . . .his sin shall he bear" (Numbers 9:13).

But if on man's journey he finds himself on a distant path, far from the source of his being; if he retains the will and the hope to reach primary and transcendent things, a second Pesah awaits him. He need not feel diminished forever, need not remain incomplete, untouched by first things. The moon wanes and recedes, but next month, at the same hour on the same day, the moon will renew itself, re-create itself, and return to its rightful place in the heavens; and man, too, will have a second chance to return to his rightful place on earth.

The Holiday in Hiding

POOR PURIM. IT HAS BECOME the Jewish mardi-gras, a day of revelry, drinking, and masquerades. But it is much more than this.

Purim is the holiday in hiding. One has to probe beneath the surface to find the spiritual dimension that lies underneath. In fact, the disguises and the masks are all designed to underscore the essential hiddenness of this day.

This theme of concealment is found in the very name of the heroine of Purim. "Esther" derives from the root *str*, which in Hebrew means "hidden." In the Torah (Dt. 31:18), God says to Israel: " I will surely hide (*haster astir*) My face from you..." The Sages see this Hebrew phrase as a subtle suggestion of the hiddenness of God during the time of Esther.

Take Esther herself. No one except Mordecai knows who she really is. Even King Ahashveros is kept in the dark. *"Ein Esther magedet moledetah,"* says the Megillah in 2:20. "Esther did not reveal her origins ..." This is the theme of the day: nothing is revealed.

Note also the lineage of the protagonists of the Purim story. It is the lineage of hiddenness. Mordecai and Esther are descendants of mother Rachel. Rachel, the mother of Yosef, is the very essence of hiddenness and concealment. When her sister Leah is substituted for her in marriage to Yaakov, why

The Holiday in Hiding

does Rachel not cry out and protest that an injustice is being done? Because to do so would have humiliated her sister: Rachel knows how to conceal things, including her bitter disappointment.

Rachel's son Joseph is also a master of concealment. His essential qualities of holiness are concealed from his brothers, who do not recognize his greatness because he effectively hides them. And when the brothers come down to Egypt 22 years later, they again fail to recognize him, for he is now concealed behind his garments. The Talmud (*Sotah* 10) underscores the hidden qualities of Joseph when it states that — in the case of Potiphar's wife — Joseph sanctified the name of God in private, in a hidden way. And Saul, from the same lineage as Joseph, feels unworthy of becoming king of Israel: he hides among the vessels when they search for him to become king.

It is thus fitting that Esther and Mordecai, who stem from this same lineage, should also do their saving work quietly, secretly, in a hidden and concealed manner. (It is also fitting, incidentally, that Haman, the descendant of the Amelekite King Agag whom Saul refused to kill, is sent to his destruction by Mordecai the descendant of Saul, for by so doing, Mordecai repairs the transgression committed by Saul.)

Even God Himself is hidden in the Purim story. Search the Megillah from beginning to end, but you find no mention of His name. Is this not strange for a Biblical book? The closest we come to a reference to God is when Mordecai says to Esther that redemption for the Jews will come from *makom aher*, "another place."

To underscore the hiddenness of God, the entire story seems to be one of chance, happenstance, and coincidence — the very things that the Bible tells us the world is not! In the Megillah, the role of God is unseen, His hand invisible. Queen Vashti just happens to refuse to appear at the royal feast; the king just happens to rid himself of her and to search for a new queen; Mordecai just happens to be in the right place at the right moment to foil a plot against the king's life; the king just happens to have a sleepless night and his courtiers remind him that Mordecai saved his life; Haman just happens to be in the Queen's chambers when the King walks in. Even the date on which the Jews are to exterminated is determined by the casting of lots: *hipil pur hu hagoral*, "he cast a *pur*, that is, the lot . . . " (Esther 3:7) and it is this *"pur"* that gives us the name of the holiday. All these echoes of randomness and chance suggest anything but the guiding hand of God.

Even the miracle of Purim is a hidden one. Contrast this with the miracle of Hanukah. There, the oil that is enough for one day burns instead for eight days, which is a *nes niglah*, an open miracle that everyone can see. But the Purim miracle — whereby the entire Jewish community is saved from destruction — is a hidden miracle, a *nes nistar*. The interceding hand of God is invisible. It could easily be ascribed to happenstance, the way everything else in the story seems to be happenstance.

Gradually we begin to understand the role of masks in the Purim story. *The entire deliverance of the Jewish people is masked.* It is a story wrapped in a disguise, hidden behind a costume, concealed behind a mask.

Even that strange dictum in the Talmud (*Megillah* 7b) that ordains us to become intoxicated on Purim *ad delo yada*, "until we know not the difference between cursed is Haman and blessed is Mordecai" — even this is part of the theme of hiddenness. For how strange is this Talmudic advice. Ours is, after all, a tradition that abhors drunkenness. We are a people of the mind, discernment, analysis — all those things that fall under the rubric of *daat*. But on Purim we are bidden to become intoxicated and conceal our vaunted *daat* — to the point of *ad delo yada* — "until there is no *daat*" — and to enter a universe where reality has no meaning and we begin to realize that it is not our intellects that guide the world but the One Intellect above that guides the world.

There is another strange hiddenness about Purim. This is the most physical of all our holidays. The festive Purim *seudah*, the sending of food gifts, the encouragement to drink to excess — these are matters that deal with the body. What, by contrast, is the most spiritual of our holy days? Obviously, it is Yom Kippur. Our observance of these two days are in diametric opposition to one another. But upon closer examination we perceive that the two are closely related in a very hidden but real way. The official name of Yom Kippur is Yom Hakippurim. Literally, that means, "a day like Purim." This is stunning. Yom Kippur is like Purim? How can this be?

It can be, because Purim and Yom Hakippurim are mirror images of one another. On Yom Kippur we are forbidden to eat or drink; on Purim we are bidden to eat and drink. Yom Kippur is overwhelmingly spiritual; Purim is overwhelmingly physical. But on each day we are required to serve God fully, with our bodies and with our souls.

The lesson is clear: God can be served not only in the solemnity of a Yom Kippur, but also in the revelry of a Purim. God is present not only in the open ark of Yom Kippur when spirituality seems so close, but also in the open food and drink of Purim when spirituality seems so remote. It is much more of a challenge to remember God amidst the revelry than to remember Him in the midst of the solemnity. To imbibe and to feast and to remember the Author of all; this is the great challenge of Purim — perhaps a greater challenge than any other holy day.

Purim is the holiday in hiding. But its message need not be concealed from us.

Why I Like Tish'a B'Av

TISH'A B'AV IS NOT EVERYONE'S favorite day, but it is one of mine — not because it is enjoyable, but because of what it represents.

I like Tish'a B'Av because of what it says to me about Jews: that we are a people that remembers and knows its past leads to a future.

There are many more Italians in the world than Jews. Yet no one laments for Rome. There are many more Greeks than Jews. The Acropolis and the Parthenon are tourist's attractions, but does anyone mourn because of their destruction?

Babylonia, Persia, Assyria, the glory of ancient Egypt — who remembers, who sheds a tear, who cares?

I like Tish'a B'Av because only a people that can weep will someday learn to laugh.

And I like Tish'a B'Av because I need it.

In the midst of all the affluence and creature comforts, I need to remove my leather shoes, and dim the lights. I need to fast and not to indulge myself. I need to read Lamentations and weep for my people's martyrdom, for its bloody history. I need to focus outward.

I need Tish'a B'Av because it reminds me of what it is to be a Jew; and that Esau hates Jacob, Pharaoh oppresses Israel, and Haman wishes to destroy us; and that the empires of the world abhor the Jew because he belongs to "a nation that dwells alone."

I like Tish'a B'Av because it teaches something profound; that for Judaism, historical events are not just history, not just events. "History" and "events" take place at a point in time — but in Judaism, once an event occurs it goes on being part of us. It is a new awareness, cognition, an ongoing perception, a new consciousness.

When you suddenly achieve a new insight, it remains part of you. On particular days in our history the awareness of joy as an element of life (Succot), or of Godliness (Rosh Hashanah), or the consciousness of nearness to God (Pesah) first entered the universe. On Tish'a B'Av the elements of tragedy and disaster were introduced to us.

A man once said to me: "Why bother with an event that took place 2,000 years ago? Why mourn, why sigh? We have modern Israel, we should rejoice."

Is there a county more concerned about daily security than Israel, or one that has more bitter experience of friendly countries growing cold and distant at the slightest provocation?

No other countries have to struggle daily over the sovereignty of their ancient capitals. No other countries are restricted in their right to visit and worship at their ancient holy sites in their own land.

One of the main reasons for the original destruction of the Temple and our exile from our land — baseless hatred among Jews — still exists among us. Tish'a B'Av is a good day to ponder unity and tolerance.

I like Tish'a B'Av because it contains a message of profound hope and faith. On this day, our Sages tell us, the Messiah was born. How profoundly insightful, how ironic, how just — on the day of destruction, redemption began. The end was also the beginning. "Give us joy in accordance with the days of our suffering," says the Psalmist.

On the Sabbath preceding Tish'a B'Av we read the first chapter of Isaiah, the chapter of rebuke. On the following Shabbat we read the fortieth chapter of Isaiah: "Comfort ye, comfort ye, My people." Just as the tears are real, so will the comfort be real.

With plain, solid assurance like that, is it any wonder that I like Tish'a B'Av?

Uncommon Connections in the Halakhot of Mourning

THE CLASSICAL JEWISH MOURNING PRACTICES such as the rending of the garment, the prohibition against cutting the hair, and, of course, the seven day mourning period, are well known. But widespread as many mourning practices are, a glance beneath the surface reveals a body of law whose legal origins and derivations are subtle, suggestive, and even paradoxical.

A case in point is the normative *shivah* period. What are its origins and sources? Joseph mourns for his father for seven days (Gen. 50:10), but the Talmud does not view this as a specific biblical commandment, because it occurred before Sinai, and Joseph's mourning precedes, rather than follows, his father's burial.[1] The Babylonian Talmud points to the communal mourning for Aaron the *kohen* (Num. 20:29), indicating that only the first day is a Torah requirement[2], while the Jerusalem Talmud states that the entire seven-day period is not a biblical

---

1. Tosefot *Mo'ed Katan* 20a, s.v. *mah hag shiv'a*
2. *Zevahim* 100a; cf. Maimonides, *Mishneh Torah, Hil. Avelut* 1:1, who cites this as the halakhah, as does Alfasi, *Mo'ed Katan* 3:13a and Ber. 2:9b-10a; cf. also *Tur, Yoreh De'ah*, 398:1, and 399:113; see also Rashi, *Nazir* 15b, s.v. ela; *Tosefot Mo'ed Katan* 14b, s.v. *aseh*; and Maimonides, *Sefer Hamitsvot, Aseh* 37. Rashba and Raavad support the concept that the first day of mourning (which coincides with the day of death and of burial) is a Torah requirement, while Rosh, Ri, and Rabbenu Tam consider it rabbinic.

commandment but was instituted as a *taqanah* by Moses himself."[3]

A specific biblical source for a seven-day mourning is cited in *Mo'ed Katan* (20a), but this, too, is not a clear directive but rather a juxtaposition of the terms "festival" and "mourning" in Amos 8:10: "*v'hafachti hageichem l'evel.... v'samti-ha k'avel yahid* ...." "I will turn your festivals into mourning, and I will make it as a mourning for an only son." From this, the Talmud deduces that just as *hag*/festival continues for seven days (Lev. 23:7, 8, so also does the mourning period continue for seven days. The equation of *hag* and *evel*, of festival and mourning, becomes the source of the seven-day *shivah*.

An additional connection between festival and mourning is found in *Mo'ed Katan* (14a and 17b). Here it is suggested that further parallels exist between the two; i.e., that most of the practices which are forbidden during the intermediate days of a festival — *hol ha-moed* — are also forbidden during the mourning. In strictly legal terms, this is a clear analogy. But in conceptual terms, the idea of a parallel or identity between two such utter opposites is both perplexing and resonant.

This is not an isolated instance. Halakha makes a number of odd analogies in the area of mourning. In several places, the Rabbis connect certain mourning practices with those related to marriage. *J. Ketubot* (1:1) states: "Just as one comforts a mourner for seven days so does one make a (newly) married couple joyous for seven days after the wedding." Maimonides codifies this in his Hilkhot Avelut (1:1): "...and Moshe Rabeinu enacted for Israel seven days of mourning and seven days of feasting (for a newly married couple)." In *Pirke de-Rabbi Eliezer* (No. 17), we find that King Solomon built two gates in the Temple, one for the bridegrooms and one for excommunicants and mourners: "Jerusalemites would gather between the two gates

---

3. *J. Ketuvot* 1:1; cf. also Maimonides, ibid. Cf.also *Nazir* 15b. The taqanot initiated by Moses, as distinct from commandments which Moses enunciates in the name of God, do not have the status of Biblical commandment. But see *Korban Ha-eda* commentary on this citation of *J. Ketubot* 1:1.

and offer condolences to the mourners at one gate, and congratulations to the married couples at the other gate." And in *Ketubot* (17a) we learn that "Torah study is interrupted both for a funeral and for a wedding." Further, regarding the practice of eating lentils, the normative food of mourning, it is evident that lentils were once used both for mourners and marriage celebrants.[4] Both *birkhat hatanim* — the blessings recited at the marriage ceremony and after meals during the seven-day celebration — and *birkhat avelim* — the blessing recited in Talmudic times after the funeral and during the *shivah* — are said over wine only, in the presence of a minyan and then only when *panim hadashot* — new faces — are present.[5] According to Rav Hanin (*Eruvin* 65a), one of the reasons for the creation of wine was so that mourners could be comforted, as indicated in Prov. 31:6, "Give strong drink to him who is ready to perish, and wine unto the bitter of soul."

Even more surprising is the fact that one of the primary legal concepts of the halakhic marriage ceremony, marriage by means of monetary consideration (*kesef*), derives from the fact that the Torah uses the identical terminology to describe both the "acquisition" of a bride and the acquisition by Abraham of the burial place for Sarah. The legal concept of *kiha kiha misdeh Efron* is so familiar to students of Talmud that few pause to reflect how odd it is that a marriage practice can be derived from an event so conceptually distant from marriage as is burial.[6]

A strange thread winds its way throughout the classical sources: feasting and lamenting, *hag* and *evel*, share much common and curious ground.

This intriguing equation of opposites continues on the level of mourning and sanctity. Thus, the requirement to remove

---

4. Cf. Rashi to Gen 25:30, s.v. *min ha'adom*, based on *Midrash Rabbah* 63:14, and *Bava Batra* 16b; see also Targum Yonatan ben Uziel to verse 29 above. For a full listing of sources dealing with this mourning food, see *Rashi Hashalem* (Ariel, Jerusalem, 1988) vol. II, p. 17, f.n. 62.
5. Cf. *Mo'ed Katan* 27a; *Ketubot* 8b; *Tur, Yoreh De'a* 378-9.
6. *Kiddushin* 2a. Rabbi Simcha Krauss first pointed out this contrast to me.

one's shoes during mourning is paralleled by the requirement to remove shoes at a sacred site, beginning with Moses who was told, "Remove your shoes, because the place on which you stand is holy" (Exodus 3:4).

An even more striking relationship between mourning and sanctity is found in the very basic mourning practices. The very law requiring mourning for the seven different relatives — father, mother, son, daughter, brother, sister, wife/husband — is derived from the *kohen*. It is precisely these seven for whom the *kohen* defiles himself by attending them at death. The *kohen's* regulations are specifically defined in Lev. 21:2-3, from which is derived the requirement of a non-*kohen* to mourn for each of these seven. (See also *Yev.* 22b concerning mourning for one's spouse.)

Almost every customary mourning practice, such as the prohibition against cutting one's hair and the requirement to rend one's garment, is obliquely derived from the Torah's directives to the *kohen*. For example, from the fact the *kohanim* involved in the Temple service are forbidden to let their hair grow long when they are in mourning (Lev. 10:6), the Talmud deduces that any other mourner may not cut his hair. Only the Temple *kohen* is forbidden to let his hair grow long in mourning, because he is *kohen*. Furthermore, the Torah forbids the *kohen* to rend his garments in mourning, implying quite clearly that every non-*kohen* does rend his garments at such an occasion.

An entire section of the Talmud (*Mo'ed Katan* 14a-16a) is devoted to such types of inverted derivations. The normative mourning practices for a non-*kohen* involving the donning of *tefillin* or the eating of one's own food on the first day of mourning, the prohibition regarding the wearing of shoes, the study of Torah, and *sh'ilat shalom* (offering greetings) are derived from the laws of the *kohen*. There are no biblical mourning laws directed specifically to the non-*kohen*. What the *kohen* is forbidden to practice in his mourning — because he is a *kohen* — the ordinary Jew must practice in his mourning — because he is not a *kohen*.

That mourning practices should be inversely derived from the *kohen* is especially intriguing because it is the *kohen* who by Jewish law is most removed from death, and is forbidden even to be within the precincts of the dead. And yet it is the same *kohen* whose non-practice of mourning is the source of our observance of mourning. (This echoes the paradox of *hag* and *evel*. Although, as we have seen, these two concepts are very much intertwined, *hag* and *evel* are so inimical that they cannot co-exist. The onset of a *hag* cancels mourning that has already commenced, and postpones mourning that would otherwise begin.)

II

Since halakhic norms are not the result of a haphazard, disjointed process, but instead are manifestations of a coherent system with its own world-view, a probe beneath this perplexing surface will suggest a connecting link between these apparent opposites.

Perhaps, in this highlighting of opposites, halakhah is suggesting that the human attitude toward the ideas of *hag* and *evel* is fundamentally out of joint. The conventional view is that feasting and lamenting are ultimate opposites: death and tragedy are times of crisis, but festivals and joy are not times of crisis. The halakha may be saying that *hag* and *evel* are in fact parallels of crisis; that the moment of *hag* is as much a watershed event as a moment of *evel*. *Hag*, like *evel*, calls for introspection, self-evaluation, contemplation. Just as the time of mourning brings on the instinctive human reaction to take stock, ask questions, and assess one's relationship with the Creator, so should it be at festive times. The essential commonality inherent in both joy and sadness is alluded to in the Mishna's declaration that "just as a person is obligated to bless [God] for the good, so must he bless for the evil." (M.

Berakhot 9:1) And *J. Ketubot* (1:1) states that "Moses instituted the seven days of feasting [after a wedding], and the seven days of mourning."

The halakhah seems to be suggesting that there is in fact an equivalence and a connection between joy and sadness, and that the authentic religious reaction at the festive moment is not dissimilar from the authentic religious reaction of the sad moment: not the tired, inevitable cliché, "What have I, who am such a good person, done to deserve this evil?" but the fresh and authentically religious response, "What have I, who am essentially undeserving, done to deserve this good?" In each situation, the Jew must cry out, "I am newly aware, O God, of Your presence, and I acknowledge Your paramount role in my life."

The ultimate purpose of the mitsvah of *hag* is to remind the celebrating Jew that there is a God Who must be acknowledged and praised. In truth, one does not comprehend the ultimate meaning of celebration any more than one comprehends the meaning of sadness. Death and tragedy inevitably bring in their wake an awareness of God's role in the universe. This is occasionally expressed in resentment or rebellion against the very idea of a just Creator, or in a deepened consciousness of one's utter dependence upon Him. In one form or another, questions dealing with God's existence and the individual's relationship to God rise to the surface almost naturally in the wake of disaster.

On the other hand, at a personal or religious festival, with the family at one's side, the moment glowing with candles and light, there is the distinct possibility that one will completely ignore God. For this is, after all, a *simchah,* and because one feels that he deserves a *simchah,* there are no searching, unsettling, or agonizing questions about bad things, good people, or the undeserved suffering of the righteous (and certainly none about the undeserved joy of the non-righteous). For we consider the moment of *hag*, and by extension any festive moment, to be our due and our right, and, unlike moments of sadness, they do not instinctively remind us, in positive or negative ways, of God's presence in the universe.

In sum, a crisis may cause us either to turn towards God or away from Him. In one way or another, God plays a key role in our reactions. We may cry out, "Why have you forsaken me?"; we may even turn away from Him — but in one form or another God is at the center of the storm. At moments of bliss, however, while there may be verbalized blessings of gratitude to the Creator, it is only the rare and truly religious personality for whom God is at the center of celebration. For most, He remains offstage, in a sad manifestation of the fear of Moses that Israel in its prosperity may some day "forget" God (Dt. 8:11), thinking that "my power and my strength hath gotten me all this wealth" (Dt. 8:17). (This is also the basis of the admonition in the second paragraph of *Shema* (Dt. 11:16): "Beware lest your heart be lured away (*pen yifte levavhem*) and you turn aside and serve other gods. . . ." which follows on the heels of the three previous verses which speak of the prosperity of Israel, on which Rashi comments: "Since you will eat and be satisfied, be especially careful (*tishmeru*) that you not buck, because a person rebels against the Holy One only when he is sated (*mitoch svi'a*), as in (Dt. 8:12 ff...)" This theme reverberates throughout Deuteronomy.

This, then is the connecting link between *hag* and *evel*: each demands acknowledgment of His presence and requires His participation. The transcending, luminous moment of the birth of a child, for example, is as much a testing ground for the lowly human being as the transcending, shattering moment of death. Seven days of feasting after a wedding are as much a trial of faith (will I remember the Author of my joy?) as are the seven days of mourning. The risks of "*vayishman yeshurun vayiv'at*, (*Jeshurun* (Israel) grew fat and rebelled)" (Dt. 32:15), are ever present. Thus, says halakhah, the idea of a seven day mourning period shall be derived from the seven day festival, to underscore the idea that these are not two discrete segments of life, but are in fact conceptually bound together.

In this regard, the salient insight of Radbaz (R. David Ibn Zimra, 1479-1573), on Maimonides, Laws of Mourning (1:1) is instructive. Explaining why Moses instituted both the seven-day feasting after a wedding and the seven-day mourning after death, as cited above, Radbaz states:

> ". . . .so that the days of mourning shall be like the days of joy; that is to say, that in the days of feasting he should keep in mind (*yiten el libo*) the day of death, as Solomon said (Kohelet 7:14): "On the day of goodness (*b'yom tova*) be in good spirits (*heyeh b'tov*) but on the day of evil, behold well (*b'yom ra'a r'eh*); God has made this in equal measure to the other." (Cf. Targum Yonatan ben Uziel on this verse.)

This interaction between sadness and joy also supplies the link between the obligation to comfort the mourner for seven days after death, and the obligation to celebrate the couple for seven days after the wedding. This also sheds some light on the matter of interrupting Torah study for either a wedding or a funeral, as well as on the curious legal derivation of marital "acquisition" from the acquisition of a burial place. Further, this suggests why King Solomon had the two gates — one for consoling and one for congratulating — built in the Temple. He, too, was pointing to this concept: both mourner and celebrant, lamenter and feaster, must know at the profoundest levels of their being that their respective weeping and laughter are separated only by a thin line. Each of these movements is a reminder of dependence on the Creator. The joy of the wedding and the despair of death, though opposites, are alike in their capacity to evoke in the human heart the realization that we are less than we thought possible (death/*evel*) and also more than we thought possible (joy/*hag*).

The seven days of the wedding celebration and the seven days of mourning both reflect another important seven: the number which represents creation. The seven day unit which is common both to death and marriage underscores the idea that we are required to experience both death and life for the full creation cycle. For it is through this unit that there is imprinted upon our being the consciousness of a Creator Who hovers over us in our seven-day sadness and our seven-day joy, just as He hovered over His universe during the first seven days of creation.[7]

III

What lies behind the connection between mourning and sanctity, and specifically between mourning practices and the *kohen*?

Among the most striking of all the laws dealing with the *kohen* are the restrictions which remove him from the precincts of death, as an examination of Lev. 21 and 22 makes quite evident. These two chapters contain the bulk of the Torah's legislation related to the *kohen*, some fifty verses concerned with whom he may or may not marry; under which circumstances he may or may not offer the sacrifices; things which defile and disqualify him, and his restrictions during his defilement; who among his immediate family may partake of the sacrificial food; and his restrictions vis-à-vis the dead. It is noteworthy that, of all these, the very first laws concern the *kohen's* requirement to remove himself from the dead, followed by the very restrictive ways in which the *kohen* may or may not engage in mourning practices. The apparent reason for these severe constraints follows immediately:

> They shall be holy unto the Lord, and shall not profane the name of the Lord,
> Because the burnt offering of their God do they offer up, and they must be holy (Lev. 21:6).

That is, the *kohen* must remove himself almost totally from death because he represents the sanctity of God. In fact, according to rabbinic tradition, Levi, son of Jacob, was directed

---

7. That a week's wait is required before approaching the *berit milah* (circumcision) is suggestive.

by his father in Egypt not to be among those who carry Jacob's bier. Levi, the progenitor of all *kohanim*, was destined some day to carry the Ark of the Lord, and therefore was enjoined from carrying the bier containing a corpse.[8] In addition, the High Priest, unlike the ordinary *kohen*, may not come in contact with, or be in the environs of, deceased members of his own family, not even his father or mother; nor may he follow the funeral cortege.

The inordinate amount of attention devoted to the removal of the *kohen* from the realm of death underscores the idea that the *kohen* is the earthly symbol of God Who is the God of Life. For example, He is explicitly referred to as *Elohim hayyim* five times in the Bible, and as *El hai* eight times. The oath most frequently used by man in the Torah — found thirty-six times — is that in which he swears by the "life of God." God swears by His own life, so to speak, some seventeen times. And when at the beginning of Genesis, God breathes into man, He gives man *nishmat hayyim*, the breath of life. The livingness of God, like His sanctity, is His primary characteristic. Life and sanctity are in fact identical. Clearly, God is Lord over the realm of the dead as well as the realm of the living, but His own Being is associated with *hayyim*. It follows, therefore, that His functionaries should be withdrawn from death.[9]

This withdrawal from the precincts of death is a subtle indication that death is an aspect of man's existence which God, as it were, had hoped would not have been necessary, and which He considers not to be a permanent aspect of His creation. Death was not present in the original divine blueprint: it was man, in the exercise of his free choice, who brought upon himself banishment from the Garden and death upon the earth, a turn of events which God "regrets" (Gen. 5:5). In the eschatological plan, however, man will ultimately be found worthy of returning to the Garden where, finally death will

---

8. CF. M. Sanhedrin 2:1; Lev. 21:11.
9. For a fuller treatment of the connection between *kedusha*/sanctity and *hayyim*/life, see Emanuel Feldman, Biblical and Post Biblical Defilement: Law as Theology (N.Y., 1977).

have no dominion. It is precisely for this reason, to help pave man's way back to the Garden and to the realm of non-death, that man was given Torah and mitsvot. These become the stepping stones from the beginning of creation, but which man must now earn on his own.

The *kohen's* radical removal from death can be viewed as a manifestation of this concept. As the representative of God's livingness, of the *Elohim* Who is *hayyim*, the very removal of the *kohen* from death underscores God's distance from death, and stresses an even more profound theme: God's knowledge that man, exercising the same free choice that originally ensnared him, can ultimately free himself from the coils of death. The *kohen*, as the representative of the God of life, is the embodiment of the ideal human being in the ideal human environment; i.e., he represents Adam in the Garden of Eden, before sin and death became realities. By requiring the withdrawal of the *kohen* from the realm of death, the Torah preserves the *kohen's* primeval link with the first man, and presents the *kohen* as the embodiment of that ultimate moment when once again death shall have no dominion, and man returns to the paradisic state of deathlessness.

It is because of this that the normative mourning laws are derived from the *kohen*. For the mourning practices are the exquisite symbols of man's mortality, and the *kohen* is the exquisite symbol of the God of life and of immortality and of a realm not subject to death. (That shoes are to be removed both during mourning and at sacred sites is thus not surprising, given this connection between death and the embodiment of sanctity). By connecting rites of mourning practices to the *kohen*, Jewish tradition underscores the eschatological idea that man is not permanently banished from Eden; he can some day return to Eden and to the deathlessness which it represents.

And by making this connection in a negative, inverted way — what is prohibited to the *kohen* is demanded of the mourner — the halakhah might be suggesting that death and mourning are negative images of reality, reversals of God's design, reversed blueprints which will some day be connected and made straight. For God, the *Elohim hayyim*, desires life for all of His creatures. Death and mourning are not congruent with His ultimate plan, and when we are found worthy, the living God will obliterate death itself, in fulfillment of Isaiah 25:8: "Death will be swallowed up forever, and God will erase the tear from every face."

Thus, the very paradoxes and convolutions, the strange connections and the juxtaposing of opposites, suggest that halakhah is articulating a subtle and profound statement about sadness and joy, mourning and sanctity, death and life.

Orthodox Feminism or Feminist Orthodoxy

IN A RECENT PANEL DISCUSSION about the Jewish feminist movement, a female Jewish academic, not observant but religiously sensitive, related that in her "egalitarian" congregation she was told that if she learned to read the Hebrew from the Torah for a certain *aliyah*, she would be called to the Torah and be invited to read aloud that portion. She practiced with a tutor for several months, and then was called to the Torah. She read her portion flawlessly. "It was a moment of supreme joy for me," she said. "I felt religiously happy." Turning to me, she added, "Why do the Orthodox deny such joy to their women?"

I quickly assured her that Orthodoxy is all in favor of joy. "But," I added, "joy is not the overarching criterion of Jewish life. There are many mitsvot we perform — such as fasting on Yom Kippur — that do not necessarily give us joy, and yet they help us to make contact with our Creator. It is fine that you were happy, but that is not the touchstone of serving God."

I went on to suggest that one surely experiences a deep inner joy reaching out to God, but it is best not to confuse joy and religion, because, while in a profound sense, things that are deeply religious are deeply joyous, not everything that is joyous is religious.

She was unconvinced. From her standpoint, halakhah would deprive her of the right to serve her Creator joyously. I tried to point out that certain mitsvot are gender-linked (mandatory *mikveh* immersion with a *berakhah* for women but not men; tefillin for men but not women); certain others are status-linked (Kohen, but not Levi, Levi but not Yisrael, Jew but not non-Jew); others are time-linked (daytime and not nighttime); and that we may not at our own discretion cross over to perform mitsvot that are limited to one gender or one status, even if those crossovers makes us happy.

But all this fell on deaf ears. Joy and personal fulfillment were the major criteria, and anything that would deny them was by definition insensitive, unegalatarian, patriarchal, and therefore wrong.

This exchange highlighted much that is problematic in today's Jewish feminism, including the loose congeries of various women's groups that describes itself as Orthodox feminism. This essay will attempt to show that Orthodox feminism has not been entirely unaffected by the tensions and consequent attitudes within feminism in general. Along the way, we will examine some of the forces that exert powerful influences on Jewish life in general, and to whose subtle overtures women's groups are not immune; and we will raise certain vexing issues that, unless they are recognized and addressed, have the potential of seriously undermining the halakhic integrity of Orthodox feminism.

In so doing, the intent is not to be critical of women who seek a deeper attachment to the Creator. Every Jewish woman who views herself as part of the halakhic community is a priceless asset to *Klal Yisrael*, all the more so when so many Jewish men and women have been lost to us through apathy, ignorance, assimilation and intermarriage. Learned, dedicated, and mitsvah-practicing women are the vital key to the future of the Jewish people, and it is not to such women that these comments are directed. Rather, they are directed at certain perceived trends within the larger circles of Orthodox feminism.

The views of my academic acquaintance are endemic to contemporary times, and it would be surprising if they had no impact on contemporary Jewish movements across the board — even the Orthodox ones. Contemporary culture emphasizes the Me and not the You. The Me focuses attention on rights; the You focuses attention on obligations. That which makes the Me feel good is good; that which makes Me feel not so good, is not so good.

When a society is based on Me-ness and on its corollary — "How much am I entitled to take?" — then it is reasonable and just that everyone should be able to take as much as possible. Since this is not feasible, society works out a system whereby everyone has equal rights to take. That is, everyone has the same rights that I do, and I have the same rights as everyone else. The focus is on Me.

The Torah is not a bill of rights, but a bill of obligations — to God and to other people. In Torah, there is no right to property; rather, there is an obligation not to steal or damage someone else's property. Torah does not mention the right to be treated decently; it stresses that we must treat others decently. In Torah we have no right to life, liberty and the pursuit of happiness; instead, we have the obligation not to diminish someone else's life, liberty or happiness. Torah is not designed to make us feel good; rather it is designed to teach us how not to make others feel bad.

Thus, it is not an accident that in Biblical or Mishnaic Hebrew one is hard pressed to find a term for the Western concept of "rights." There is a classical Hebrew word for "obligation": *hov*. (In an effort to translate the Western concept of "rights," modern Hebrew has coined the term *zekhuyot* - which derives from *zekhut*, meaning "merit," not "rights.")

Obviously, the end result of Torah is that it helps to achieve a close relationship with God, which in turn infuses life with meaning, fulfillment and a deep inner satisfaction that can be called joy. But even if, theoretically, Torah were not to lead to meaning and purpose, even if it were to make us miserable, a Jew would still be obligated to live by it.

But when one peruses Orthodox feminist literature, or listens to its conference speakers and panelists, one still hears persistent voices that express religious yearnings in the accents of contemporary society. An *aliyah* to the Torah is fulfilling, as is wearing a *tallit*. Having separate women's *tefillah* group is self-actualizing. A woman reading the *ketubah*, the bride breaking the glass — all are significant because they presumably enhance the status of the woman.

The halakhic legitimacy of these examples is not crucial to this discussion (though many of them are being actively promoted among Orthodox women's groups, as will be noted below). But a highly visible thread weaves its way through Orthodox feminism's halakhic innovations, and the thread invariably bears the imprint of self-absorption: How can my needs and requirements be expressed, and my status and prestige enhanced? Not what doth the Lord require me, but what do I require of the Lord?

While self-concern is natural and often healthful, it is clear that in the context of serving God, the spiritually healthful way stresses the You and not the Me. A preoccupation with, say, what worship does for me, or whether it makes me feel good, is in full harmony with contemporary culture. It reflects today's penchant for the narcissistic pulse-taking that affects us all: am-I-happy-today-am-I-feeling-good-about-myself-do-I-still-love-him/her?

Within the context of genuine service of God, however, it strikes a discordant note. Concerns like "How do I feel about this mitsvah? Is halakhah being fair to me?" unwittingly tend to transform the Torah into an instrument for self-gratification and a tool for satisfying one's needs and for making one feel good.

No less than Jews of any gender or any group, the Orthodox feminist's desire to achieve a spiritual relationship with the Creator can only be met by striving for the highest standards of religious devotion. A program that carries the residue of the old shibboleths of autonomy and self-hood is incongruous with such high standards. Pristine faith demands that the will of the self be subordinate to the will of God.

A recent issue of an Orthodox feminist newsletter provides a vivid case in point (*JOFA Journal*, 1:3, Summer, 1999). This particular eight-page issue is devoted to Jewish marriage. With one exception, every single article is focused on ways to rectify the perceived inequality of the bride and to right the "imbalance." We are told about making "her voice heard on a par with that of the *hatan*," the need to demonstrate that "Jewish women are a vibrant and essential part of the greater Jewish community," and that the traditional wedding ceremony, "silenced women's voices and excluded the participation of other women." The feature entitled "Thirteen Ways to Enrich Your Wedding" suggests that a woman translate the *sheva brachot* under the *hupah*, or read the *ketubah*, or hold the poles to the canopy, or "preside under the *hupah*."

One article does deal thoughtfully with the *agunah* issue and the role of prenuptial agreements. The lead article stresses the importance of marriage, but the presentation is marred by what has become *de rigueur* in today's overheated Jewish climate: the inevitable out-of-context citation from Rav Soloveitchik, z'l — in which he refers to the "equal rights of both parties concerned with the covenant" — as an implied justification for the suggested innovations.

Clearly, a sense of having suffered from inept and unfair treatment prompts such proposals. When a group feels that in the broader areas of religious life it is not regarded with the requisite dignity and respect, pain and resentment are aroused. Such treatment is, of course, by no means universal, but even an occasional occurrence is inexcusable. Contemporary women, for good or ill, are not our grandmothers of old. They have contemporary sensibilities that need to be recognized and addressed. It should be possible, even within the framework of the strictest reading of halakhic norms, to give women the sense that they are a vital and necessary part of Jewish religious life.

This is not always conveyed effectively. To be sure, the lasting impression inadvertently made on some women that they are second-class Jews, disenfranchised and excluded from religious life, does not stem for the norms of Torah and *halakhah* whose ways are ways of pleasantness: it stems, rather, from disregard of that "fifth" *Shulkhan Arukh* that includes *sechel*, standards of *mentshlichkeit*, and old-fashioned sensitivity.

Nevertheless, the proper response to perceived wrongs does not lie in mounting an assault on the halakhic ramparts. A deeply spiritual response is called for, one that would, for example, address the inchoate yearnings for closeness to God that apparently underlie the demands for activities like separate minyanim or dancing with the *Sefer Torah*: how to approach God more closely, to serve the Creator with more fidelity. Instead, we read about ways to achieve parity with men. "Whatever can enhance equality," says the lead editorial of the above-mentioned newsletter, "should be instituted." Since this newsletter features several leading Orthodox feminist writers, it is fair to say that its tone is an accurate reflection of today's Orthodox feminist leadership.

One is in general hard-pressed to find Orthodox feminist studies and discourses that treat halakhah as means for reaching out to the Creator without the precondition that it must do something for Me. To cite one notable example: In vain does one search Orthodox feminist literature or conclaves for an objective discussion of one crucial term: *tseniut*. This untranslatable word exemplifies another lexical void, this time a word that exists in Hebrew and has no English equivalent, for *tseniut* reflects a Weltanschauung that is foreign to contemporary society. To put it simply as "modesty" or to limit it only to sleeve lengths is to deprive it of texture and nuance. Orthodox feminists may cover their hair and wear modest clothing, but in the anxious rush to right perceived wrongs, that aspect of *tseniut* that transcends clothing but is concerned with matters spiritual and intellectual is often overlooked.

Spiritual and intellectual *tseniut* is not for women only; it includes men. It calls for a certain attitude of mind that is cognate to humility. It shuns even the whiff of pride. It suggests a certain reticence and reverence towards classical elements of Judaism such as halakhah — qualities not easily achieved by either gender. To demonstrate restraint, to be circumspect in attitude, to be guarded in language, to exercise discretion and not to seek to attract attention in dress, behavior or speech — this is classic *tseniut*. These are qualities not easily achieved by either gender in today's shrill and strident world.

A spiritually *tsanua* person will, for example, eschew the slogan-filled lexicon of a feminism that shoots from the hip at the Sages; a *tsanua* will refrain from discussing halakhah in clichés that take the discredited paradigms of class struggle and apply them to gender; he or she will not discuss halakhah in the tired slogans that echo the themes of male domination and redistribution of power and repression and hegemony and patriarchy and exclusion and control and oppression and victimization — for the *tsanua* will sense the rhetoric of revolution is not only banal but is an incongruous intrusion into halakhic discourse.

This is not to suggest that this alien vocabulary dominates the Orthodox feminist lexicon; it is to suggest that when it does occasionally surface, those who would employ the terminology should be sensitive to its origins in the past and to its destructive potential for the future.

It is indicative of how far Orthodox feminism tends to drift from those pristine concepts of *tseniut* that is not uncommon to find within its discourse the astounding idea — accepted almost as a fact of halakhic life — that *tseniut* is a rabbinic device whose purpose to derogate women and keep them in their place. One rarely encounters a serious discussion by Orthodox feminism about the *ko-kevuda bat melech penima*, "the glory of the king's daughter is within" (Psalm 45), which is one of the underpinnings of classical *tseniut*. When an entire lecture was devoted to this verse at the International Conference on

Feminism and Orthodoxy (February, 1997), its use as a basis for *tseniut* was referred to as a "sound-byte" whose time had passed, and there was a call for newer sound-bytes. Apparently, the newer sound-bytes include terms like servitude, exploitation, deprivation and empowerment. It is unclear why those who seek objective truth would sweep a basic concept like *tseniut* under the rug, there to be consigned to oblivion with other unsavory words.

And most puzzling: Surely Orthodox feminism does not deny that women have different roles from men, that they are different not only biologically but spiritually, and that as a consequence their approach to God is different. Somehow, however, Orthodox feminism presents an incoherent message in this area. It claims that women are not being given their due as full-fledged participants of the halakhic community, and that, because they are women, they are being denied the opportunity to attain a state of closeness to their Creator. But instead of searching for ways by which women as women can affect this, Orthodox feminism proffers the concurrent claim that it is only in the emulation and adoption of male roles that women can find that closeness.

This is indeed wondrous strange, for what emerges is that a religious Jewish woman can serve her God only by being called to the Torah like a male, by being encircled by the groom at the *bedeken* just like the groom is encircled by the bride, by having an *aufruf* and reading the *haftarah* like a male, by celebrating "*shalom nekevot*" on Friday nights like a male, or by placing a *tallit* over the groom just like the groom places the veil over the bride.

Again, the halakhic legitimacy of these "me-too" practices, most of which are advocated in the newsletter cited above, is not the issue here. Rather it is the conscious mimicry of men. From one vantage point, such overt emulation of the male comes across as a serious denigration of women, for the inescapable message is that without these masculine accouterments a woman remains religiously inferior. It is hard to think of a more hurtful diminution of a bride than to advise her that the only form of self-respect available to her is to become a pseudo-groom.

Is it far-fetched to detect in the "groomification" of the bride a subliminal echo of the radical feminist assault on the fundamentals of male/female behavior that have been part of humanity since Creation? Has a whiff of some of these old notions unwittingly insinuated itself into the rhetoric of some Orthodox feminist circles? Perhaps it is a far-fetched analogy, but the thought does intrude — especially when it is recalled that radical feminism was in essence an attempt to remake the human past and to reconstitute the nature of men and women.

One also has the disconcerting sense that Orthodox feminists tend to push the halakhic envelope very far. Somehow, their search engines seek out behaviors that, while not expressly forbidden, are invariably marginal. In a particularly striking example of the rush to the edges, a recently published book, "Jewish Legal Writings by Women," (edited by Halperin and Safrai, Jerusalem, 1998, pp. 445-72 in the Hebrew section) contains a paper by a prominent Orthodox feminist that unconsciously resonates with the distant echo of the early radical feminist motto of "Who needs men?" In her paper, the author attempts to demonstrate halakhically that, under certain circumstances, single Jewish women should be permitted to bear children through artificial insemination.

Such a discussion is rather poignant. It mirrors the reality of an Orthodox community where there are more single women than men, where many Orthodox single men are not ready to make life commitments, and where the Orthodox community has not addressed itself successfully to this issue.

Nevertheless, with all due awareness of the social realities that may impel it, the proposal reflects a mind-set in which things that are not explicitly forbidden are candidates for a seal of approval.

While this idea at least has the refreshing appeal of not miming masculinity, its destructive potential for the institutions of marriage and the Jewish family — over and above the issues of consciously creating fatherless children — should be self-evident. But an Orthodox feminism that does not want to appear judgmental apparently receives such proposals with equanimity.

An oddly shaped pattern emerges from all this. Orthodox feminism, despite its declared allegiance to the halakhic process, gives the consistent impression that it has difficulty resisting both the anti-halakhic winds that buffet it, and the anti-halakhic models of contemporary society that tempt it.

Most confusing is the tableau of an halakhically oriented group that seems to disregard classic halakhic parameters in setting priorities. Halakhah, after all, is not a subjective matter reflecting the whims or prejudices of this or that *posek*. It contains its own objective methodology for arriving at halakhic decisions. But it is difficult to reconcile a group's declared loyalty to a system of law with that same group's complaint that the system is male-dominated and therefore stacked against it. When universally recognized world-class *poskim* are by-passed for whatever reason — an assumption that they will not give woman a fair hearing, or that they are men who have no sympathy for women — the fundamentals of halakhic discourse are undercut. When end runs are made around the halakhic judicial system, and calls are heard for women *poskot* who will be more sympathetic to feminist causes, fealty to that system cannot be fairly claimed.

It is one thing to seek to redress perceived injustices against women. But it is quite another to view halakhic history and its decisors from the times of the Talmud to the present as purveyors of female exploitation and of male empowerment.

The obvious — if naïve — question is: Orthodox feminists have certain serious halakhic issues that require resolution. Do they discuss with universally recognized *poskim* their long-term priorities, or solicit their views about what practices are appropriate or inappropriate? It is important here to rise above the "my-*posek*-is-more-authentic-than-your-*posek*" syndrome. I refer to the towering, world-class figures in halakhah who set the Jewish agenda, and about whose authority and eminence there is no disagreement. Until recently we had such poskim in Rav Mose Feinstein, Rav Joseph B. Soloveitchik, Rav Shlomo Zalman Auerbach, Rav Shaul Yisraeli, z'l. We are bereft without them, but there are such figures today — Rav Yosef Eliashiv and his younger counterparts come to mind — who are rising to take their place and to become their spiritual heirs.

How is it that this integral element of the halakhic process in consistently ignored? An intellectually honest search for Godliness must perforce involve the guidance of halakhic specialists whose entire life span is devoted to full-time Jewish learning and service to *Klal Yisrael*. When such *poskim* are leapfrogged because of the pre-judgment that they will not listen, an essential element in halakhah is overlooked. Of course, it is more reassuring to allow the Orthodox feminist agenda to be approved by rabbis who are known in advance to be favorable, but this obviously devitalizes the objective nature of halakhic decision-making. A wedding, for example, is an halakhic event. But there is no evidence that any of the thirteen ways to enrich the wedding was ever submitted for adjudication to a world-class decisor — be he labeled centrist or rightist.

Thus it is that an observer finds Orthodox feminism to be internally conflicted. In its one hand it bears the exemplary desire of Jewish women to reach out for more connectedness to their Creator, and in its other hand it bears the deadening baggage of thinking and attitudes that stem from a world where God-connectedness has no currency.

This is not good for the Jews, because we desperately need the talents and insights of committed Jewish women. Who can quantify the positive results for the Jewish future if Jewish women were to use their considerable energies and talents in a focused assault on those issues which threaten to undermine our people, and in which the organized community of men has failed so badly: Jewish ignorance, runaway intermarriage, the breakdown of the Jewish family, and — most importantly — the disappearing disciplines and sliding boundaries of contemporary Jewish life?

This is where the future lies and where the action is — not in who breaks what glass in what context. It would be a pity if this generation of Orthodox women — well educated, dedicated and committed to halakhic living — were to be sidetracked from the opportunities to enhance the Jewish future, and instead were to focus on ways that might give them status or gratification.

There is work to be done, a generation to be rescued. Placing a *tallit* on the groom's head is clever and will achieve a certain notoriety, but so what? Outside the brightly lit wedding hall a generation is withering away, and precisely those women who have the ability to help are being urged to prove that they, too, can hold the poles to the *hupah* (suggestion #5 "....Ways To Enrich Your Wedding").

A delicate issue must be raised: If the halakhic process is given little credence, and rabbinic authority is regularly being challenged or simply ignored, will Orthodox feminism remain a stream with Orthodox Judaism, or will it become the forerunner of a meandering tributary of non-Orthodox movements? They, too, began with efforts to save Judaism from what they called the halakhic deep-freeze, made a powerful impact for a short while, but ultimately drained themselves as they eschewed classical halakhic guidelines and fell under the thrall of contemporary intellectual fads. (It may or may not be significant, but a leading Orthodox feminist in Israel and a founder of the Israeli feminist network has followed her extreme views to their logical conclusion: she abandoned Orthodoxy and accepted the rectorship of the [Conservative] Schechter Institute in Jerusalem. And in what could be read as a further blurring of the lines, the religious feminist conference in Jerusalem this past July [which called itself "Kolech: the Religious Women's Forum/Forum *Nashim Datiot*"] featured a strong Conservative presence, with four of the presenters listing the same Institute as their affiliation. The absence of the word "Orthodox" in the title and in the abstracts of the conference, as well as in the section discussing the goals of the conference, is also worthy of note.

In assessing its future direction, Orthodox feminism — which has not flinched from asking painful questions of the Orthodox community — would do well to ask a painful question of itself: Is sufficient heed being given to ideas like *avodat Hashem* and *kedushah* and *tseniut* and *mesorah* and *ahavat Hashem* and *yirat Hashem*, or are these being devalued by the dross of more stylish concepts like empowerment, self-realization and the other rhetorical shards of the politics of resentment? A Jewish movement, after all, can preserve its integrity and become historically effective only when it is able to identify and fend off the subtle incursions of the dominant culture. This kind of serious self-assessment would sensitize Jewish women to these incursions that hover over all of us, Jewish women and men. More specifically, it could persuade Orthodox feminists to be more alert to the influences of feminist orthodoxy.

※※※

Every sensitive Jew and Jewess strives constantly for enhanced spirituality. But the Jewish spiritual tradition itself teaches that only within the parameters of halakhic practice can true spirituality be realized. Amorphous spiritual hunger, unframed by halakhah, leads nowhere.

Each Jew and Jewess is bidden to walk towards God in his or her own way, at his or her own pace, across an halakhic bridge that is clearly marked with guardrails and directions. The bridges are not identical. Adjacent bridges may seem more inviting or may seem to offer faster or more secure passage, but this is an illusion. Kohen, Levi, Yisrael, male, female — each crosses a unique bridge that is prepared for him or her alone. The Kohen who jumps to the bridge of the Levi will only delay his passage, and vice versa. For every single bridge, as long as it is traversed in faith, in love and in discipline, leads inexorably to the other side — the side of the Other — where God waits patiently.

Vice and Virtue:
Today's Vice-Versa

ADULTERY! BIG DEAL, SAY MOST Americans. Let's not be prudish and puritanical. Everyone is involved in it. Even the chairman of the House Judiciary Committee, which recently sat in judgment of Bill Clinton, did it. Even Bob Livingston, potential Speaker of the House, who pressed the impeachment proceedings, did it. Of course, to hear them say it, they were not involved in real adultery per se. They were guilty only of "youthful indiscretions."

It is normal and commonplace, says everyone, so why all the fuss about Bill Clinton? Why can't we be like the French, whose late President Mitterand was publicly mourned by both his wife and his mistress? (Appropriate enough, for this is why France, which gives political support both to Iraq's Saddam and Lybian dictator Quaddafi, holds the title of world's oldest professional.) Why can't we be sophisticated like they are?

Of course, it is unnecessary to belabor the fact that in Judaism, the normal and the commonplace are not necessarily permissible. On the contrary, Judaism takes all the normal and commonplace impulses — the instinct to murder, to lie, to steal, to wound, to destroy — and tries to help us discipline and control them. This is the very underpinning of Torah: *Barati yetser hara, barati Torah tavlin (Kiddushin* 30b). The Torah is the antidote to the evil inclination.

But contemporary society maintains that if everyone engages in an act, then that act is acceptable. Everyone drinks Coca-Cola, therefore Coca-Cola is good. Everyone drives a GM car, therefore a GM car is good. Everyone commits adultery, therefore adultery is... well, if not good, at least it's not that terrible. So many customers can't all be wrong.

In his syndicated column, Richard Cohen of the *Washington Post* decried the sentiment of certain House members that just because the Hon. Mr. Livingston had committed adultery that he is unfit to be Speaker of the House. And then Cohen writes the following line that I had to read twice to make certain that I was not hallucinating: "It was as if he had committed a crime," lamented Cohen.

Why adultery is less of a crime than, say, pick-pocketing is not made clear. If everyone were to begin stealing from other people's pockets, would that, too, having become normal and commonplace, cease being a crime? If the honorable Congressmen were to admit that they had been common thieves, but that this thievery was a youthful indiscretion, would there not be demands for their resignations? But they only admit to adultery. Big deal.

Admittedly, the act of adultery is in one major respect different from stealing. Sexual temptation is much more difficult to withstand. (See the commentary of R. David Kimchi to Psalms 51:7: *Hen be'avon holalti, u-vehet yehemasni imi* / "Behold, in iniquity was I brought forth, and in sin was I conceived.")

This may account for today's permissive view of adultery as opposed to piddling little sins such as theft. Sex is difficult for many to resist. Theft is relatively easy to resist for most people. Therefore, in our perverted scale of values, we condemn stealing but condone sexual impropriety. That which is difficult to resist we make no effort to resist; we simply call them "indiscretions," cluck over them a bit, and continue on our indiscretionary way.

This is how society slides down the slippery slope of contemporary morality. There are no absolutes. Everything is relative. Even religion no longer demands strong belief and absolute commitment, but is now more a matter of the individual's preference and choice. I prefer chocolate to vanilla. I prefer Judaism to paganism. Do you wish to know what is right and what is wrong? The answer lies not in your Bible but in the latest polls. In our time, the old joke about Moses and the Ten Suggestions has been apotheosized.

We are experiencing the strange phenomenon of a society that instinctively senses that what the president has done was morally wrong, but does not know precisely why. For a generation we have been taught that nothing is wrong per se, that it all depends on the circumstances, that all is relative, and that one must not judge others. We must not repress our instincts or be prudish about sex; unrestricted sex is acceptable and even desirable as long as it is consensual; discipline is for nuns and monks; adultery is not so terrible and in fact is sometimes helpful to a marriage, and nothing is intrinsically wrong as long as no one gets hurt. We must not be intolerant of homosexuality; people must be given free choices; and abortion on demand will help free women from the chains of feminine bondage.

For a generation we have been taught by our opinion makers that anything goes, and for a generation the courts have codified this. Before our very eyes there was revealed a topsy-turvy world in which right became wrong and wrong became right; marriage, family, home, self-reliance, accountability, and discipline all became vices, and in what may be termed a manifestation of "vices-virtue," self-indulgence, hedonism, sexual license, and a no-holds-barred "self-actualization" became virtues. And so when the president behaved in ways that shamed us and offended our deepest instincts of decency and morality, in our confusion we continued to give him high marks as president while at the same time proclaiming our distaste with his actions.

It was not, as so many have theorized, that because the economy was good we were willing to overlook his behavior. Rather, it was the inability to frame our discomfort in any articulate manner and to place it in any specific context that forced us to look the other way. To state that his violation of his marriage bonds was a violation of religious principles and of essential Biblical morality would be intolerant, benighted, judgmental and — worst of all — fundamentalist. It would be to impose our personal standards of behavior on others, and this, we have been incessantly taught, is the worst sin of all. We knew within us that something was not right, but somehow no one ever bothered to tell us that morality was not a reflection of how things are but of how they should be.

There are, in other word, no absolutes.

※❈※

In the midst of all this, the Torah in its anachronistic way tells us that adultery, like idolatry and murder, is one of the three sins for which one must be prepared to surrender one's own life before violating them: *ye-hareg va-al ya-avor.*

How quaint of the ancients, how very bizarre — to demand that one choose death rather than enjoy what his instincts and his society proclaim to be perfectly acceptable. I mean, religion is a good thing and all, but to surrender your life rather than commit adultery? Please!

Judaism demurs: Why these three and no others? Because each of these three, more than other *mitsvah*, represents a rebellion against the essence of God.

The taking of life from someone to whom God granted life is an act of rebellion against the Giver of life. We are not by any means on the same level as God.

The worship of idols is an act of rebellion against the One God. When other deities are substituted for Him or allied with

Him, this represents an assault on the very essence of the One God.

The breaking of the marriage bond is a rebellion against the gift of the creative power of sexuality which God has granted us. This gift, which transforms us into a potential creator like the Creator, is God's most wondrous gift to us, for with it we become partners in the miraculous act of creation. But it is given to us with certain restrictions and safeguards. Marriage is one of these restrictions. To use one's sexual power outside of marriage is to distort and misuse this most awesome gift of God, and constitutes a rebellion against His conduct of the universe.

There are other reasons why these three are a formidable triad of transgressions. The murderer says: There is no other beside me. The idolater says: There is no Other above me. The adulterer says: There is no Other above me and there is no other beside me; it is only I who matters, and therefore there are no restraints upon my impulses, and whatever I desire I can do. Thus is the *ein od mi-levado* of Deut. 4:35, "There is none other than He," effectively changed to *ein od mi-levadi*, "There is none other than I."

From every perspective, the three should be grouped together. Murder may be commonplace, and various forms of idolatry widespread, and adultery widely practiced, but to commit these acts is to encroach upon God's essence and to challenge Him frontally.

Better to surrender your life.

For a tiny minority of the world's population — the Jews — these are the three restrictions that represent subservience to God and our acceptance of His sovereignty. As such, they impinge on the essence and nucleus of a holy society. And more than any other mitsvot, these three affirm that there are absolutes in life.

So it has finally come down to this. At a time when no one is shocked by it, when it is considered a perfectly normal part of life, when Congressmen shrug their shoulders at it, when the

Vice and Virtue: Today's Vice-Versa

president of the United States trivializes it, when the citizenry is not sure how to deal with it, an Orthodox rabbi must underscore his continuing belief that there are absolute rules of conduct in life. As R. Moshe Haim Luzzatto states in the Introduction to his *Mesillat Yesharim,* "...the more widely something is known, the more does it tend to be ignored." And so this rabbi makes a statement that, in our day, will surely be considered outrageous: adultery is a cardinal sin, and we are definitely and clearly against it.

Reform of Reform?
A Talmudic Reading

THE 1999 PITTSBURGH STATEMENT OF Principles issued by the Central Conference of American Rabbis is a fascinating document on its own, but one must read it in tandem with the three previous major Reform statements: the Pittsburgh Platform of 1885; the Columbus Guiding Principles of 1937; and the Centenary Perspective of 1976. It is in this context that it becomes especially intriguing.

1885

In the 1885 statement — which appeared shortly after the infamous "treife dinner" which was the catalyst for the Conservative split away from Reform — the words "Torah," "*mitsvot*," "revelation" and "commandment" are kept off stage. Instead of Torah, we find "Bible," Holy Scriptures," and euphemisms like "Mosaic legislation," and instead of *mitsvot* and commandments we have "ceremonies." Only the "moral laws" of the Mosaic legislation, and only "such ceremonies as elevate and sanctify our lives" are binding; "all such as are not adapted to views and habits of modern civilization are rejected." Laws that "regulate diet, priestly purity and dress originated... .under ideas entirely foreign to our present mental and spiritual state. . . .[and] obstruct rather that further modern spiritual elevation. . . .The Bible represents the primitive ideas of its own age." Since "we consider ourselves no longer a nation but a religious community," we do not expect "a return to Palestine...." The platform "rejects. . .belief in bodily resurrection and in Hell and Paradise as abodes for everlasting punishment and reward." In fact, anything not in "accord with the postulates of reason" is rejected.

With such self-confident and assertive tropes did American Reform leaders set out on what was to become a Sisyphean climb towards spiritual elevation.

1937

By 1937, nineteenth century meliorism had gone up in the smoke of Kristallnacht, Fascism was in full swing, and reality was no longer as simple as it had once been conceived. The tone of the 1937 statement, though still in thrall of the general culture, reflects a tentative recognition of Jewish uniqueness. The word "Torah" takes a full bow, albeit with firm strings attached from backstage. In an echo of Pittsburgh, "certain of its laws have lost their binding force with the passing of the conditions that called them forth"; and "each age has the obligation to adapt the teachings of the Torah to its basic needs...." Sabbath and holy days are to be "preserved," prayer is to be "cultivated," and "such customs, symbols and ceremonies as possess inspirational value" are to be "retained and developed," as is "the use of Hebrew in worship together with the vernacular...." Revelation makes a cameo appearance, albeit in the guise of "a continuous process, confined to no one group and to no one age."

Still absent are *mitsvah* and commandment. Significantly, the statement stresses that it is being presented "not as a fixed creed but as a guide for the progressive elements of Jewry." But the 1937 statement eschews the 1885 repudiation of Jewish tradition. In fact, it features two major reversals: a) Palestine — the return to which was spurned in 1885 — is mentioned positively as a "Jewish homeland" and as a "promise of renewed life for many of our brethren"; and b) the earlier pronouncement that Judaism is only a religious community is rejected.

Although there is philosophical movement between 1885 and 1937, Reform still equivocates in its calls for observance and Jewish identity. Western culture is still the avatar of spiritual living, and individual Reform Jews are still encouraged to make their own decisions about which customs and ceremonies they should perform.

1976

Forty years later, in 1976 — after the Depression, World War II, and the murder of six million Jews — Western culture had lost much of its glow. Thus the San Francisco "Centenary Perspective" avers that "the spiritual emptiness of Western culture has taught us to be less dependent on the values of our society and to reassert what remains perennially valid in Judaism's teachings." But in the same breath it asserts that "this past century [has] confirmed the essential wisdom of our movement."

(Flying in the face of the assimilation, intermarriage, and Jewish ignorance that even in 1976 was already rampant within Reform; oblivious to its early categoric repudiation of the idea of a Jewish homeland, and its stubborn rejections of Jewish uniqueness in favor of the now morally bankrupt Western culture; unmindful of consistently having bet on so many wrong horses in the past century — this calm confidence about the wisdom of Reform is a bit jarring.)

Nevertheless, the 1976 Reform model inches closer to the classical Jewish tradition. To be sure, it still shies away from commandment and *mitsvah*, but "emphasis on duty and obligation," enters the scene, and these include "daily religious observance, keeping the Sabbath and holy days. . . ." But this is not to be viewed as an abandonment of the historic devotion to personal freedom of choice, for the section quickly backtracks: "Jewish observance" is a "differently perceived" by individual

Reform Jews, who are called upon to "exercise their individual autonomy, choosing and creating. . . ." The term "autonomy," hinted at in earlier statements but never specified, has in the world of 1976 become a PC buzzword in liberal circles, and appears for the first time in this statement. But the inclusion of phrases like duty, obligation, daily religious observance, Sabbath and holy days — even if fuzzy and undefined — is significant. And, in a further turnaround, the state of Israel here looms larger than ever before. The state must be assisted in every way. Even *aliyah* is encouraged.

1999

As the century winds down, an ideological barrier looms directly in front of Reform. While it claims millions of adherents in the USA alone, and while the other movements can learn much from its organizational strengths, these virtues have not been sufficient to stem the ravages of indifference, defections, and an astonishing rate of intermarriage. This internal hemorrhaging has not been stemmed by the recognition of patrilineal descent and by large-scale conversions. So powerful have been the inroads of assimilation, and so widespread are Reform's relatively easy conversion procedures, that numerous Reform communities today are being led by individuals whose Jewishness is not recognized by two-thirds of the Jewish people; i.e., not by Conservative Jewry, and certainly not by the Orthodox. Reform leadership is not entirely blind to this phenomenon, and there is a struggle within the Reform movement between those who want to return to a more traditional stance, and those who are pushing for even further liberalization.

The 1999 statement's Preamble "affirms the central tenets of Judaism — God, Torah, and Israel," but these are left ambiguous. God's "reality and oneness" are affirmed in the next paragraph, but whether this is a personal God, a God Who commands, a God to Whom one can pray, Who sees and observes and cares and Who exercises reward and punishment (and whether this God requires upper case letters for its pronouns) is not addressed. These issues are in fact avoided, and in deference to those whose personal autonomy is threatened even by this modicum of affirmation, the very next sentence dilutes it to acceptable strength: ". . . even as we may differ in our understanding of the Divine presence."

This is the singular thread that runs through the four Statements. Whenever certain principles of Judaism are affirmed, every individual Reform Jew retains the right to his or her own understanding of those principles, the right to decide what he or she should or should not believe, and how he or she should behave as a Jew. The one echo that resounds throughout is the predictable escape clause: "differ in our understanding," "our varied understandings," "differently perceived," "obligations to choose," "adapt Torah to our needs," or "exercise individual autonomy." (I now understand why a Reform college student once told me that he "loves Judaism: it makes no demands on anyone and allows you to pick and choose what is important.")

It is difficult to avoid the conclusion that while God, Torah, and Israel play significant roles in Reform, there is only one belief that is truly central and has attained canonical sanctity: the notion of personal autonomy. Any central tenet is subject to one's personal right to accept or reject, but what cannot be rejected, what is the absolute, cardinal and unalterable principle — a virtual *yehareg v'al ya'avor* — is autonomy. This is transcendent; its august presence hovers over every set of principles from 1885 until 1999.

So central a credo is this that any phrasing that even whispers of authority are immediately rectified. Thus, on the one hand, "the Torah remains [our] dynamic source of life"; but on the other hand, we have "the obligation to adapt the Torah to our basic needs .. ." There is an "emphasis on duty and obligation. . .daily religious observance. . .Sabbath and holy days"; but Reform Jews are "called upon to exercise their individual autonomy, choosing and creating. . ." (1976). "The whole array of *mitsvot*" is to be studied; but only those *mitsvot* "that address us as individuals and as a community...." need to fulfilled (1999). No one is ever told how to behave: Micah's "*ma Hashem doresh mimekha* / what doth the Lord require of you") is transformed into "what doth the Lord (Who is open to "varied understanding") recommend as a good idea if it addresses you or inspires you."

The dialectic between autonomy and authority, of course, is not limited to Reform. It is the common lot of all those who seek God. Orthodox Jews who strive to submit their lives to the authority of God, Torah, and halakhah are not immune to the tension that is exerted by autonomy, and to the inevitable internal — and eternal — struggle between the two. Ultimately, however, halakhah insists that autonomy yield to authority. The very opposite has prevailed in Reform.

More on 1999

That this is now changing and that there is in fact a struggle within Reform between autonomy and authority is evident from a careful parsing of the delicately worded language of the 1999 statement. Although the statement contains the boilerplate that is endemic to all documents-by-committee, there is evidence between the lines of the push and pull between the two elements.

The section on God is revealing. "We encounter God's presence in moments of awe and wonder, in acts of justice and compassion, in loving relationships, and in the experience of everyday life." This is generic theology which sidesteps the central issues of the God-human relationship. But then we encounter a significant line: we should respond to God daily through public and private prayer, "through study and through performance of other *mitsvot* . . . ." Here there is no qualifier about choosing which *mitsvot* — a nod to traditionalists.

It goes on blandly to affirm faith despite the evil in the world, and a trust in the "tradition's promise" that though we are finite, "the spirit within us is eternal." It concludes, "God gives us meaning and purpose to our lives." Lofty sentiments, but what is not spelled out is crucial: affirmation of God's presence does not necessarily obligate anyone, as a believing Jew, to perform any particular deeds.

The autonomists can take heart again.

The parry and thrust of this document is most apparent in the section on Torah, in which divine revelation is sidestepped by "we cherish the truths revealed in Torah, God's ongoing revelation to our people. . . . (One wonders about the word "cherish". Was there a debate about using a more appropriate word like "revere," with its echoes of responsibility and obligation?) Obviously, the revelation here is not Sinaitic, a special and singular point in time when God revealed Himself to all Israel, but a continuing revelation of God. Ongoing revelation certainly exists, but without the pinnacle of Sinai, the ongoing kind loses force and power.

Mitsvot are referred to again in 1999: "We are committed to the ongoing study of the whole array of *mitsvot,* and to the fulfillment of *those that address us as individuals and as community."* (emphasis added). It is not specified who determines which *mitsvot* "address us" and which do not — although the same section recognizes that *"mitsvot* [are] the means by which we make our lives holy." Nor is it made clear whether our lives are made more holy by *mitsvot* which do not "address us." While autonomists can take heart in this, there is an obvious curtsy to the traditionalists when it goes on to suggest that "although some *mitsvot,* sacred obligations, have long been observed by Reform Jews, others, both ancient and modern, demand renewed attention as the result of the unique context of our own times."

To wend one's way through this statement is difficult because of the underlying, and probably unavoidable, ambiguities. Is "demand renewed attention" designed to encourage one to perform additional *mitsvot* that were heretofore neglected, or merely to examine them and consider them? It is not clear why it should be that, although "some *mitsvot* have long been observed by Reform Jews, other *mitsvot* now deserve only "renewed attention." Beyond this, what is an ancient *mitsvah* and what is a modern one? And does "the unique context or our own times" suggest that sacred obligations gain or lose sanctity depending on the context of one's time? Further, are not all times unique?

To be sure, the cobbling together of a statement that will satisfy competing agendas is a major diplomatic achievement. That the final version will lack laser-like coherence and will contain some platitudes is a hazard faced by every group. But this should not detract from the fact that such traditional verbiage has issued forth from the spiritual grandchildren of the framers of the 1885 statement. Better pro-Jewish than anti.

The 1999 statement represents a recognition of the realities of contemporary Jewish life. For the last generation Reform, together with Conservative Judaism, have held the reins of Jewish life in America. Theirs has been the influence and the power to affect Jewish life. On their watch, American Judaism gained unprecedented acceptance and respect among non-Jews, while at the same time sinking to historically low levels of religious literacy. To be sure, the internal condition of American Judaism cannot all be laid at their doorstep. But certainly part of the cause was their fierce desire to be in the vanguard of liberal American life, and not to revert to the outmoded ways of the past. They strove mightily to attain the position they now occupy in American life, but along the way they surrendered much of Jewish particularity. Having achieved acceptance by the Nations, they have willy-nilly ignored the Biblical warning about becoming "like the Nations."

Simultaneously, Orthodox Judaism, although small and unfashionable, grew in influence, stature and power, and has gained the upper ideological hand in the battle for Jewish souls. While there is no justification for the triumphalism of some Orthodox circles, and while Orthodoxy suffers from a many internal problems, it cannot be gainsaid that the Orthodox have dramatically lower rates of intermarriage and assimilation, a more stable family life, and that the products of its networks of schools and yeshivot are literate, learned, and self-confident Jews.

Thus it is that Reform — underneath its anti-Orthodox belligerency — seems to have begun, very quietly, to emulate the ways of the Orthodox. There is movement towards textual studies and towards *mitsvah* observance in many Reform Temples in the USA; there are Reform day schools, talk of Reform *kollelim*, and Reform schools advertise that they learn *Bet Midrash* style complete with *havrutot*. Militant anti-Orthodox rhetoric may emanate from some Reform pulpits, but downstairs, in the boardrooms and classrooms, there is a candid recognition that the maybe-yes-maybe-no program for Jewish life has failed, and we see occasional evidence of a search for new-old approaches.

This is not to deny the unpleasant facts on the ground. Reform rabbis officiate at marriages between Jews and non-Jews, sometimes together with non-Jewish clergy; lesbian and homosexual spiritual leaders are found in Reform pulpits; and of course, the quickie Reform conversion procedures still cannot be taken seriously by anyone committed to halakhic standards. In fact, the 1999 statement in effect concedes the futility of these conversions when it officially welcomes the intermarried, even the non-converted, into the fold. ("We are an inclusive community, opening doors to Jewish life . . . to all . . . including the intermarried, who strive to create a Jewish life." How a Jew who marries out of the faith can strive with a non-Jewish spouse — who has not even undergone a pro-forma conversion — to create a Jewish life is an interesting oxymoron.) It is altogether a rather unbecoming scene.

Before such a confusing backdrop, one is hard-pressed to decipher the signs. In whose hands lies the future shape of Reform: with those who call for holiness and *mitsvah* observance, or with those who pay the inevitable homage to the mindless *mantras du jour;* with those Reform rabbinical students at New York's Hebrew Union College — Jewish Institute of Religion who observe Shabbat and *kashrut* and pray daily with *tallit* and *tefillin*, or with those who are enraged by such traditional practices?

That there are stirrings beneath the surface is apparent, but whether these stirrings are strong enough to reverse Reform's slide into religious oblivion is beyond the ken of ordinary morals.

The heirs of 1885 have embarked on a long journey, but clearly have a long way to go if they are to return to the palimpsest of classical Judaism. An Orthodox Jew who loves both practicing and non-practicing Jews can only pray to the God of us all that in the next century Reform leadership will follow its better instincts, step back from the precipice, and bring back to the sacred discipline of Torah their many followers who will surely respond to courageous and visionary direction. The 1999 statement indicates that it is still possible to do so.

Postscript: Just as this essay was being completed on a hopeful note, the Reform rabbinate approved a resolution permitting its member rabbis to officiate at homosexual weddings. My hope has now been shown to have been credulous and naïve. Rather than turning back towards classical Judaism, Reform has now lurched into a morass from which it will be difficult to extricate itself. To grant an official imprimatur to such liaisons is not only an outright rejection of Leviticus 18; and a severe blow to the institution of family in Jewish life; and a crippling assault on Jewish unity; and a stunning setback for the traditionalist elements within Reform. It also rips into tatters the remaining threads that once connected Reform to classical Judaism. It is one thing to tolerate anti-Torah behavior; it is quite another to give it a *hechsher*. This is what *Midrash Rabbah (Bereishit* 26:5) has in mind when it states that God did not seal the doom of the Generation of the Flood until they began writing *"ketubot"* contracts (*gumamsiot*) for sodomic relationships. It is very likely self-delusion, but not one must pray even at this critical juncture that saner heads will prevail, and that Reform's pell-mell slide into self-immolation — which will drag with it millions of innocent Jews — will somehow be stemmed.

PART FIVE

Smiling at Ourselves

First Class Musings, Second Class Conclusions

> *Deceitful is the heart above all things, and grievously frail; who can know it?*   JEREMIAH 17:19

I WAS RECENTLY BUMPED UP to first class on an overseas flight to Israel. El Al had oversold the coach section, and I was one of the fortunate few to be given complimentary seats upstairs. I am not certain that it is worth the extra thousand dollars normally charged for this pleasure, but I must admit that I loved it. The ambience was luxurious, the service gracious, the seat wide and comfortable. But something strange happened to me when I entered that first class compartment.

I confess that before very long I sensed within me the beginnings of an attitude towards those unfortunates in coach that was quite unbecoming: a blend of pride, hauteur, and what can only be described as something akin to condescension towards those huddled masses yearning to breathe free.

It was at first a deliciously wicked feeling, but soon enough I was troubled by it. *Parvenu that you are*, I scolded myself. *Shameless arriviste. One short flight of stairs on a plane have you climbed, and look to what level you have sunk. By what alchemy have you suddenly been transmogrified into an aristocrat, and they into riffraff? Had it not been for the sheer accident of your being at the right point in the line, you too would be down there rubbing shoulders with screaming children, irritated parents, and harassed flight attendants. Countless times have you preached about the sin of forgetting our origins, and how the Torah constantly reminds us to remember where we came from. But in the time it takes to climb nine short steps you have forgotten your origins.*

But as quickly as the twinges of guilt settled upon me, just as quickly did they dissipate. Pampered by the luxury, I let myself melt into the hedonistic ambience of eat, drink and be merry for tomorrow we arrive in Israel.

Now and then I wondered about the great unwashed who were sitting downstairs. Was it noisy there, were the tourists already standing and chatting loudly in the aisles, had the attendants by now become impatient, had the saran-wrapped meals and the plastic cutlery been served, were the aisles already impassable and the rest rooms all occupied?

Thus enclosed in a cocoon of self-satisfaction, I dozed off in my soft leather chair. It had enough leg room and tilted back deeply enough for me to fall into the semi-somnolent airline state that resembles actual sleep.

And then I dreamed a dream. In the dream an old question was posed to me: *If a tree falls in a forest, does it make a sound?* Without hesitation, I answered firmly: *Yes. A sound is a sound independent of its listeners. The existence of a sound is not dependent on who hears it.*

A second question was posed to me: *If you are in the first class compartment of a plane, and there are no passengers at all in the coach section, are you still in first class?*

Now this was a more complex question. If there is no second class, there can be no first class. First class-ness itself depends on second class-ness. So if no one at all is in the coach section, by what definition is my section first class?

And yet, the same level of luxury obtains in first class whether or not there are people sitting in coach. Like the tree that falls in the forest, first class-ness is its own entity: it is a state unto itself, independent of any thing else, unrelated to other sections.

Or is it? One of the items the airlines sell with their first class tickets is the unsavory little pleasure of knowing that there are passengers on the same plane who are not in first class — who are sitting in a separate, curtained-off compartment behind you or beneath you in a place euphemistically called "coach," in a section more crowded that yours, in seats narrower than yours, receiving service less frequent than you, attended by stewardesses more harried than yours, eating on table trays not covered by linen tablecloths like yours, and — if you don't observe *kashrut* — eating food that is much less varied than yours.

But if the coach section is empty, that means that all the passengers are in first class. If everyone is in first class, that means that the first class passenger is being deprived of his unsavory first class pleasure. First implies a second. (See Rashi to Gen. 1:5, s.v. "*Yom ehad*.") After all, as the incisive old adage puts it, it is not what we have that gives us pleasure; it the knowledge that our neighbor lacks what we have that gives us true pleasure.

So bemused, I spent the next few hours in semi-sleep. Soon enough the questions dissolved in the steady hum of the engines, the quiet in the compartment, the whispering attendants, the dim lights, the thick blankets, the oversized pillows. Coach class, first class — why all this *pilpul?* I was, for a change, having a comfortable trip to Israel, period.

The sun came up, and with it, breakfast. Entrée, juice, eggs, warm bagels, lox, cream cheese, cereal, coffee, Danish, chocolate, milk — an endless array of goodies. I stretched, yawned, washed, *davened*, and sat down to enjoy the feast.

But the night-time question hung in the air. In the dawn's early light it occurred to me that a truly pious Jew would not have had a difficult time answering it. *Al te-hi baz le-khol adam*, says *Avot*, "Do not look down at anyone." And Ramban in his famous letter warns about humility and the evils of haughtiness and pride:

"... Humility is the finest quality among all the fine qualities....- Know, my son, that he whose heart is arrogant toward other beings is in fact a rebel against God's kingdom, for he is utilizing God's garments to glorify himself — for it is written (Psalms 93:1): "God reigns, he is robed in pride...."

Ramban goes on to demonstrate that in whatever man would be proud — be it his wealth, his glory, his wisdom — he is foolish and sinful, for all these things are God's alone.

Beyond this, the Torah itself (Deut. 17:20) warns a king not to multiply chariots or sessions *le-vilti rum levavo*" so that his heart not be lifted up among his brethren." A king — who has authority and majesty — is warned against the pride which is his due; how much more so ordinary people.

Only two more luxurious hours remained before landing, and I would not allow vexing reveries to disturb my tranquility. Not for me these trivial exercises in pettiness. Thus purified and cleansed, I awaited our arrival in the Holy Land.

And yet.... what if no one was in fact down there in coach?

I was only curious. It had nothing to do with my being upstairs; I was simply wondering. Could there be such a thing as a coach compartment without any passengers at all? An entirely empty coach cabin: that would be something to see. Just theoretically, of course.

I don't recall exactly what happened next — was I dreaming again or not? — but I found myself arising from my chair, walking to the cabin exit, and descending the circular stairwell. Nine steps. Once on the lower level I turned towards the back of the plane, parted the curtain and peered inside. Before me were unruly children, impatient flight attendants, a long line before the restrooms, papers and refuse on the floor, mothers diapering babies, two hundred passengers pressed closely together.

I slid back the curtain, climbed back up the stairwell, entered the first class compartment, and sank into my seat. The compartment was tranquil, and the attendant plied me with more Danish and asked me how I would like my coffee.

But my mind was elsewhere. Dream or not, I knew that Ramban would never have experienced the tiny surge of reassurance that coursed through me as I beheld the multitude overflowing the coach sections.

It was then that I became aware of four unvarnished facts of life:

1. For ordinary people who have not attained Ramban's heights, first class does require a second class.
2. The *rum levavo* warning of the Torah is directed not only to a king who is tempted daily by pride, but is directed at every human being; for anything — even a seat that is three inches wider with leg room four inches longer — can generate an attitude of *rum levavo*.
3. The frail human heart not only needs someone to look up to, but also someone to look down at.
4. It is much easier for a religious Jew to be in a first class compartment than to be first class religious Jew.

Of Pennants and Penitents

I COULD NOT HAVE FORESEEN what it would all lead to. It was a friendly call from one of my Atlanta congregants. He had World Series tickets; would I like to go with him to the game? They're great seats, he said. Right behind third base, field level.

I hesitated, because there are many more important things to do with one's time. But the sports juices of my youth began to stir with me, and the rationalizations fell quickly into place: it will be a study of Americana in the raw; it will be a moment of relaxation; you have always liked baseball, its non-violence, its patience, the solitary struggle of lonely pitcher against lonely batter. And consider its religious undertones: the goal is to circle the infield and then come back to the starting point, to return to beginnings. Unlike football or basketball, where the clock ultimately runs out, baseball is timeless: a tie game can theoretically continue into eternity. Besides, this particular layman is a solid supporter of all the important communal causes, and he would be very pleased if you went. Go. It's not so terrible.

So did the *yetser ha-ra* work its cunning upon my soul. And I, author of a dozen exhortations against yielding to temptation and another dozen urging strength and fortitude in the face of Clever Enticer, succumbed. Thus innocuously begins this morality tale.

I hung on every pitch and every Atlanta Brave hit, but a vague sense of discomfort hovered over me: why are you here among these rabid fans, who are doing "tomahawk chops" and Indian chants and who growl "Rrrruff Rrrruff" whenever cleanup man Fred McGriff, dubbed the "crime dog" by the press, comes to bat. You with the black yarmulke on your head and the non-so-black beard on your face, do you really belong here? You, a veteran rabbi, a person who attends *daf yomi* early every morning in Jersualem and *shiurim* at night, who is from a family of *talmidei hakhamim* and the son of a European Rav who was a respected *baki beShas* and *posekim* — do you really belong here among these sixty thousand screaming people who are passionately following the flight of a little round ball? And why are you avidly watching these nine young men who are multimillionaires simply because they are able to catch and throw a ball, strike it with a piece of wood, run swiftly, and slide in the dust? Why does it matter to you when your home team scores? (Home team: if they are offered more money tomorrow, they will play for another team, until they sell themselves to still another team.) Why does it please you when one of these boys strikes a ball that sails high over the fence for a home run? In the eternal scheme of things, does it matter? Does it even matter in the non-eternal, temporal scheme of things?

The self-flagellation ebbed and flowed as the game progressed, but I dismissed it. It was the eighth inning, Atlanta had taken the lead, six more outs and we — did I say we? — are winners.

A high pop fly is veering foul this side of third base. Slowly it heads toward my section of the stands, gracefully it completes its parabolic arc, hangs in the air, and begins its descent. The ball comes closer; it is heading toward me. Suddenly I am eighteen years old again, and instinctively I find myself on my feet. I leap from the ground, reach backward for the ball, and feel the satisfying slap into my outstretched palm. I clutch it and tumble down into the row of seats behind me, where a dozen hands and arms break my fall.

As soon as I sit down, the flagellation intensifies: What have you wrought here? You don't belong here in the first place, and now you've gone and made a fool of yourself in front of thousands of people. This is probably the beginning of a genuine, old-fashioned, major-league, World Series-quality *hillul haShem*.

The people around me cheer and applaud: "Great, Rabbi.....Attaboy....Sign him up." They ask to see the ball. It is emblazoned with the words, "Official Ball, 1995 World Series." The usher comes over and smilingly hands me a certificate which reads, "Contract: Grandstand Outfielder for The Atlanta Braves." I am sitting in my yarmulke and beard and am the hero of the grandstand. As I walk up the aisle to stretch my legs, people raise their fists in triumph, waving to me and shouting, "Way to go....Great grab...." Could it be, I ask myself, that this is really a *kiddush haShem*?

The next morning at the *minyan*, the *Gabbai* greets me. "Was that you who caught the ball last night at the game? Saw it on TV. Great going, Rabbi!" He is genuinely proud. All week long I am the celebrity of the Shul, the block, the community. Friends who have not spoken to me in years call from around the country. By the end of the week, I manage to convince myself that I have in fact brought glory to the name of the God of Israel.

But how fickle is the roar of the crowd; how swiftly does acclaim become mortification; how rapidly is the elixir of triumph reduced to dregs. Our daughter from Jerusalem called. "Abba," she asked quizzically, "I don't believe this, but people here are saying that you caught a ball at a World Series game. Is that true?"

I was stunned. They heard about it in Jerusalem? In Mattersdorf, in Har Nof, in Bayit Vegan, they heard about it? "I think it's funny, Abba. It's hysterical."

Akhen noda ha-davar, the deed has become known. In a month, I was to return to Jerusalem. My Jerusalem neighborhood is not America. That which in America brings approval can in my Jerusalem neighborhood bring ignominy. In my neighborhood, entertainment is serious business: it consists primarily of *melava malkas, sheva berakhos, shalom zakhars, brissin,* bar mitsvahs, weddings, and listening to the occasional visiting *maggid*. Ball games are for the vulgar.

How could I face these people in Jerusalem? How would I explain to them if (when!) they ask? How would I daven in the Shul on Shabbat? I sit in the front row next to my late father's seat, and bask there in his reflected glory and that of my brother the Rosh Yeshiva, who sits nearby. What will happen to their good name when the true nature of this American rabbi becomes known?

On the first Shabbat after my return to Jerusalem, I walk with a certain trepidation into the Shul. I am comforted by one thought: the Shul is comprised of Israeli, Swiss, South African, British, French, Dutch, and some American Jews. They are a fine group of people, very proper, staid and upright. Sports and frivolity are not in the lexicon. I am hoping that they have never heard of something called a World Series.

After davening, I greet my friends and walk with them to the door. No one seems to know.

An elderly Swiss gentleman approaches me with a smile. "Nice to have you back among us. By the way, I heard you caught a ball at a baseball game in America."

I started to say that it wasn't just a baseball game, it was World Series game, but thought better of it. "Oh?" I said nonchalantly, "Where did you hear that?"

"Everybody knows about it. That's quite exceptional, I must say."

"Well, yes, it's true. In a weak moment I went to a game. You know how we Americans are."

"I didn't realize you were such an athlete." There was a twinkle in his eye. Whether it was an amused twinkle I cannot say. In this Shul, athlete is not a term of endearment. In the hierarchy of adjectives, it rests somewhere between barbarian and lout. "Ha, ha," I laugh weakly, "in my youth I used to play a little ball."

"Well, everybody here thinks it was quite a feat."

"Everybody here"? How do these TV-less, baseball-less people know of a World Series game in Atlanta, Ga., seven thousand miles away? Is there nothing secret any more, nothing hidden, nothing just between us? Because the eye of a camera caught me for an instant, am I now condemned to lose my good name and that of my family for eternity? (Thank God my children are all married.)

To be sure, these good people will not talk behind my back, for these are seriously religious Jews: they do not gossip. But who can control one's thoughts? "There goes the son of a *talmid hakham* and the brother of *talmidei hakhamim*. What a pity; he's the one who catches baseballs on television at American baseball games." Will they wonder how it can be that the selfsame person can say the *Shema* with *tallit* over his head, listen attentively to the Rav's *divrei Torah*, never talk during davening — and then go to the USA and attend sporting events and catch baseballs on television? Well may they wonder.

I am, please God, heading back to Atlanta before very long. I am hoping that in this new baseball season, those nine boys of summer will do as well as they did last year. But this time, it is not for the usual reasons that I cheer them on, but for personal religious reasons. I am praying that they win the pennant and go on to the World Series and then, when a friendly congregant calls to invite me to the game, I will have the strength to beg off and thereby become a true penitent in fulfillment of Rambam's *Hilkhot Teshuva*, 2:1:

> "What is complete repentance? When something which a person has previously transgressed presents itself to him again under the same circumstances, and he has the option to transgress once again, but withdraws from the transgression.... this is complete repentance."

But if perchance the Enticer works his cunning on me once again and I fail the test and somehow find myself at the game, I humbly pray for two things: (1) that no balls, fair or foul, come my way; and (2) if one does happen to come my way and I instinctively leap for it, that I have the good sense at the very least to drop the ball.

A Simple Driving Test

THE NOTICE IN THE PAPERS was innocuous enough. Under new regulations, all those who had been driving in Israel under foreign driver's licenses are now required to obtain an Israeli license, after taking a simple test.

Where bureaucracy is king, nothing is simple. I called the Motor Vehicles Bureau to find out the details. After nine attempts over a span of two days — getting nothing but busy signals or endless ringing — a very courteous man, who had finally finished his tea, picked up the phone. The procedure would be simple, he assured me. Just show your foreign driver's license and, after a simple test to establish your driving ability, an Israeli license will be issued.

"How do I go about taking the simple test?" That too, I was told, is simple.
You just go to the Motor Vehicles Bureau and take the test.
Can I go any time? Are the lines long?
No, it's very simple. You just schedule the test at a certain time. There's nothing to it.
How do I schedule the test?
You go to a licensed driving school and pick up the necessary forms there.
And bring the test forms with me to the test?

A Simple Driving Test

Yes. But first you have to take the forms to a licensed eye doctor for an eye test, and he has to sign and stamp the form. They charge about 20 shekels.

And then I bring that form to the driving test?

Yes, but first you go to a licensed medical doctor to have a physical examination. He won't charge more than 100 shekel.

And then I bring the forms to the driving test?

No, first you go to a licensed driving school to take driving lessons.

But I've been driving for 30 years! Why do I suddenly need lessons?

To learn Middle Eastern techniques. You may need to take only a few lessons, but those are the regulations. You have to go to driving school and they will tell you what you need.

How much are the lessons?

80 shekel each.

And the test — does it cost anything?

Not much. 80 shekel.

After my lessons, when do I take the test?

The driving school schedules your lesson. But first you pay 40 shekel to the Motor Vehicles Bureau for administering the test.

And if I fail the test?

Who said you would fail the test? Who told you that? Should that somehow happen, you just have to take additional lessons at 80 shekel per lesson, plus another 80 shekel for retaking the test, plus another 40 shekel for administration, of course.

Sir, with all due apologies, is it not in your interest, and the driving school's that I fail the test?

Our only interest is in making driving safer.

And if I pass the test?

It's very simple. You come back the next day to pick up your temporary license.

And when do I get my permanent license?

You come back four weeks later to pick it up.

Must I stand in line each time?

Well, the lines are not very long. Bring a book. Maybe two.

Thanks, you've been very helpful.

Like I said, it's very simple.

I am proud to report that I'm now licensed to drive like an Israeli. That means I can weave in and out of traffic, blow my horn at red lights, be churlish and rude, make illegal U-turns, speed in reverse, never give another person the right of way, and in general, throw civilized behavior out the window as soon as I turn the key in the ignition.

All this cost me only 15 hours and 900 shekalim. Yet when I consider that surge of unbridled ferocity that comes with getting behind the wheel just like a *sabra*, it was, plainly speaking, a bargain.

An Imagined Symposium

The Messianic issue continues to exercise the imagination of present-day Jewry. We present here the imagined responses of six Orthodox publications to a fanciful symposium on the question: "What is the Role of Messianism in Contemporary Orthodoxy?"

Artscroll Overview

It is the challenge of our contemporary, confused, frightened, baffled generation to strip away the veils that obscure our vision of HASHEM. Better still — it is the very veils which are given existence by the One Above (see Overview to Artscroll "G-d"). If man were only to recognize this, he would know that nature itself is but an illusory veil that conceals the One Above only from those who are blinded by the artificial sham and ersatz glitter of this-worldliness.

Does modern man have less need for the Mashiach than his forebears? No, just the opposite. Because man thinks he is modern, he has more need for Mashiach than ever before. Once the messenger of HASHEM arrives, however, it will be clear that it is our neglect of our total dependence on HASHEM which beclouded the Image, and allowed a barrier to conceal His true anointed redeemer from our visage. Nevertheless, he whom we call the anointed one, the Mashiach, is still there, waiting for the Overview to end so that he can finally appear.

The Jewish Observer

The Yeshiva world, the world of pure, unadultered Torah, takes every aspect of Emunah seriously, and unlike others among us, does not pick and choose beliefs and principles which are currently fashionable or convenient.

No matter what the prevailing sentiment in the outside world is, the answer for us is clear; we believe in the coming of the Mashiach. Not — we must make clear — the second coming, or the third coming, but the one and only coming, the first coming. (Although we see eye to eye with traditional Christians on many SOCIAL issues). It should, however, be noted that the term in the question — "contemporary Orthodoxy" — leaves us rather puzzled, because Orthodoxy, like Torah, is eternal, and there can be no contemporary Orthodoxy any more than there can be a contemporary God. We will try not be shrill, but it is difficult to be silent about such a serious matter which goes to the very roots of our beliefs as they have been taught to us by our revered leaders — who, history shows, have been, once again, right.

Yated Ne-eman

Despite the attempts of certain elements of the Jewish word to say that the Mashiach belongs to them exclusively, it is clear that this is only the voice of the *yetser hara* speaking. The Mashiach belongs to every Jew, not to just one extreme group which claims that all of Yiddishkeit was invented by it and its leaders. We believe in the coming of the Mashiach every day, and even though he tarries we will nevertheless wait for him that he comes. There is much loose talk about the Mashiach these days, but we have it on the highest authority, from unimpeachable sources, that everyone who speaks with too much familiarity about this subject will not be worthy of receiving his holy presence when he arrives, speedily, soon, and in our day. Amen.

Algemeiner Journal

We know who the Mashiach truly is, he is among us, even though he does not publicly admit it, it can be seen every day clearly who he is, and if we will but be worthy of him, our wishes that Mashiach will come now will definitely be fulfilled. If certain people in Bene Berak have problems with such matters as we are describing them here, well and good. Everyone knows what happens to those who do not believe such things. As to the question of the symposium, everyone knows that the Mashiach and his arrival is the only major question in Yiddishkeit in our day. There is nothing else to talk about.

Journal of Halacha and Contemporary Society

Meiri in his comment to Bava Kama 51a, reacting to the Tosafos in Bava Kama 51a (loc cit) in which Tosafos takes issue with Rashi's comment on Devarim 14:7 in which the Rambam takes strong issue with Rashi citing Onkelos in Bereshis 24:9 as a support, renders the entire issue moot by pointing to a *taus hadefus* supported by the Rosh's emendation to the locutionary error discovered by the Gaon in his classic dispute with the Baal Hatanya who, far from disagreeing with the original premise, in fact lends credence to Rambam's reading of the annotated version of the text as pointed out so perceptively by the Ravad in his gloss to the Mishneh Torah.

Tradition

In strictly teleogical terms, it is quite apparent that it is the ontological aspect which requires scrutiny, if not — *mutatis mutandis* — some serious reevaluation and reassessment of previously sacrosanct positions. Despite the clarion calls coming from Bene Beraq and Eastern Parkway, one should give a rational Maimonidian glance at the primary sources before rushing off to conclusions. A sober, analytical examination of the central (though not exclusively centrist) halakhic parameters is definitely called for. Hubris would be self-destructive, not least in axiological terms. Some historic oversight is mandatory if we are not to fall into the trap of quintessential misunderstanding. While it is true that Maimonides and Nahmanides have somewhat differing meta-historical thrusts on this issue, Rav Kook has stated that the poetry of the spheres is the telos of the "yet-to-come." It is quite apparent to whom he refers. The locus of these comments must therefore be clearly understood: we do not push the End; the End pushes us.

In any case, it is clear that the strategies employed must avoid the meta-halakhic polarities which are so endemic to the dimensions of redemptive and existential angst (corresponding to the categories of Berdyaev and Kierkegaard, respectively) which finds its focus in the constructs of contemporaneous Orthodoxy. These constructs hardly induce the paradisical anterior — not to mention interior — locus for which all of us strive.

Eschatologically, teleologically, and axiologically, the Messiah's coming is the consummation of world history devoutly to be wished. We can only hope that our hope is not a fond one because, as John Milton put it, "he also serves who only stands and waits."

Haim and Ita and the Communications Revolution

THEY SAT THERE, HAIM AND Ita, over their supper. He was engrossed in the evening paper, she stared into her salad. Fifteen minutes passed without a word between them.

"Haim," said Ita.

"Mmm," said Haim, his eyes on the print.

"So how are things in general?" asked Ita.

"Mmm."

Silence.

"And at work? Are things going OK?"

"Mmm. OK, I guess."

Silence.

"What do you think of the Hebron deal? Is it good for the Jews?"

"Mmm. Maybe yes, maybe no."

Silence.

Ita opened her purse. She took out her cellphone and dialed a number. Haim suddenly looked up from his paper. His cellphone was ringing. He picked it up from his belt. "Hello?"

"Haim, how are you," said the voice. "This is your wife. You know, Ita. How are things in general?"

"Ita! Great to hear from you." Haim put down his newspaper. "I haven't heard from you in such a long time. I am really happy you called, because there are lots of things I want to talk with you about."

"Nu, so here I am, let's talk."

"Well for one thing, things at the office are not going so well and I really need your input. Yossi, my assistant is trying to undermine me every step of the way. Not only does he not do his job well, but he has the hutspah to bad-mouth me to the boss and to the other workers. And I can't have a heart to heart talk with Yossi because he's so hypersensitive. Right away he gets insulted and pouts and even gets tears in his eyes. He is really impossible to work with. I need some advice from you on how to handle this. It just can't go on like this forever. It's driving me crazy. My stomach is constantly churning. And there's no one to talk to about it. I tried talking to the boss, but he doesn't listen. He just sits there and looks at his financial statements and says *Mmm*. Soon I'll need a psychiatrist. I'm just lucky I've got someone like you to talk to, otherwise there's no telling what would happen to me. . . And there's one other thing. I think this whole so-called peace process is a big joke. All right, Sharon is a little tougher than Barak was, but basically we are still giving things away for nothing. And this guy Arafat, this murderer, why is the world so taken with him? Look how far he's gotten with terror and killing. And the world gives him money, and we give him weapons — which he uses against us! I tell you, crime does pay in this world of ours. Oh Ita, it's so good to pour out my heart to you. If it weren't for you I would go completely crazy. Thanks for calling me."

Haim put his phone back in its case and resumed reading his paper.

"Haim," said Ita.

"Mmm," said Haim, his eyes on the print.

"So how are things in general?"

"Mmm."

Silence.

"And at work? Are things doing OK?"

"Mmm. OK, I guess."

Silence.

"What do you think of the Hebron deal? Is it good for the Jews?"

"Mmm. Maybe yes, maybe no."

Silence.

Ita opened her purse. She took out her cellphone and dialed a number. Haim suddenly looked up from his paper. His cellphone was ringing. He picked it up from his belt. "Hello?"

"Haim, how are you?" said the voice. "This is Ita. You know, your wife. How are things in general?"

"Ita, great to hear from you! Thank God for these cellular phones, otherwise people would never communicate. I am so glad you called. Oy, have I got problems. Listen, the situation at the office has gotten worse and I need to talk to you about it..."

The Heavenly Editor

BENEATH THE UNRELENTING PYRAMID OF articles on every editor's desk there lies buried a secret at once comforting and daunting: the act of editing can involve more than reading manuscripts. In its pristine, ideal state, it is a crucible in which one's character can be molded — a touchstone for what the *baalei musar* call the eternal struggle for personal *shelemut*. It bears in it the daily challenge of Abba Shaul (Shabbat 133b), "*Ma hu rahum af ata rahum*...(Just as He is merciful, so shall you be merciful; as He is patient, so shall you be patient. . .)" And above all, it provides a measure of one's ability to temper the quality of pride with humility, to exercise patience and forbearance, to balance kindness and truth.

Consider the interplay between pride and humility. Editors are free to criticize someone else's work — nay, expected to do so — to point out the faults of others, to instruct them with impunity to change this, delete that, abbreviate this, expand that. Few activities in this temporal world have the same capacity to induce pride as does the invitation to correct others.

And few activities have its capacity to nurture humility. Editors may completely re-write a manuscript, spend weeks negotiating with the author, make sense out of nonsense and English out of who knows what — and when the final product appears, the editors, faceless and anonymous, lurk backstage as the author takes the curtain calls. This is the ultimate exercise in humility, in *hitbatlut ha-yesh*. Changing and molding and shaping may be redolent of divine power, but editors are reminded daily that God also has the ability to be *metzamtzem:* He willingly restricts His power, narrows it, withdraws it.

And if this challenge is not enough, there is the problem created by the inherent resonance of the written word. Say something, and in time its impact dissipates. Write something, and the stark, black letters refuse to vanish. This is why any published article can engender intense and widely differing reactions. From time to time, for example, every Jewish journal finds itself described as closet right-wing or (for the same article) closet left-wing. When we are simultaneously seen as both black and white, there looms before us another divine attribute: to strive to be an *erekh apayim* — long-suffering, forbearing, and patient with those who suspect us of possessing, heaven forfend, opinions which are not in full consonance with their own.

Perhaps the most vexing of all the challenges to imitate God occurs when editors have to inform an author that his or her article is not accepted for publication. For although no journal can possibly publish every manuscript — even some very fine ones — to tell this to an author is like telling a mother that her baby is not the most beautiful you have ever seen.

The analogy is not inapt. Giving birth to a manuscript is in some ways similar to giving birth to a child. Writing involves the conception of an idea, its gestation for a period of time, the pangs of writing a first draft, a second, a third. And then, when the product of this labor finally sees the light of day, along comes a stranger, a midwife who calls himself an editor, and declares that what has been brought into the world with such effort is just not good enough.

A mother would be very upset by such a reaction to her offspring; so is an author. Having in my lifetime often experienced the wounds of rejection slips, I genuinely identify with every author. Therefore we eschew form-letter rejections, attempting instead to inform the author gently, with tact and great regret, that we cannot use his article. But however compassionate the message, the truth must out: we are not going to publish it.

Is it possible to be simultaneously kind and honest? It is surely not a happenstance that in the Thirteen Divine Attributes, *hesed* and *emet* stand side by side. Perhaps the lesson is that only the Divine Editor of us all can successfully combine the two. For when human editors try to do so, the resulting meta-rational logic is vivid evidence of the limits of mortal reasoning: your article is brilliant; we are unable to publish it.

In a moment of desperation, we even considered adopting the rejection letter attributed to a certain Chinese journal:

> We have read your manuscript with boundless delight. If we were to publish your paper it would be impossible for us to publish any work of a lower standard. As it is unthinkable that, in the next thousand years, we shall see its equal, we are, to our regret, compelled to return your divine composition, and to beg you a thousand times to overlook our short sight and timidity.

To receive such a letter is almost as good as being published, but the letter lacks one major ingredient: while it is *rav hesed,* it contains no *emet.*

On any level, mundane or transcendent, the business of editing is not for the faint of heart. The dilemmas of pride, humility, forbearance, *hesed* and *emet* — and the need to be a loving midwife — are enough to intimidate even the most hopelessly deluded editor. But since there is no easy way out, we will simply have to continue the struggle. We will keep you informed (humbly, of course,) about our progress. In the interim, we pray with Hillel that what is hateful unto you, you will not do unto editors. Be kind to us, patient, loving, understanding. And, if you insist, honest.

The Cruelest Month

T. S. ELIOT NOTWITHSTANDING, OCTOBER and not April is the cruelest month. Let Eliot have his illusions about April: what does the man who wrote about Bleistein with a cigar know, anyway?

This October has been both cruel and depressing. First came the news that once again I had been overlooked for the Nobel Prize in literature. Instead, it was given to one Dario Fo, an obscure Italian comic playwright whom no one ever heard of. Do you know anyone who reads Italian? Last year it was given to an obscure Polish female poet whom no one ever heard of. Do you know anyone who reads Polish? To add salt to my wounds, I wasn't even on the short list of finalists — even though, if obscurity is a criterion, I am as obscure as they come.

There is no longer any point in keeping it quiet. It must finally be said clearly and unequivocally: This repeated annual snubbing by the Nobel Committee is motivated by nothing other than anti-Jewish animus. (I have written several strong letters to the Anti-Defamation League about this; for some unexplained reason they never responded.)

Once the Nobel committee set the tone, it was no surprise that this year's Pulitzer Prizes also overlooked me. Nor was this the first time. They have ignored me for the past thirty years. With all the different categories they have, one would think that during all this time I would have qualified for at least one of their prizes. If not non-fiction, then fiction; if not fiction, then poetry; if not poetry, then criticism; if not criticism, then translation. But such is the power of prejudice that not once in the past thirty years have I received any recognition whatsoever. In the future I will not even bother searching the prize lists. It is too depressing.

Even the lesser awards like the National Book Awards and England's Booker Prize have overlooked me once again. Well, one becomes inured to such things. Besides, can one really expect the Brits to give an award to an Orthodox Jew? But the bottom line remains unchanged: I don't stand a chance with any of these people, and we all know the reason.

Just when I was getting over the literary insults, I came across an issue of a Jewish magazine which features on its cover "The Greatest Minds of the Twentieth Century." I opened it eagerly, certain that my name and an annotated bibliography by a suitably sycophantic disciple would be there. It wasn't the Nobel Prize, but it was at least some recognition that would help tide me over this cruel month.

I thumbed the pages carefully: my name was not there.

All these deliberate snubs in one month were a little hard to bear. It was depressing to discover that even a Jewish journal, sponsored by an Orthodox organization, could fall victim to the same kind of prejudice that animates the Nobel Committee. How they could overlook an Orthodox person is beyond me. What other reason can there be for not including me in that select list than the subtle and pernicious influence of a hostile world that now has even penetrated the ranks of Orthodox to the extent that they have denied me a place among the greatest minds of the twentieth century. But I comfort myself with the knowledge that there is always the twenty-first century. . . .

Blind prejudice has even penetrated the world of athletics. I have been playing tennis, for example, all my life. One would think that by now the international rankings would have listed me. But no: I have never even made the world's top 500!

So pervasive is anti-Semitism that even the world of chess, so long dominated by Jews, has fallen victim to its poison. Just today I checked this year's world chess ranking. I am not even in last place.

I try not to grow bitter and cynical, and I remind myself that Delacroix never won a prize and Cezanne never sold a picture, but what is one to do after these deliberate snubs in every field of endeavor, year after painful year?

The Nobels and the Pulitzers and the world rankings might ignore me, but despite them, I am still creative, and an idea has begun to germinate in my mind. I am happy to announce that during this year *Tradition* magazine (of which I happen to be the editor) will institute its own awards — which, like all awards, will of course be coveted. It will be called The Tradition Prize, awarded to the most unrecognized talents in the world in every field of human endeavor. There are only two qualifications: (*a*) applicants must be Jewish; (*b*) applicants must be obscure. (Obscurely Jewish or Jewishly obscure candidates do not qualify.) An unusually large number of candidates is expected.

It is only fair to warn our dear readers that someone is already in the lead for the first year's major award. His name cannot as yet be revealed, but rumor has it that, in keeping with the standards set by the committee, he is an extremely obscure editor.

The Last Bus Stop

IN 2006 IT FINALLY HAPPENED: Israel and Syria signed a treaty giving Israel undisputed sovereignty over Jerusalem's newly constructed Central Bus Station, including one outgoing lane.

President Bush, in a ceremony on the White House lawn, praised Israel for not allowing petty details like territory to stand in the way of peace, adding that "to attain full jurisdiction over this revered bus station is a fitting climax to the history of the wandering Jew."

The Israeli Prime Minister declared: "It has been a long journey, but we finally have a homeland the world can live with — and the outgoing lane will guarantee safe passage if we have to wander again."

Syria's Assad publicly renounced all attempts to wrest land by terrorism, since it was much easier to do so by negotiation. He pledged that those Jews who could not be squeezed into the bus station would be repatriated to friendly regimes like Syria and Iraq.

Shimon Peres stated that "this accord proves to all the world that for us, 'Land For Peace' is not just a slogan. Unfortunately, we have no more land to surrender — but if we did, we would give that up, too. We hope the world will now see what really fine people we are once you get to know us."

Then Assad declared that it was intolerable for a foreign power to have full sovereignty over so hallowed an Arab site as the Jerusalem Bus Station. But as a gesture of goodwill he would allow Israel to retain a lower level, plus the concession stands, since "they do so well at concessions."

Peres agreed: "The fewer buses we have, the more difficult it will be for terrorists to blow them up."

The world was ecstatic. *The New York Times* declared that "Assad is to be commended for his patience that overcame paranoid Israeli fears."

Said *Ha'aretz*: "No longer will we have to dominate other people through might and power." *Ma'ariv's* cover featured a full-color picture of the new, compact bus station under a banner headline: "If you will it, it is no dream."

In the Knesset, the Prime Minister was challenged about the bus station referendum he had promised. "I will hold it," he pledged, "the day after the implementation of the treaty. Stop whining," he said.

Shulamit Aloni was livid at the opposition. "Only the *haredim* are opposed to peace. It will serve them right to have to live in a crowded bus station. Who tells them to have such large families? We have pledged to build them a brand new western wall at the western side of the station — and they're still not satisfied."

Intoned Peres: "It is always the religious who oppose progress. They are living in medieval times. They should come into the 20th century, where there is compromise and tolerance. I have read the Bible, and nowhere does God promise the Jews both upper and lower levels of bus stations. Any religious Jew who doesn't like it can go back to Brooklyn."

Terror intensified. As a goodwill gesture, the government gave Syria 50 military trucks. It also released 400 convicted terrorists, and changed the words of Hatikva so that Arab sensibilities would not be offended.

As anti-government demonstrations erupted, the Knesset pushed through a bill sponsored by the Party to Prevent

Religious Coercion labeling all anti-government statements subversive. All protesters were placed under house arrest.

Terror increased. Peres flew off to Damascus. Two days later he returned in triumph.

"In my hand are twenty-five post-dated letters from the president, in which he regrets in advance the next twenty-five terrorist attacks. No longer need we worry whether we have his regrets — for I hold them firmly in my hand. And as an additional good-faith gesture, he has pledged that as soon as we run out of these, he will issue new ones. He is prepared to do this for as long as necessary."

The next day Syria declared that the term, "Central," as in Central Bus Station, was offensive to Arab sensibilities. He demanded that the new Jewish homeland be known as "The Final Station."

The Prime Minister's response was unequivocal: "We must not falter over a mere name after finally arriving at a solution. But I faithfully vow: This lower level of our beloved bus station, which carries so many memories for all us, will forever remain eternal and undivided."

In Any Image Createth He Them

NEIMAN-MARCUS HAS LONG BEEN FAMOUS for its annual His and Her gifts. There have been His and Her camels, His and Her yachts, His and Her airplanes. For 2002 they offer something very special: His and Her people: full-dimensional life-size facsimiles of — yourself. A life-size model will be done of you (you can specify the sitting or standing model), and you can have him (or her) as a constant companion. The model can be programmed to respond vocally at your beck and call. If you like appreciative listeners, she/he/it will laugh heartily at your jokes; or if you are the authoritative type, the model will say, "Yes sir" at the touch of a remote control button. And when it runs down and gets tired, you simply plug in the accompanying cord to charge it up again. All this for only $7,000.00 (Clothes and sculptor's air fare are extra.)

The idea has infinite possibilities. For a rabbi — if he could afford it — it might well be worth the investment.

For example, I have often wished I could be two people. Now I can. When Organization X wants me to sit at the dais for their annual banquet and I would rather be elsewhere, I can now be elsewhere and send my $7,000.00 facsimile to the dinner. When I have to be present at a meeting when I'd rather be doing something else, I can send my double and do something else. When I am expected at an interminable cocktail party my counterpart (the standing model) can go and smile affably, while I study. Certainly it would be the kind of spiritual leader who offends no one: a true model rabbi.

The possibilities are dizzying: I could purchase a few models of synagogue officers and program them to say, "Yes, Rabbi," and all my requests for new projects and ideas would pass without a dissenting vote.

Or perhaps I should order a few dozen synagogue worshippers and place them strategically throughout the congregation on Shabbus. I would have them sculpted with eyes wide open, mouths closed, understanding looks in their eyes, expressions of sheer delight and joy on their faces as the rabbi delivers his sermon. They could even be programmed to say, "You didn't speak long enough."

But then again, things would probably soon get very dull with all those robots around. Genuine people are much more exciting, cost much less (at least initially), and come in many more interesting models. They are pre-programmed to speak softly or loudly, politely or rudely, honestly or deceptively. They have built-in souls, minds, characters — which even Nieman-Marcus cannot provide — and they come with various degrees of integrity, ethics and morality. They do need an occasional re-charge, and there is no handy cord to plug into the nearest socket — but there is always Shabbat, which is much more effective.

The live model does not always laugh at your jokes, occasionally says no, opens his mouth when it should be closed, closes his eyes when they should be open, and sometimes tells you that you spoke too long. They can be very vexing, these live models, but they are much more fascinating.

No, this year I'll have to pass up the His and Hers gift. Yachts yes; camels yes; airplanes yes; but people facsimiles? Not just yet.

At least not until Neiman-Marcus develops a model that can be counted towards a minyan.

Prime Minister Jones and the New Middle East

IN THE YEAR 2009, JOHN Paul Jones II, an immigrant from California, was elected the first Christian prime minister of Israel.

The event caused hardly a ripple. Israel had long since lost its uniquely Jewish character, its society was more American than America, and Arabs were a controlling bloc in the Knesset. Most Israelis simply ho-hummed and went back to their Palm Pilots and cellular phones.

The press reacted predictably. *Ha'aretz* intoned: "This demonstrates our allegiance to the ideals of democracy. When Moslem Arabs determine Knesset legislation, and the leader of this Jewish land is a Christian, we are witness to the fulfillment of the prophetic vision." *Yated Ne'eman* opined: "Better a goy who keeps no Torah than a Jew who keeps no Torah."

Abba Eban wrote that it as not unusual for democracies to have Christian leaders, and since Israel was above all else a democracy, it was logical for her to have a Christian PM.

In the Knesset, Yossi Sarid declared, "We have much in common with Christianity. They have long claimed that Judaism is outmoded, and so have we. They don't follow Judaism, and neither do we. It is appropriate for us to have a Christian leader."

In America, the Conference of Presidents of Major Jewish Organizations issued a press release: "While this is most unusual, we Jews have never flinched from our trailblazing tradition. We eagerly anticipate that the Vatican, in view of this dramatic new step, will reevaluate its role in the Holocaust."

In his acceptance speech, PM Jones thanked God for having brought him to this day, spoke of spiritual strength of the Jewish people, and asked the entire country to pray for him. He then went to church for evening vespers to ask for divine guidance.

There was some disquiet at the religious content of his speech, but the media quickly dismissed it as a foreign relations ploy. There was more unease when it was revealed that PM Jones not only attended church regularly, but that he visited a different synagogue every Shabbat morning, and that out of respect for Judaism he did not work on Shabbat or Yom Tov.

Sniffed *Ha'aretz*: "Jones is clearly a religious man. It remains to be seen whether he can maintain public trust despite this break with the traditions of Israeli leadership." PM Jones, however, maintained not only public trust but public love.

Rarely had Israelis seen such a prime minister. He listened attentively to everyone, was unfailingly courteous and was scrupulously fair and honest in all his dealings. In a few months, he became the most popular PM in Israel's history. Instead of naming their sons Nimrod and Tuval, Israelis began naming them John Paul.

When the PM formed a special Religious Enhancement Commission, there was more unease, but it was dismissed as a gimmick to impress the religious bloc.

But in a speech to the nation, Jones stated: "God did not return Jews to their ancestral home so that Judaism should be forgotten. He surely wants Judaism to be strengthened in His Jewish state. This new commission will be empowered to recommend the proper course of action for Israel's continued spiritual growth."

When Jones announced that members of the commission would include the chief rabbis and major yeshiva heads, panic gripped the secular leadership.

Ma'ariv declared: "Jones has gone too far. This could undermine the character of the Jewish state. Religion is fine, but it should be confined to the synagogue. This is the 21st century, not the benighted Middle Ages."

The Jerusalem Post worried that the PM might antagonize the secular Western countries. Shulamit Aloni cried out: "This is against Jewish tradition. It is unthinkable that rabbis should determine the future of the Jewish people."

But it was all without effect. Jones was too beloved and respected by the masses of Israelis.

Under the gentle prodding of their PM, a wave of Jewish consciousness swept over the land. New synagogues were built in north Tel Aviv to meet the demand. The daily Knesset sessions began with Torah study. Yom Ha'atzmaut opened with a massive *ma'ariv* service in Teddy Stadium.

Shimon Peres begged religious Jews to come from Brooklyn to Israel: "Come to the land of your fathers. We need your religious intensity and piety. This is a new Middle East."

Haredim began looking at secular Israelis as human beings, and secularists found that *haredim* were really pleasant people. Rav Ovadia Yosef scheduled personal meetings with secularist leadership, and they in turn declared that they appreciated a spiritual leader so forthright and courageous.

Jones called a press conference. "I am grateful that Judaism has been brought back to the Jews. Now that my mission has been accomplished, I hereby tender my resignation. May God bless this holy land."

From somewhere in the Galilee, the media reported strange happenings. A woman claimed that her infant had placed his hand in a nest of scorpions and escaped unharmed. The media discounted this as a mother's hysteria.

But then a motorist reported in amazement that he had seen lambs lying down with wolves. A shepherd swore that his goats were cavorting peacefully with leopards, and that his young calves were frolicking with ferocious mountain lions.

Finally, an angelic looking man on a white donkey was seen entering Jerusalem.

No one was quite sure what to make of it.

Glossary

The following glossary provides a partial explanation of the Hebrew and Yiddish (Y.) words and phrases used in this book. The spellings and explanations reflect the way the specific word is used herein. Often there are alternate spellings and meanings for the words.

AGGADAH: the homiletic, non-legal portion of the Talmud.

AGUNAH: lit., "chained one." A wife unable to obtain a religious divorce from her husband and thus prevented from marrying another.

AHARONIM: the later decisors of Jewish law, from fifteenth century onward.

AL HANISSIM: special prayer recited on Hanukah and Purim festivals.

AM SEGULAH: chosen people.

AMIDAH: the central portion of the liturgy.

ANINUT: the legal status of a mourner during the interval between death and burial.

ASHREI: part of the daily worship.

AUFRUF: (Y.) the soon-to-be-married groom is called to the Torah on the Shabbat before his wedding.

AVODAH SHEBALEV: divine service of the heart.

BAKI BESHAS: one who knows the entire Talmud by heart.

BARUKH ATA: "Blessed art Thou"; the beginning of every blessing.

BAT KOL: a divine echo.

BEDEKEN: (Y.) lit., "covering." Prior to the wedding ceremony, the groom places the veil over the bride's face.

BEHUKOTEIHEM LO TELEKHU: the Biblical injunction not to walk in the ways of the heathens.

BEIN ADAM LAHAVEIRO: laws between man and his fellow man.

BEIN ADAM LAMAKOM: laws between man and God.
BERIT MILA: ritual circumcision.
BET KNESSET: synagogue.
BIRKAT HAMAZON: prayer after meals.
BIRKAT KOHANIM: priestly blessing.
BITAHON: faith, trust.

DAVEN: engaging in prayer.
DERAKHEHA DARKHEI NOAM: "her (the Torah's) ways are ways of pleasantness."

EMET: truth.
EREKH APAYIM: patient, long-suffering.
EVEL: mourning.

GALUT: diaspora.
GASHMIYUT: physicality, materialism.
GILUI SHEKHINAH: revelation of the heavenly Presence.

HAFTARAH: the prophetic portion read in synagogue on Shabbat and festivals following the regular reading from the Five Books.
HALVAYAT HAMET: funeral.
HAR HABAYIT: Temple Mount.
HASHEM ROI LO ECHSAR: "The Lord is my shepherd, I shall not want....".
HASTARAT PANIM: the concealment of God's face.
HATAN: the wedding groom.
HATZIONUT PASHTAH REGEL: "Zionism is bankrupt."
HATSNEA LECHET IM ELOHECHA: "walk humbly with thy God."
HEICHAL HASPORT: temple of sport.
HILLUL HASHEM: desecration of God's name.
HOL HA-MOED: intermediate days of a festival.
HUMRA: strict interpretation of Jewish law.

Glossary

HUPAH: wedding canopy.

IM YIRTZE HASHEM: please God.
IR HA-ATIQA: the Old City.
ISH EMET: a man of truth.

KAKH DARKAH SHEL TORAH: "this is the way of the Torah."
KARET: excision.
KAVANNAH: concentration in worship.
KAVOD: prestige, honor.
KE-AKUM NIDMEH LO: "he appeared to him like an idolator."
KE-TALMID HAKHAM NIDMEH LO: "he appeared to him like a Torah scholar."
KEKHOL HA-GOYIM BEIT YISRAEL: "let Israel be like all the nations."
KELAL YISROEL: the community of Israel; the Jewish people.
KIDDUSH HASHEM: sanctification of God's name.
KITSUR SHULHAN ARUKH: the Code of Jewish Law.
KOL KEVUDA BAT MELECH PENIMA: "the honor of the princess is within."
LE-AVDO BEKHOL LEVAVKHEM: "to serve Him with all your heart...".
LEHODOT ULEHALLEL LESHIMCHA HAGADOL: "to praise and extol Thy great name."
LEKHA DODI NIGGUN: a Friday night melody marking the entrance of the Shabbat Queen.
LIMNOT YAMEINU KEN HODA: "teach us to number our days....".
LIFNEI SHEVER GAON: "pride goeth before the fall....".
LO BARA'ASH HASHEM: "God was not in the thunder....".

MA HASHEM DORESH MIMEKHA: "what doth the Lord require of thee....".
MA HU RAHUM AF ATA RAHUM: "as He is merciful, so shall you be merciful...".
MAYVIN: connoisseur.
MENTSCHLICHKEIT: (Y.) interpersonal decency.
METZUYAN. KOL HAKAVOD: "excellent; more power to you."

MI BIKESH ZOT MIYEDCHEM: "who asks this of you?"
MI HU YEHUDI: who is a Jew?
MI-MAAMAKIM: "out of the depths."
MIPNEI SEIVAH TAKUM: "you shall stand up before the elderly...".
MISTAPEK BE-MUAT: to be satisfied with the minimum.
MITZVAT ANASHIM MELUMADAH: serving God by rote.
MUSAR SHMUESS: (Y.) ethical discourse.

NA'AR HAYITI GAM ZAKANTI: "I was young, and have grown old....".
NES NIGLAH: an open miracle.
NES NISTAR: a hidden miracle.
NISHMAT HAYYIM: the breath of life.
NUSCHAOT: versions (of prayer).

OHEV ET HABRIOT UM'KARVAN LA-TORAH: "loves people and brings them close to Torah....".

PESUKEI DEZIMRAH: the Halleluya section of the morning prayers..
PITHO SHEL GEHINNOM: the entrance to hell.

RAV HESED: abundant mercy.
RISHONIM: the early decisors of Jewish law (tenth to fifteenth century).
RUAH HAKODESH: divine spirit.
RUHNIYUT: spirituality.

SEDER HA-TEFILLAH: the order of prayer.
SHAHARIT: the morning prayers.
SHALIAH TSIBBUR: the leader of a prayer service.
SHELEMUT: perfection.
SHEMONEH ESREI: lit., "eighteen." The central portion of the liturgy; also "amidah."

Glossary

SHEVA BRACHOT: the seven blessings of the marriage service recited at special meals for bride and groom during the post-wedding week.

SHOMER DELATOT YISROEL: "Protector of the doors of Israel."

SHTREIMEL: (Y.) fur hat worn by hassidic Jews on holy days.

SIDDUR: prayer book.

SIMCHA: happy event.

TAHANUN: a section of the daily service.

TAHARAT HAMISHPACHAH: laws of family purity.

TAQANAH: rabbinic ordinance.

TAUS HADFUS: printer's error.

TEFILLAH LAMEDINAH: prayer for the State of Israel.

TICHEL: head covering worn by observant Jewish women.

TIKKUN HA-OLAM: repairing the world.

TIKKUN ATSMI: repairing oneself.

TSANUA: humble, reticent.

TSENIUT: modesty.

VOS VILL GOTT?: (Y.) "What does God want?"

YA-ALEH VEYAVO: a special prayer for holy days.

YADEINU LO SHAFKHU ET HA-DAM HA-ZEH: "our hands have not spilled this blood....".

YAHADUT: Judaism.

YALDEI: children of ....

YE-HAREG V'AL YA-AVOR: a commandment for which one must give one's life before violating it.

YEHEI SHMEI RABBAH: communal response to the Kaddish.

YETSER HARA: the evil inclination.

YIRAT HASHEM: fear of the Lord.

YOM ZE MEKHUBAD: the name of a Shabbat table hymn.

Z"L - ZIKHRONO LIVERAKHA: "may his memory be for a blessing."
ZECHER L'HURBAN: a remembrance of the Temple's destruction.
ZEMIROT: Shabbat table hymns.